Horatio Balch Hackett

Christian Memorials of the War

Vol. 1

Horatio Balch Hackett

Christian Memorials of the War
Vol. 1

ISBN/EAN: 9783337307639

Printed in Europe, USA, Canada, Australia, Japan

Cover: Foto ©Lupo / pixelio.de

More available books at **www.hansebooks.com**

CHRISTIAN MEMORIALS OF THE WAR:

OR,

SCENES AND INCIDENTS

ILLUSTRATIVE OF

RELIGIOUS FAITH AND PRINCIPLE, PATRIOTISM AND BRAVERY IN OUR ARMY.

WITH

HISTORICAL NOTES.

BY

HORATIO B. HACKETT,

PROFESSOR OF BIBLICAL LITERATURE AND INTERPRETATION IN NEWTON THEOL. INST.;
AUTHOR OF "ILLUSTRATIONS OF SCRIPTURE," "COMMENTARY
ON THE ACTS OF THE APOSTLES," ETC.

BOSTON:
GOULD AND LINCOLN,
59 WASHINGTON STREET.
NEW YORK: SHELDON AND COMPANY.
CINCINNATI: GEORGE S. BLANCHARD.
1864.

PREFACE.

It is hardly possible that too many books should be written in illustration of the objects and spirit of the present war. Among them all, may there not be room also for one like this?

The object has been simply to gather up some fragments of this great history that otherwise might be lost. Most persons will agree that the incidents recorded in these pages are worth preserving; and yet from their nature, as not falling distinctly within the province of biography or history, and from their being scattered in so many different quarters, they are liable, after having been read at the moment, to pass out of sight and be forgotten.

I have put these materials together in this manner because I thought it might be a grateful service to the friends of our brave soldiers, as well as an act of justice to the soldiers themselves, and because I felt a hearty interest in the work. Facts like those here spread before us are adapted to give us our strongest impression of the intelligence, the earnestness, the Christian principle and heroism of so large a class of men, who have come forward to support the Government in this great emergency, and to give us also our strongest conviction that a cause which such men support cannot and will not fail. The least we can do for those who thus lay themselves on the altar of sacrifice for us is, to show ourselves grateful to them, and to cherish the memory of what they have done and suffered. History, in due time, will render to many of them its fitting tribute of commemoration; but not to all. Such imperfect memorials as these form the only record that will ever be made of names not a few, and of deeds of suffering and valor never surpassed, which we and those after us should not "willingly let die."

Nothing has been inserted here that I have not reason to suppose to be strictly true. It will be seen that the names of persons, the names of places and dates, have been freely given; and when they are not given, it will be seen that the statements themselves bear with them the marks of their truthfulness. The interest of the facts lies in their sober reality. Accounts that might be thought by some very interesting, and entitled to a place here, have been excluded, if they were drawn up in such a manner as to seem to be written for effect.

I have endeavored to give to the selections as much variety as the scope of the book allowed. The events related take place under circumstances more or less different, and serve in each instance to illustrate, to some extent, a new class of ideas or a new phase of character. This fact will account for the absence of some narratives which the reader may have seen elsewhere and may be disappointed not to find here. It was impossible, of course, where the noteworthy incidents are so many, to insert them all; and it was unnecessary to mention those which are so similar to others that to insert them would be to repeat very nearly the same things.

The author's task has been chiefly that of selection and arrangement, but not without some additional labor. I have inserted explanatory remarks here and there, sometimes in the text, and sometimes at the bottom of the page. I have made some of the articles fuller, where the means of information enabled me to do so, and have abridged other articles, as it seemed, in the one case or the other, to agree best with the object of the present publication. It was necessary to give some uniformity to the style of the book. I have felt at liberty to make occasional changes in the language, such as the writers themselves, with an opportunity for revision, might be supposed to make; yet taking care always never to interfere with the facts, or the spirit and tone of the original articles. With this exception, the articles verbally, as well as in respect of the subject-matter, have been left in the state in which their authors wrote them in the presence of the scenes and events which they describe; and which, in consequence of being thus written, will be found to be distinguished often by touches of pathos and a vigor of expression which no skill of rhetoric could heighten or improve.

H. B. H.

NEWTON CENTRE, March 18th, 1864.

CONTENTS.

CHAPTER I.

FIGHTING FOR THE GOVERNMENT ACKNOWLEDGED AS A CHRISTIAN DUTY.

		PAGE
1.	The first Ohio Volunteer,	16
2.	First Christ's, then our Country's,	17
3.	Songs on the Battle-field,	18
4.	The Missionary's Son,	20
5.	Pastor and People enlist together,	21
6.	He made his Will before Battle,	22
7.	The Two Brothers,	25
8.	The Bible in the Knapsack,	26
9.	The Pennsylvania Roundheads,	27
10.	The Prayers at Home the Soldiers' Defence,	29
11.	Last Words of a Dying Hero,	31
12.	Dying for his Country a Privilege,	32
13.	A Chapel Under-ground,	34
14.	The Commodore in the Pulpit,	35
15.	They ask God's Blessing,	36
16.	The Indiana Hero Boy,	37

CHAPTER II.

SOLDIERS OF THE CROSS IN THE ARMY.

1. The Aged Volunteer, ... 40
2. John Lorenze, ... 41
3. General Mitchell as a Preacher, ... 44
4. The Model Prayer-meeting, ... 44
5. A Starless Crown, ... 47
6. Baptism in the Mountains, ... 48
7. The Log Church, ... 49
8. The Blind Soldier, ... 53
9. The Silent Prayer, ... 53
10. Foote's Farewell to his Sailors, ... 54
11. The Soldier's greatest Fear, ... 57
12. Sorrow in the Homestead, ... 58
13. Last Interview of the Heroes, ... 60
14. Jesus will take me Home, ... 61
15. The Story of Nolan, ... 63
16. The Dying Hand on the Bible, ... 65
17. Suddenly at Rest, ... 65
18. Such are Ministering Spirits, ... 66
19. The First Sabbath in Camp, ... 68

CHAPTER III.

COURAGE PROMOTED BY TRUST IN GOD.

1. A Message from the Bible, ... 70
2. A Word in Season, ... 71
3. March of the Seventh N. Y. to Washington, ... 72
4. The Dying Soldier's Prayer for the President, ... 74

5. A Scene in the Log Church,................................... 76
6. Prayer in Time of Battle,................................... 78
7. He was only a Private, ... 79
8. Relics from the Battle-field,................................ 83
9. Words of the Martyr Stephen,................................ 84
10. The Soldier-boy's last Hymn, ... 85
11. The Tract—"Come to Jesus,"................................. 86
12. The Model of a Chaplain,.................................... 87
13. Worship on the Flat-boat,................................... 89
14. Garments rolled in Blood,................................... 91
15. The Cabin a Bethel,... 91
16. Strength of the Ruling Passion, ... 93

CHAPTER IV.

CHEERFUL SUBMISSION TO HARDSHIPS AND SUFFERINGS.

1. Heroism in the Hospital,.................................... 95
2. A Funeral in the Forest,.................................... 97
3. Wiping the Tears from their Eyes,........................... 99
4. The Soldier's Farewell, ... 101
5. True to the Flag, ... 102
6. Is that Mother?... 104
7. Little Eddie the Drummer,................................... 104
8. What a Physician saw,....................................... 108
9. The Hospital Tree near Fair Oaks,........................... 111
10. The Wounded at Fort Wagner,................................ 112
11. The African Standard-bearer, ... 115
12. A Singular Death, ... 117
13. The Last Duty to his Country,.............................. 119

CHAPTER V.

EFFORTS FOR THE SPIRITUAL WELFARE OF THE SOLDIERS.

1. Prayer in a Churchyard, ... 121
2. Regimental Churches, ... 122
3. The last Soul-cheering Word, ... 124
4. All One in Christ Jesus, ... 125
5. Worship in Camp, ... 126
6. A Regimental Revival, ... 128
7. Preaching by Moonlight, ... 131
8. A Soul brought to Jesus, ... 132
9. A Mother's Thank-offering, ... 135
10. A New Thing in the Army, ... 137
11. The Lord's Supper in Camp, ... 138
12. The First Sabbath at Beaufort, ... 139
13. A Leaf from his Journal, ... 140
14. Gift of the Prayer-books, ... 142
15. Fortunes of a Bible, ... 143
16. An Answer to Prayer, ... 145
17. A Sabbath with the Contrabands, ... 147
18. The Power of Sympathy, ... 149
19. A Religious Service for the Veterans, ... 151

CHAPTER VI.

HAPPY DEATHS OF BRAVE MEN.

1. Death of General Mitchell, ... 154
2. The Child's Prayer that of the Man, ... 156
3. So the young Soldier died, ... 157
4. The last Message, ... 158
5. Surprised but Ready, ... 159

6. Looking Up, ... 161
7. Not dumb, though Speechless, ... 161
8. The Doctor's youthful Patient, ... 162
9. Surely I come quickly, ... 166
10. The Student's last Wishes, ... 166
11. The favorite Hymn, ... 168
12. Asleep in Jesus, blessed Sleep, ... 169
13. The Lowly Exalted, ... 173
14. Waiting for Day-break, ... 175

CHAPTER VII.

OUR DEPENDENCE ON GOD FOR SUCCESS.

1. The President's Journey to Washington, ... 180
2. The Prayer at Fort Sumter, ... 182
3. An Altar in the Tent, ... 184
4. The Puritan Spirit, ... 185
5. A Regiment on their Knees, ... 186
6. National Fast in the Army, ... 187
7. The Army Hymn, ... 189
8. General Anderson in the Sunday School, ... 190
9. Pray for the President, ... 192
10. Faith and Works, ... 193

CHAPTER VIII

INCIDENTS OF THE CAMP AND BATTLE-FIELD.

1. How a Body was Identified, ... 195
2. Dread of Temptation, ... 196
3. Use Your Talents, ... 197
4. Early Impressions revived, ... 198
5. Unmarked Graves, ... 199
6. Spirit of Sire and Son, ... 200

7. The Unknown Children, ... 201
8. A Mother's Love, ... 202
9. The Value of Seconds, ... 203
10. Old Hundred at Night, ... 204
11. A precious Testimony, ... 205
12. Anecdote of General Sedgwick, ... 205
13. A brave Confession, ... 207
14. The Soldier's last Watch, ... 207
15. Power of Forgiveness, ... 210
16. Seals of his Ministry, ... 211
17. A Step Onward, ... 212
18. Generosity of a Slave, ... 213
19. Principle stronger than Nature, ... 217
20. Sights after Battle, ... 218
21. Dying for a Benefactor, ... 221
22. The last Victory, ... 222
23. Do you remember Eckington? 224
24. The Book will tell, ... 225
25. A Soldier's Pocket Diary, ... 227
26. Gentle as well as Brave, ... 230
27. Picket Duty, ... 231
28. The young Color-Sergeant, ... 233
29. Lock of Hair for Mother, ... 234
30. Not yet too late, ... 235
31. Soldier, are you Hungry? 236
32. Our good-hearted President, ... 237
33. Brought back to the Fold, ... 239
34. The Current between Camp and Home, ... 242
35. Home-links of the War, ... 243
36. A Plea for the Christian Commission, ... 246

MEMORIALS OF THE WAR.

CHAPTER I.

FIGHTING FOR THE GOVERNMENT ACKNOWLEDGED AS A CHRISTIAN DUTY.

The examples of our motto in this chapter show, among other proofs, how strongly the Christian sentiment of the country has been aroused by the object and issues of the present war, and illustrate the true connection between loyalty to God and loyalty to the government. The examples have been selected with impartiality, from a wide range of religious and social life. They are specimens only (which is true also of other portions of the book) of the many similar incidents that have appeared from day to day in the public journals since the outbreak of the rebellion. They are instances of an unselfish, heroic devotion to the claims of patriotism and humanity, which, instead of being admired and praised merely, should rebuke our apathy if we are not in sympathy with such ideas of public duty; which, at all events, should strengthen the universal determination to crush the rebellion, and save from overthrow our institutions of liberty, self-government, and law, to which these costly sacrifices are giving, if it were possible, new sacredness and value. On subjects of this nature facts supply the most effective teaching, and those presented here may as well be left to make their own impression, without amplification or comment.

I. THE FIRST OHIO VOLUNTEER.

The name to which this enviable distinction belongs is never to perish. Colonel Lorin Andrews, late President of Kenyon College, in Ohio, was the first man in that State to offer his services to the governor. Having raised a company by his own efforts, he was elected captain, and afterwards was appointed colonel of the Fourth Regiment of the Ohio Volunteers. At the expiration of the three months for which he had been called out, he enlisted for the war, and commanded his regiment until disease, contracted in camp, compelled him to resign. He then went home, already death-stricken, and soon ended his days. Though he had no opportunity to share in any actual fighting, he was considered a very efficient and brave officer, as well as a devoted, exemplary Christian.[1]

"I well remember," says Bishop McIlvaine, in the address at his funeral, "with what pleasure he related to me a circumstance that had just occurred, which put his decision as a Christian to a severe test. On the previous Sunday, some good minister of the Methodist denomination had preached to them. At the close of his discourse, very unexpectedly to Col. Andrews, he called on him to pray. It was a trial. But immediately he saw what an opening it afforded him at once, in the sight of the whole thousand, officers and soldiers, — to the far greater portion of whom he was as yet personally a stranger, — to take his stand as a

[1] The compiler has learned these facts from a private letter.

Christian, and as one who intended to walk before them in the confession of Christ. He therefore, without hesitation, stood up and prayed, — praying for his men and their families. The impression was very strong and general; and he was happy and thankful. About this time, in expectation of soon taking the field, he said to me, 'I have no fear that I shall not have courage enough for the dangers of battle. All my anxiety is that I may have firmness enough to be faithful and decided as a Christian in all the various circumstances in which I may be placed. I feel that to do *that* requires higher courage than to stand unmoved before the mouth of cannon.

"Such a man," continues the bishop, "was fitted to have command in our army. He could be trusted. In writing to me about the motives which led him to become a soldier, he said he had no love or desire for a military life. It was not his taste. He did not covet military distinction. He was a man of peace and quietness. But he was moved entirely by the consideration of duty to his country, in the time of her great and awful trial. He said he had carefully and solemnly, before God, considered his duty; and he had prayerfully arrived at the conviction on which he was acting.".

"He died," says his successor in the college, "in the full enjoyment of his faith, and trust in his Redeemer, and, I believe, has gone to that perfect rest prepared for the saints in heaven."

II. FIRST CHRIST'S, THEN OUR COUNTRY'S.

Bishop Simpson, of the Methodist church, soon after the outbreak of the great treachery, delivered a sermon on the national crisis, at Chicago. It is represented as one of the ablest efforts of this clergyman, so distinguished for his power in the pulpit. As it was one of the anniversaries of the denomination, thousands were present to hear the discourse. Suddenly, at one point in the sermon, and as the fitting close of a most impassioned paragraph, he gave utterance to the following noble sentiment: "We will take our glorious flag — the flag of our country — and nail it *just below the cross!* That is high enough! There let it wave as it waved of old. Around it let us gather: 'First Christ's, then our country's.'"

The effect was electrical. Every heart responded to the appeal. The sentiment, the preacher's manner, the solemnity of the crisis, moved the great assembly as men are seldom moved under the power of human speech.

III. SONGS ON THE BATTLE-FIELD.

The sanguinary battle of Shiloh was fought on the sixth and the seventh of April, 1862. The ordinary scene which presents itself, after the strife of arms has ceased, is familiar to every one. Heaps of the slain, where friend and foe lie by the side of each other; bodies mangled and bleeding; shrieks of the wounded and dying, are things which we always associate with the victories and defeats of war. But seldom do we read that voices of prayer, that hymns of exultant faith and thanksgiving, have been heard at such times and in such places.

The following account was received from the lips of a brave and pious captain in one of the Western regiments, as some friends who visited Shiloh on the morning after the battle were conveying him to the hospital.

The man had been shot through both thighs with a rifle bullet; it was a wound from which he could not recover. While lying on the field, he suffered intense agony from thirst. He supported his head upon his hand, and the rain from heaven was falling around him. In a short time, a little pool of water collected near his elbow and he thought if he could only reach that spot he might allay his raging thirst. He tried to get into a position which would enable him to obtain a mouthful, at least, of the muddy water; but in vain, and he must suffer the torture of seeing the means of relief within sight, while all his efforts were unavailing. "Never," said he, "did I feel so much the loss of any earthly blessing. By and by the shades of night fell around us, and the stars shone out clear and beautiful above the dark field, where so many had sunk down in death, and so many others lay wounded, writhing in pain, or faint with the loss of blood. Thus situated, I began to think of the great God who had given his Son to die a death of agony for me, and that he was in the heavens to which my eyes were turned, — that he was there, above that scene of suffering, and above those glorious stars; and I felt that I was hastening home to meet him, and praise him there; and I felt that I ought to praise him then, even wounded as I was, on the battle-field. I could not help singing that beautiful hymn: —

> ' When I can read my title clear
> To mansions in the skies,
> I'll bid farewell to every fear,
> And wipe my weeping eyes.'

And though I was not aware of it till then," said he, "it proved there was a Christian brother in the thicket near me. I could not see him, but was near enough to hear him. He took up the strain from me; and beyond him another, and then another, caught the words, and made them resound far and wide over the terrible battle-field of Shiloh. There was a peculiar echo in the place, and that added to the effect, as we made the night vocal with our hymns of praise to God."

It is certain that men animated by such faith have the consciousness of serving God in serving their country, and that their presence in the army adds to it some of its most important elements of strength and success.

IV. THE MISSIONARY'S SON.

The memory of the devoted missionary, Rev. William H. Pohlman,[1] of his saintly life and martyr death, is yet fragrant in all the churches. Let them add to this treasured memory still another as fresh and beautiful, — that of his only son, Lieutenant William Henry Pohlman, Assistant Adjutant of the Fifty-ninth Regiment of the New York Volunteers, who died July 21st, 1863, aged twenty-one years, of wounds received in the battle of Gettysburg.

Late in the afternoon of Friday, the eventful third of July, his left arm was frightfully shattered by a Minie ball; but the brave spirit did not quail. "No," he answered those who urged him to withdraw from the front, "never, while I have a sword-arm left to fight with!" An hour later, his sword-arm failed him too. Another ball, glancing from his sword-hilt, which it shattered, pierced his right wrist, severing an artery, and his battle-work was done. But not for him should the great work of the hour, the salvation of the republic, suffer interruption for a moment. "Boys," he said to the soldiers who would have borne him from the field already almost won, "stay in your places; your country needs every man of you." And so he left them, regretting most of all that he could not recover the sword his mother gave him. Its empty scabbard, battered and blood-stained, but with its glorious legend, the key-note of his life, unmarred, "For God and your Country,"

---

[1] He was a missionary of the American Board in China, and lost his life by shipwreck in 1849.

is now the most cherished treasure of her who filled a mother's place to the orphan boy. He reached the camp at last, fainting on the way from loss of blood, and was laid beside his beloved colonel.

And now a new phase in the character of this knightly, nay, *Christian* hero, was to be developed. A trial, heavy for such as he, so full of exuberant vitality and rejoicing in his strength, was laid upon him, and he was cast into the fiery crucible of bodily anguish and bodily weakness. Sustained by strength beyond his own, nobly did he endure the test. His beautiful unselfishness and utter freedom from degrading vanity were most conspicuous. Withholding his name from the newspaper reporters, lest the sight of it among the killed and wounded might too rudely shock the tender hearts which he fain would spare all needless pain, his first care was to break the news of his condition as gently as possible. For this purpose he dictated a characteristic note on the day succeeding the battle. Beginning, not with his own achievements or sufferings, but with an exultant announcement of the victory won, he adds: "But the usual good fortune which has attended me in thirteen battles of the war has forsaken me in the fourteenth engagement. I bear honorable wounds in my country's cause."

V. PASTOR AND PEOPLE ENLIST TOGETHER.

A pastor in one of the Western States had in his congregation fifty-one men who had enlisted in the service of their country. They assembled to listen as they supposed to his parting address; but when he saw their patriotic zeal, he said to them, that if they were all going he should go too. At the door of the church they chose him as their captain, and now pastor and people are fighting together in this great struggle for the national life and the rights of humanity.

It is estimated that the churches of the different Christian denominations throughout the country have been represented in the army, on the average, in the proportion of one to every seven of their male members. They have gone as volunteers, and not as drafted men. The churches in the older States, it is to be remembered, contain large numbers beyond the military age, and thus, of those liable to serve, this proportion is greater than that of one to seven. Many of the Western churches have exceeded this ratio of membership, in the contributions which they have made to the ranks of the army. Not a few of the smaller churches, in the less populated regions, have been left almost without any men at home, clergy or laity.

VI. HE MADE HIS WILL BEFORE BATTLE.

I transcribe the following sketch, with slight changes, from the Boston "Journal," under date of June 18th, 1862. Alas, that one so full of promise, more than a Marcellus in every augury of civic and private virtue, should only "be shown to us," and then be withdrawn!

Yesterday, the remains of the late Major Edwin M. Smith passed through Boston on their way to Maine. He was the son of the late governor of that State, and was of a character so charming and so rare that public testimony should be borne to his virtues and services. He fell at the battle of Fair Oaks, in the van, leading the Fifth Michigan Regiment of Berry's Brigade, in their splendid work of that day. "Better," said his general, "better that I had lost a hundred men than that brave boy!" He was acting as the chief of that general's staff, and that true officer knew him well. Young Smith had just returned from Europe, at the age of twenty-one, when the war commenced. Having gained much credit for his bravery and discretion, he was soon commissioned as major in the Maine Fourth, but at the urgent request of General Berry, finally accepted a place upon his staff, and acted as chief of his staff at the battles of Williamsburg and Fair Oaks. In fact, he led one wing, while General Berry commanded the other, in that brilliant charge and fight which saved Hooker's division, at Williamsburg. Smith there dashed forward with his Michigan regiment, and the Thirty-seventh New York, and, leaping the enemy's rifle-pits, forced his way through the abatis into the strongholds with an impetuosity which astonished all. Four of the enemy's bullets passed through his clothing, but left him unharmed! So popular and beloved did he become with these regiments, that they would often cheer him as he passed. His heart though brave was tender as a woman's: His hand was always open to the needy; and the sick found him the gentlest of all who breathed around them. Fond of all befitting sports, and active as a child, he was nevertheless of a mature and thoughtful nature; having a real love of country and the highest reverence for truth and law. Frail in body, he had an exalted spirit and an energetic will, and won the love of all who knew him. When his horse was brought to the White House to be sent home, a Michigan soldier said, "There goes the noble horse that leaped the rifle-pits at Williamsburg!" "Yes," said his comrade, "he had a noble rider then, but he has gone!" and the sturdy warrior could hardly utter his name.

It was Berry's brigade which at the battle of Williamsburg came up just in time to save the day, after Hooker's division had been fighting at terrible odds for several hours, had exhausted their ammunition, and were on the point of giving way. At this critical moment, the newly-arrived soldiers, having fired five deadly rounds into the enemy, and repulsed five of their desperate charges, made that memorable charge, which recaptured all the lost artillery and the ground which the exhausted soldiers of Hooker's division had yielded.

During the night of the fifth of May, which followed the battle, young Smith wrote in his journal: "We stood in arms amidst the enemy's dead and dying, cold, wet and weary enough. For all this bravery and skill our noble general was publicly thanked by General Heintzelman, and eulogized by General McClellan." But the modest journalist does not say, what was the fact, that one of the most distinguished generals openly pronounced the youthful officer himself "one of the bravest of the brave, one of the heroes of the day, from whom we might expect a future of great usefulness and honor."

Before the attack on Yorktown he made a short will, yet in all the haste of a camp, he closed it by adding this remarkable paragraph: "And now, having arranged for the disposition of my worldly estate, I must say that, possessing a full confidence in the Christian religion, and believing in the righteousness of the cause in which I am engaged, I am ready to offer my poor life in vindicating that cause, and in sustaining a government the mildest and most beneficent the world has ever known."

So he gave that life to his country. Let his memory and that of our kindred martyrs be embalmed forever in the nation's heart. He was fit to live and fit to die, and his crown was ready for him.

VII. THE TWO BROTHERS.

The following simple and touching letter is from the brother of John W. Chase, a member of Co. G, of the Fourth Rhode Island Regiment, who recently died in the hospital in Carolina City. James and John were twins, and both members of the same regiment, — noble boys, of whom a friend writes very justly : " This letter will convey a touching idea of the loss which the mother has experienced in the death of one of these Christian youth, who might truly be called 'Cromwellian soldiers.'" With genuine patriotism, childlike faith in God, a filial and fraternal affection, James conveys the sad news to his mother; and this is another instance, in the humble classes, of that genuine heroism which has been brought to light by this war.

CAROLINA CITY, Saturday, 26th.

DEAR MOTHER : — I now take my pen to say that there has been a great change since I wrote last. John has got through with fighting, and with all his hardships and trials. He has gone to rest. His sickness was short. He was seized with typhoid fever, and soon followed Denham and William. This makes three deaths in our company.

John wrote you a letter two or three days before he was sick. Then, mother, he was as well as I was; so you see we cannot tell what to-morrow will bring forth. Death is certain, and life is uncertain. But the Lord knows best about these things; and when he calls us, we have to go. Oh! I wish that I was in John's place! Thank God, mother, there is one consolation, that if we do not see each other again in this world, we shall in the one above.

I prayed every night while John was sick for the Lord to bless him. I left him in His hands. It was so ordered that John was not to be shot in the battle-field, but to be taken by sickness; and it has turned out all for the best.

I have tried to do my duty since I have been in the war. I have felt that this was the place to remember and look to Him who is our best Friend. And he has proved so. He brought John and me both safe out of danger in the field, and now he has called one of us to go to him. He may call for me next. I do not care, mother, how quick; for I can say that I am ready to go when God calls me, and I believe I shall meet John with the angels above.

He died at four o'clock this morning. I send you a lock of his hair. Remember, mother, if we part with our friends here, we shall sooner or later meet them before God.

I close by saying, do not take it too hard. The Lord bless you.

From your dear son, J. S. C.

VIII. THE BIBLE IN THE KNAPSACK.

A gentleman from one of the Western cities, says the "Banner of the Covenant," at a recent prayer-meeting in New York, rose and said, —

A few days ago, I was present where a body of soldiers, an entire regiment, having been drawn up in line, were asked if they would accept of copies of the Bible. The question was put to them by the commanding officer, after having stated that the citizens of the place, anxious to show their interest in them and to promote their welfare, would be happy to supply each one of them with a Bible if they were willing to receive it. "Now," said he, "as many of you as are willing to receive the Bibles are requested to raise your right hands." The result was, (said he,) every hand was raised, and many tears were falling as they responded to the proposition. In addition to this, as the commander stood on the steps of the hotel, one of the distributors approached him, and gave to him, also, with appropriate remarks, an expensive and elegant copy of the Scriptures, in the sight and hearing of all the men. It so happened that one of the spectators in the crowd was a missionary from Turkey. "Oh," said the missionary, "I never expected to live to see such a day as this! I never expected to see such a sight as this. I never expected to see the legions of an army going out to battle, voting the word of God into their knapsacks." The men declared, by this act, that they needed the Lord of hosts as their ally, and that, in performing their duty, they could look to him for his blessing on them.

IX. THE PENNSYLVANIA ROUNDHEADS.

The interesting sketch which follows is from Rev. Solomon Peck, D. D., so well known for his philanthropic labors in behalf of the freedmen at Beaufort, S. C.: —

It was said by Cromwell of his regiment of "Ironsides," who "were never beaten," "I raised such men as had the fear of God before them; as made some conscience of what they did." It is from them the "Roundheads of Western Pennsylvania, descendants of Scotch Covenanters and English Puritans, derive their name — a name first given in derision by the "Cavaliers," but afterward well understood to be a synonyme for Invincibles.

Soon after the battle of Bull Run, and on the expiration of the "three months" service, application was made to the Secretary of War, by Colonel D. Leasure, for leave to raise a regiment for the war. The Pennsylvania "Reserves" by that time had been filled out. "Can you bring Roundheads, Bible-men?" asked the Secretary. "I can bring no other," was the reply.

It was my lot to meet the Roundheads, officers and men, for the first time in the house of God, the Sabbath after I landed in Beaufort, December twenty-second. The chaplain of the regiment, Rev. Robert A. Brown, of Newcastle, Pa., lay ill of fever at that time, and the colonel had invited me to preach to them at the usual hour of morning worship. The appointment was made accordingly; and at bell-ringing the colonel marched his men, nine hundred strong, into the Baptist meeting-house, under arms, and with measured tread; but quiet and reverent, as became the place, the service, and the day.

It was an impressive spectacle. The soldiery, intermingled with members of other corps, filled the entire area of the lower floor, and most of the spacious galleries, which projected on either side. At the end stood, close crowded together, groups of "colored people." There, listening to the word of God, or rising in prayer, or singing, after their ancient metrical version, some of the Psalms of David, the Roundheads joined in worshipping the God of their fathers, — their God and our God, — just as they had been wont to worship, in their several sanctuaries, with kindred and friends at home. What added to the interest of the occasion was the presence of two other ministers, who took part in conducting the services, one of them the chaplain of the Eighth Michigan Regiment, Rev. Mr. Mahon. The service, moreover, was only the second had by the Roundheads, in Sabbath public worship, since coming to the South.

X. THE PRAYERS AT HOME THE SOLDIERS' DEFENCE.

At the close of the preceding service, says Dr. Peck, and after the benediction had been pronounced, an incident occurred, not less inspiriting at the moment than it was matter of earnest gratulation afterwards, as a token of Christian alertness and tact in days to come.

The congregation was on the point of moving out, when one word " Steady ! " clear and sharp, arrested every foot. Silence the most profound ensued ; while Colonel Leasure advanced to the foot of the pulpit stairs, and spoke to his Roundheads, whose very breath seemed to hang upon his words, in nearly the following terms : —

" By the waters of the Yough, the Monongahela, the Slippery-rock, the Conoquanessing, the Neshannock, the Shenango, the Mahoning, the Hantaba, and the Sunny Beavers, those dearer to us than the lives we have come here to lay down, if need be, to preserve for their inheritance a country worthy of them, are met to-day in their holy places, their sanctuaries, to worship the God of our country and our salvation. I need not ask any one here *whose* names are graven on their hearts, while their united prayers ascend to heaven for their absent soldiers. In the midst of peace and rest, they pray for the dear absent, who, for aught they know, may be enduring the hardness of toil or battle at this hour. Does any soldier here feel that he is less a man, less patriotic, or less brave to endure or dare whatever duty may command, because he feels that a column of prayer, reaching to heaven, constantly follows to support our advance ?

" In the times that are past, we have occupied our appropriate places at their side in the sanctuary. To-day, far separated, our prayers and devotions blend harmoniously before the face of our common Father. In the midst of a hostile people, on an enemy's coast, with our foemen menacing us, in their very presence, we, too, have a sacred, peaceful day of Sabbath rest and worship. Contrary to anything we could have hoped for, we have sat in a house dedicated to the worship of God, and have had his word expounded to us by a chosen minister, while two other ministers of the gospel sit on either side, and assist in the solemn services. To-day is, to us, a day of peace and rest, literally, a Sabbath. We know not when we may have another. Another Sabbath may find us on the march; or we know not where, nor in what circumstances of toil or danger. It is good to serve God while we have the opportunity, in his appointed way, according to his chosen ordinances.

"We have here present a minister of the gospel, the Rev. Mr. Evans, of Stamford, Connecticut, — 'the land of steady habits,' — who visits us from his distant home, and returns to-morrow. He can meet us here this afternoon, if you so desire; and we may again join in the worship of God and hearing of the Word, at the same hour when our dear ones at home shall be engaged in like service. It will not lessen our devotions to know *whose* prayers for us meet ours for them in the ear of our heavenly Father.

"So many as are in favor of afternoon service at three o'clock will raise their right hands."

On the instant, as if by word of military command, every right hand was above the shoulder. The colonel proceeded with rapid but clear utterance: —

"There will be service in this house at three o'clock this afternoon. At half-past two, companies will form on their company parades; the captains will carefully inspect the arms, accoutrements and ammunition, and see that all are in perfect order, and in a state of readiness for instant use;

for we must remember that we are soldiers, as well as worshippers; and that, while we pray to God to prosper our arms, we must also keep our powder dry. After inspection, the regiment will form under arms, in line of battle, on the regimental parade, and march to this place, to join in the further religious observance of the day.

"Silently now, without haste, without delay, file from the left of companies to the street, form into columns, the right resting northward, and take, at the word, the line of march to your quarters."

XI. LAST WORDS OF A DYING HERO.

The following letter of Colonel Brodhead, killed in one of Pope's battles, in front of Washington, in the summer of 1862, written to his wife in his dying moments, has been published at the request of friends who believe that it belongs to the nation as well as to his family. It recalls to us one of the darkest hours through which we have passed amid the alternations of the war. Its touching pathos and high-toned patriotism will awaken fresh regrets for the death of this noble soldier and true man. He was a colonel, we believe, of one of the Pennsylvania regiments.[1]

My Dearest Wife: — I write to you, mortally wounded, from the battle-field. We are again defeated, and ere this reaches you, your children will be fatherless. Had all those in command done their duty as I did mine, and led their forces bravely, loyally, the dear old flag had waved in triumph.

[1] Colonel Brodhead was the son of Rev. John Brodhead, a Methodist clergyman, whom many will still remember for his unwearied and useful labors in different parts of New England. He died in New Hampshire in 1838, after a ministry of forty-four years.

I wrote to you yesterday morning. To-day is Sunday, and to-day I sink to the green couch of our final rest. I have fought well, my darling, and I was shot in the endeavor to rally our broken battalions. I could have escaped, but would not until all hope was gone, and I was shot, — about the only one of our forces left on the field. Our cause is just, and *our* generals, not those of the enemy, have defeated us. In God's good time he will give us victory.

And now, good-by, wife and children. Bring them up, I know you will, in the fear of God and love for the Saviour. But for you and the dear ones dependent, I should die happy. I know the blow will fall with crushing weight on you. Trust in Him who gave manna in the wilderness.

Dr. Nash is with me. It is now after midnight, and I have spent most of the night in sending messages to you.

Two bullets have gone through my chest, and directly through the lungs. I suffer but little now, but at first the pain was acute. I have won the soldier's name, and am ready to meet now, as I must, the soldier's fate. I hope that from heaven I may see the glorious old flag wave again over the undivided Union I have loved so well.

Farewell, wife and babes, and friends. We shall meet again.

Your loving Thornton.

XII. DYING FOR HIS COUNTRY A PRIVILEGE.

In the sanguinary battle of Antietam an officer of a Massachusetts regiment was mortally wounded. He had passed unhurt through the thickest of the fight. At one time, when his regiment had captured a flag from the enemy, he seized it, and, waving it proudly in the air, galloped fearlessly up and down the lines, his men cheering most lustily, and the bullets falling about him like hail. Later in the day, and when in a comparatively sheltered position, a random shot struck him, from the effects of which he died two days afterward.

As he lay near to death, and conscious of his approaching end, the musicians of the regiment happened to pass by. He called to them with a cheerful voice, and asked them to play the "Star-Spangled Banner." They played the grand old tune, and as he listened, the countenance of the dying soldier beamed with joy. He heard no more music until he heard that of heaven, where "there shall be no more death, neither sorrow, nor crying, neither shall there be any more pain." He inquired the result of the battle, and, when told it was a victory, triumphantly exclaimed, "Oh! it is glorious to die for one's country at such a time as this!" Then, speaking in the most affecting manner to his chaplain, who was with him to the last moment, he said, "Tell my mother I love her. Tell her I feel I have a God and Father in heaven. Tell her I trust fully in my Lord Jesus Christ." These were the last words he uttered. Thus he died, a noble example of a soldier, a patriot, and a Christian.

When such sacrifices are laid upon the altar of our country, we have surely new incentives to uphold the cause for which they are made, and, with God's help, not to allow the treason which has slain so many victims, to accomplish its purpose. And, through this bloody baptism, shall not our nation be purified at length, and fitted to act a nobler part in the world's history?

XIII. A CHAPEL UNDER-GROUND.

The Fourteenth Massachusetts Regiment had for a time the very honorable but laborious duty of guarding the Long Bridge, at Washington, and the approaches to it from the Virginia side. A gentleman, who visited the army in relation to their spiritual wants, asked a member of this regiment if they had any praying men among them.

"Oh, yes, a great many!" was the answer.

"And do you ever meet for prayer?" he inquired.

"Every day," said the soldier.

"Where do you meet?"

"Just come here," said he, leading the way as he spoke. They stood in a new fort which the regiment had been building.

"I can see no place for prayer," said the stranger.

"Just down there," said the soldier, lifting up a rude trap-door at their feet.

"What is down there?" asked the other, who could see nothing but a dark hole before them.

"That is the bomb-proof, and down there is the place where we hold the daily prayer-meeting. Down there," continued the soldier, "the men go every day to lift up their hearts to God in prayer." It was not yet furnished with the implements of death, and these praying men, sixty in number, were accustomed to go down twelve feet underground, in the dark, to hold communion with God.

The same person said to a soldier whom he met in the camp, —

"Are you prepared to fight in this cause?"

"I am, sir," said he.

"What makes you say you are prepared to fight? What do you mean by it?"

"I mean this, sir," answered the soldier. "I have made my peace with God, through faith in our Lord Jesus Christ. I have the friendship of Christ, and so I am prepared for anything,— life or death."

"Do you mean that you can have the friendship of Christ, and fight?"

"Exactly so," said the brave man. "I mean just that. I could not fight without a consciousness of my interest in the love of Christ."

XIV. THE COMMODORE IN THE PULPIT.

It has been mentioned as characteristic of Commodore Foote, that he prayed as if everything depended on God, and fought as if everything depended on man. On a certain occasion, says the correspondent of a St. Louis paper,[1] the commodore was present at a meeting on the Sabbath, shortly after one of his signal victories, when the minister of the church failed to appear, and the audience was kept waiting for the opening of the service. It seemed as if the opportunity for instruction and worship would be lost. The elder of the church was unwilling to officiate. Under these circumstances, Commodore Foote, on the impulse of the moment, went up to the pulpit, read a chapter in the Bible, prayed, and delivered a short discourse from the text, "Let not your heart be troubled. Ye believe in God, believe also in me." (John xiv. 1.)

It was unexpected to the people; nor was their wonder less when they saw his self-possession, his readiness, and the pertinence of his remarks. He seemed to be as much at home in the pulpit as he was on the deck of the Cincinnati during the bombardment of Fort Henry. The audi-

[1] I have combined two reports of this occurrence.

tors were much affected at hearing the voice from which so lately rang out the word of command,

> "In worst extreme, and on the perilous edge
> Of battle, when it raged,"

lifted up in humble acknowledgment to Heaven for the recent victory, and in earnest supplication for protection and success in days to come. Some of his own soldiers were among the hearers. They were expecting to be called to go into battle again at any moment. They could have heard nothing from any one better fitted to tranquillize their minds, and nerve them for the conflict.

On coming down from the pulpit, the minister, who had arrived just after the prayer, approached and tendered his thanks; but the commodore rebuked him for his tardiness, and also for his neglect to take the pulpit immediately on his arrival.

XV. THEY ASK GOD'S BLESSING.

A lieutenant of the New York Seventh tells a story to which no one can listen without emotion and a glow of pride in our New England soldiers. He says: "While encamped in Maryland, I wandered off one day, and came to a farmhouse, where I saw a party of soldiers, who I supposed were Massachusetts boys, but who proved to be (though it is all the same) Rhode Islanders, who were talking with a woman who was greatly frightened. They tried in vain to quiet her apprehensions. They asked for food, and she cried, 'Oh, take all I have, take everything, but spare my sick husband.' 'Oh,' said one of the men, 'we are not going to hurt you; we are nearly famished and want something to eat.'

"But the woman persisted in being frightened in spite

of all efforts to reassure her, and hurried whatever food she had on the table. But when she saw this company stand about the table with bowed heads, and a tall, gaunt man raise his hand and invoke God's blessing on the bounties spread before them, the poor woman broke down with a fit of sobbing and crying. She had no longer any fears, but bade them wait, and in a few moments had coffee and other needed refreshments ready for them. She then emptied their canteens of the muddy water they contained, and filled them with coffee. Her astonishment increased when they insisted upon paying her. Their asking a blessing," said the officer, "took me by surprise; and when I saw that, I said, 'Our country is safe, when such men go forth in the fear of God to fight for her.'"

XVI. THE INDIANA HERO BOY.

The narrative which follows appeared in the Cincinnati "Gazette." Some verbal changes only have been made in the language.

On the cars running from Evansville to Indianapolis, (says the writer,) I fell into conversation with a soldier, who, though young in years, carried, as I found, the heart of a man, and a hero in his bosom. He was returning home on a discharge furlough. Having found others destitute, I inquired into his condition. He had started without breakfast, had neither food nor money to go to Elkhart, on the Southern Michigan road, a distance of over three hundred miles, and with the probability before him of being over two days on the way. His voice was gone, and he was obliged to talk in a whisper. On seeing what the prospect before him was, he said to me, with childish simplicity, "I shall be nearly starved when I reach home,—

shall I not?" I inquired for his haversack, in order to supply him with something to eat, when we stopped. He replied that "it had been stolen from him." Yet he was indifferent about the haversack; it was the Bible contained in it that he felt to be the great loss to him. His parents were religious, as I learned, and had brought him up to habits of rectitude, and in the fear of God.

He had an impression that he should not live long; and I remarked to him, "Death is no calamity to a good boy." His countenance brightened as I said that to him, and he answered with much earnestness, "No, sir; and I am not afraid to die. I made up my mind that it was my duty to go and fight for my country, and my parents consented. Through exposure, I lost my health early in the winter; and on the Sunday morning of the battle of Shiloh, I was in my tent sick, and the physician ordered me to remain there. I had been unfit for duty for two months. The physician was very kind to me. The news kept coming back to us near the river that our army was giving way everywhere, and I thought it my duty to take my gun and go to their assistance. I went to the front, and during four hours loaded and fired as fast as I could. But the exertion was too much for me; my lungs took to bleeding, and I came near dying before the bleeding could be stopped. But I was glad I did what I could. I have never spoken since above a whisper, and I fear I never shall. But it is all right; our country must be saved at any sacrifice." At the first eating-station, the boy was seated at the table, and his dinner paid for by a stranger; and his thanks were so cordial and heartfelt, that tears filled the stranger's eyes as he turned away, receiving, as he did it, the sick boy's "God bless you, stranger!"

Time for supper would bring him to Indianapolis. What would he do there? Who would befriend him there? He was told to go to Gov. Morton, and inform him he was on his way home from Shiloh, with ruined health, and had neither money nor food. He answered that he would do it if he had strength to walk. He was then told to send him a line; any one would carry it for him. He said he would do so, and added, "It would not be improper. Surely the governor would not let me starve. It seems to me almost anybody would help a sick soldier."

When he arrived at Elkhart, he would still be several miles from home. That occurred to him, and perplexed his thoughts for a moment; and, then, smiling, he said, "Our family physician lives there, and he will take me in his carriage, and carry me home, and, oh! does not a welcome await me when my mother sees me coming? I shall take her by surprise. She is not prepared for that." Here the train started with the sick boy, who seemed revived by his food, and the words of encouragement spoken to him, and the thoughts of home.

CHAPTER II.

SOLDIERS OF THE CROSS IN THE ARMY.

I. THE AGED VOLUNTEER.

John Henry, of Indiana, is the name of one of the martyr heroes of the war. Although fifty-six years of age, he enlisted as a volunteer in the Seventy-eighth Indiana Regiment. He was not influenced by ambition, for he went as a private; nor by the love of money, for he was not destitute of means, and the soldier's stipend of thirteen dollars a month was little to him; nor yet by patriotism alone, although he loved his country well enough to die for it. He was a teacher in the Sabbath school, and went from love to the members of his class, and from a sense of duty to his Lord and Master, who had committed them to his care. He said "The Great Shepherd will demand them at my hands. I wish to give a good account of my trust. I must care for the souls for whom He cared, and be able, if I can, to present them among the saved, in the day when the throne shall be set, and the books be opened." So he enlisted.

He fell in a skirmish on Monday morning, at Uniontown, Kentucky, mortally wounded. A ball passed through his face, inflicting a terrible wound. It entered just below the left cheek-bone, cut his tongue almost off, shattered the right cheek-bone, and so passed out. He was still able after this, to make himself understood, and was full of joy in spite of the pains of death. On Sunday, the day before his end, he had spent the forenoon in a neighboring orchard, in meditation and prayer. Toward noon he had this thought impressed deeply on him, "Work to-day, for the time is short." And he did work. He passed from tent to tent, praying, praising, and exhorting, not only during the remainder of the day, but late into the night.

The next morning, he was among the first to fall, and soon his mutilated tongue was silent in death. Among his last words were these: "Oh, I am happy, for when the Master came, he found me at my appointed work!" He entered into the full conception of those words of Christ, which we hear with a new emphasis from such a grave. " Blessed are those servants whom the Lord, when he cometh, shall find watching: verily I say unto you, that he shall gird himself, and make them to sit down to meat, and will come forth and serve them. And if he shall come in the second watch, or come in the third watch, and find them so, blessed are those servants."

II. JOHN LORENZE.

The following is a remarkable example of fortitude and of the power of Christian faith. It is an illustration of those virtues that would adorn the martyrology of the brightest ages of the church. The account is from the chaplain of the Eighth Regiment of Connecticut Volunteers. It was written from

"ROANOKE ISLAND, February 22, 1862.

"We are encamped on the battle-field, and the incident I relate is fresh in my mind. John Lorenze, a resident of Mullica Hill, Gloster County, New Jersey, enlisted as a private in the Ninth Regiment of the New Jersey Volunteers, and with his regiment was engaged in the fight at

Roanoke Island, February 8, 1862. During the engagement, which lasted for a number of hours, Mr. Lorenze had both his legs shot away just below the knees, and his comrades bore him from the field. But he did not lose his consciousness nor self-control. In speaking of his sensations as he was shot, he said that a something came and took away his legs, dropping him suddenly to the ground. While he was being borne on the litter to the hospital, as if indifferent to his own sufferings, he sought to cheer his comrades, and all whom he met, by his encouraging words and happy manner. In answer to questions regarding himself and his wounds, he returned cheerful answers. During the amputation of the fragments of his limbs necessary to be removed, he retained his spirits, and encouraged the surgeons by his pleasant frame of mind. His countenance was an index of the composure, almost transport, of his feelings: so much so that all who saw him remarked at once its beaming expression.

"I first observed him as he lay on the floor of the hospital on the day that he suffered the terrible injury. I went to him and asked him where he was wounded. He told me that both his legs were shot away just below the knees. I then conversed with him a few moments about his wounds, the suffering he endured, and spoke to him of the Saviour, — of his love and sustaining grace. The tears filled his eyes. 'Oh,' said he, 'Jesus is all my trust. Blessed be his holy name! I do not know what would sustain me, if it were not for the consciousness of his presence.' I asked him if he was a professor of religion. He replied that he had tried to serve God for a number of years. 'I have tried to serve him in the camp, and now he is all my trust.' The tears rolled down his cheeks while he talked. I left him, promising to see him again, and pray with him, and also to write to his wife, informing her of his situation. In the course of our conversation he spoke of his family, consisting of a wife and two young children, and said he did not know whether he should live or die; but if it was God's will that he should live, he thought he might be of some little service to those dependent on him; but immediately added, 'God's will be done.' All this time the same heavenly smile rested on his face. I called to see him again the next day, which was Sabbath, but found him asleep, and did not awake him. I called again on Monday, and conversed with him, finding him still in possession of the same peace and cheerfulness. I then read to him the fifth chapter of Second Corinthians, and prayed with him. Before the prayer closed, the room was filled with the surgeons and attendants, all of whom were in tears; and the hearty amen which came from the lips of the wounded man was audible to all in the room.

"While I was writing the letter to his wife, he said, 'Tell her I am comfortable and cheerful; but as she is very nervous, do not tell her how severely I am wounded.' And then he spoke of the surgeons and those who attended him, expressing gratitude for their kindness. 'Oh,' he said, 'they are all so kind to me.' I think I never before witnessed such an instance of Christian fortitude and heroic faith; his loss was so great, and yet under it all he was so happy and confident.

"A very profane man called to see him, and in speaking of him afterward in my presence, remarked, 'It would do any one's heart good to look at that man's face. I never saw such a face since I was born. If I had a regiment of such men, I could conquer the whole South;' and turning to me, he asked, 'What sustains that man?' It was a fitting opportunity, and I told him Mr. Lorenze's testimony respecting his faith in Christ, and its power to lift him thus above pain and the fear of death. The scorner dropped his head and was silent."

III. GENERAL MITCHELL AS A PREACHER.

This lamented officer was an eloquent man, as well as learned and brave, and often addressed his men on religious subjects. He did not esteem it beneath his dignity, or subversive of military discipline, to endeavor to bring his command under the lead of the great Captain of our salvation. On one occasion, at the conclusion of a sermon preached to the Ninth Ohio Brigade, near Shelbyville, Tennessee, the general took his stand on a huge rock as a pulpit, and occupied half an hour in delivering what is described as one of the best religious discourses ever heard. He commenced by saying that he did not appear there as the general commanding, but in a higher capacity; that he would address them as a man his fellow-men, as one striving with them for the same eternal happiness for which all are candidates in this probationary life. He insisted that the highest duty of a soldier was to be a Christian; religion heightened every enjoyment, and prepared him to discharge better all his obligations. A chaplain who was present says, "It was a sublime scene; he left an impression on the minds of his auditors never to be forgotten." The effect of this sermon was heightened by the fact that the services were held on the mountain-top, amid the rugged grandeur of East Tennessee.

IV. THE MODEL PRAYER-MEETING.

It is an instructive fact certainly, as the author of the subjoined communication in the "Boston Recorder," the Rev. William Barrows, of Reading, Mass., suggests, that the camp, and not the vestry, should furnish our "best model of a prayer-meeting." The scene is near Stoneman's Station, in the army of the Potomac, in the camp of the Twenty-second Massachusetts Regiment, and the time the evening of April 3d, 1863.

A Sibley tent, warmed by an army cooking-stove, lighted by three candles, and furnished with a long mess-table, was the "upper-room." One real chair, and several real boxes, chests, etc., furnished seats for twenty or more soldiers. A strange minister, fresh from home, had the meeting in charge. With no ado about agreeing on the tune and "pitching" it, some one began the service, when a hymn was called for, by striking up the words, —

"Nearer, my God, to thee."

Then the minister prayed; and before he could find his passage for reading, they started off with

"My days are gliding swiftly by,"

singing two stanzas. Then was read the account of the blind beggar Bartimeus, and how Jesus healed him, and how he followed the Master afterward. A few words were spoken, showing how poor our estate is by nature, sitting by the way-side of life, and how blind we are to our own good and God's glory, till we call on Jesus. Then somebody began to sing, —

"I love to steal awhile away,"

and almost all joined, singing but one verse. This was followed by a prayer, short and fervent. Then came an exhortation from a weather-worn soldier of the Cross and the government.

"Jesus, lover of my soul,"

next filled the tent and died away on the hill-side and among the pines in which the regiment has so charming a location.

Here one rose simply to testify, as he said, that he loved Jesus. He did not use five sentences, but it was all testimony. Then came a prayer for loved ones at home, the family, the church, the Sabbath school and prayer-meeting; and so still were all, that you would have supposed the praying man to be alone in the tent. The voice trembled somewhat, and if we wiped away a tear or two when he said amen, we were not ashamed to be seen doing it, for some others did so. Our thoughts went home also,—how could we help the tear?

And then, as if some of them in the chances of battle might miss the earthly home, a verse was sung beginning,

"Sweet fields beyond the swelling flood."

Next followed a practical talk about following Christ in the army. The good ideas were briefly, bluntly put, and full of the love of the Lord Jesus. Then a stanza went swelling out among the pines again:—

"Come we that love the Lord."

An exhortation was now addressed to any who had not enlisted under the Captain of our Salvation, and it was pressed home by the sweet words and, then, familiar air,—

"O happy day that fixed my choice."

Now one kneels down on the clay floor, and prays in the first person singular. It was a short broken prayer, probably by the brother who, they said, had lately learned to pray, and in that tent. We have all heard such prayers, and none ever affected us so much. An exhortation followed by a sailor on the difficulties of being a Christian in the army. He showed how they tried to do that at sea, and illustrated it by an incident.

Then came the hymn,—

"Thus far the Lord hath led me on."

The minister here remarked that if we would follow Christ successfully, we must keep in the ranks, and own to everybody at proper times, that Christ is our Captain. Following him by side-marches and obscure paths exposes us to the lurking enemy.

Now the hour was almost gone and so followed the doxology —
"Praise God from whom all blessings flow,"
and the benediction.

We thought it worth a trip to the Army of the Potomac to learn from the soldiers how to have a good prayer-meeting. No one was called on to pray or speak, and no hymn was given out. No one said he had nothing to say, and then talked long enough to prove it. No one excused his inability to "edify." No one waited to be called on; no time was lost by delay, and the entire meeting was less than an hour.

We shall always remember that prayer-meeting in the Massachusetts Twenty-second.

V. A STARLESS CROWN.

A private letter from Rev. Dr. Spaulding of Newburyport, Mass., written at Baton Rouge, mentions a rare instance of the union of patriotic zeal and tender religious sensibility: —

Yesterday Dr. Dolson told me that a man in the General Hospital greatly desired to see a chaplain, and accordingly I went to see him. When the nurse had put aside the mosquito netting, the patient began to converse with me very freely, speaking of his home in Hopkinton, N. H., where he had a wife and two children. He had once been a member of a Freewill Baptist Church in that vicinity.

He asked me if I thought it possible that his great desire would be gratified before he died. I told him I could hardly judge, without knowing what it was. "Oh," said he, "I want to be the instrument of the conversion of one soul. I cannot die and wear a starless crown, — a *starless crown!*" There was a depth of earnestness in his expression and manner very affecting, and the whole fear of the man in dying was, not that he was an unforgiven sinner, not that he should fail of heaven, not that his friends would not come to Jesus, but that he should wear a starless crown.

VI. BAPTISM IN THE MOUNTAINS.

On Tuesday of last week, says the editor of the "Christian Advocate," we had a call from Rev. Joseph Cotton, of the southeastern Indiana Conference, now chaplain of the Thirteenth Indiana Regiment. He was on his way from Indiana to his post at Huttonsville, Western Virginia. In an hour's conversation he detailed to us a chapter of stirring camp-life incidents. After one of the severest battles recently had there, and while the men of his regiment were exulting over their victory, a young man, a private who had participated in the fight, came to him, and said that he wished to talk with him on a subject the most important to him in the world — that relating to his soul and its salvation. "The tears," said the chaplain, "were in his eyes, and his lips were trembling with emotion. I knew he was in earnest. We immediately retired to a secluded valley in the woods, and I prayed with him and for him, and he prayed for himself, with great propriety and fervor. Shortly afterward, during another interview which we had together, light broke upon his darkness. The penitent felt that the burden of guilt unforgiven was gone, that he had found the peace which comes from faith in the Redeemer; and, wishing to declare his attachment to Christ, he asked to be baptized by immersion. I told his captain," said the brother; "and he, though a wicked fellow, assented to my request of having us pass the lines to a convenient place in a river close at hand, where the ordinance could be administered."

"And may not I and my men go along?" inquired the captain.

"Certainly," said Chaplain Cotton, and at a short notice they went. The scene was a most solemn one, and, as the baptism was completed, there was not a dry eye amongst all the men of the company. "That man has courage to go anywhere or do anything that is right," said a bystander; "and a regiment composed of men like him would be, like Havelock's Highlanders, invincible to all opposition."

VII. THE LOG CHURCH.

The account which follows is from the Rev. Mr. Alvord, whose self-denying labors for the soldier have so endeared his name to the hearts of all good people. The incident occurred in Virginia, during the campaign under General Burnside. It was a communication sent to one of the publications of the American Tract Society.

There are no chapel tents now, and everything has to be done usually in the open air, where but two or three can be gathered together. The chaplains and other Christian men are not inclined to spend much time in erecting any permanent buildings, as the army is constantly liable to move. But certain boys of the New York Twenty-fourth (who have no chaplain), determined that they would have a better place for their meetings. They had been held hitherto, as one of them said, by the side of a stump. Two of them especially, although only privates, seemed almost inspired on the subject. They obtained permission of the colonel to build a cabin of logs. These had to be drawn a mile, trimmed, framed, and piled up. The dimensions were to be sixteen by thirty-two feet, sufficiently large to hold a hundred and sixty persons.

The first logs were heavy, and hardly any one helped them. Their plan at first was not very definite. They would lay down a log, and then look and plan by the eye. Another log was then wearily drawn and placed on the other. To most of their comrades, the affair gave occasion only for jests and merriment. "Are you to have it finished before the world ends?" they asked. "Are you fixing up to leave?" "How does your saloon get on?" Even the more serious felt pity for them, rather than sympathy. There was already an order out to move. "What is the use?" "Who wants meetings now?" But these two Christian soldiers (S. and L.) toiled on like Noah amidst the scoffs of the multitude. The edifice slowly rose; volunteers lent a hand. The Christian men of the regiment, forty or fifty in all, became interested; some of them at length aided in the work. The structure reached at last a proper height; and a roof of brush first, and then of patched ponchos having been put on, the meeting began, — or rather they *began* when it was only an open pen. In a few days, Burnside's advance took place, and the regiment left for the field.

In their absence, plunderers stripped the cabin, and carried off a portion of its material; but on the return of our troops, the same busy hands and hearts of faith were again at work. A sutler gave them the old canvas cover of his large tent, which he was about to cut up to serve as a shelter for his horses, and lo, it precisely fitted the roof of the meeting-house, — not an inch to spare! This was drawn over the neat rafters and lashed at the edges, making a transparency by day, and reflecting the light most pleasantly by night. The boys, when they saw this, thought it almost a miracle; and were hardly less pleased when the door, with its latch and string, was fitted so nicely in its place. But they had no lock as yet to preserve the interior of their house from depredations, and when, having inquired and sent everywhere for one in vain, they were out for their last load of poles for benches, they had to tell me how, just upon their pathside in the forest, a lock was found with a key in it, all ready to be fitted to their door! I thought myself it was a little strange, that far out here in Virginia, at such a time, an article of this description, by just these eyes, should have been discovered. But I concluded that the God who had helped these feeble workmen to build his house could help them finish it.

Well, there it stands, a monument to his glory, and the credit of their perseverance. You should have seen their eyes shine, as, here in my tent for tracts, they were one day giving me its history, and you should have been with us last evening. The little pulpit from which I spoke is made of empty box boards. Two chandeliers hang suspended from the ridgepole of cross sticks, wreathed with ivy, and in the socketed ends are four adamant candles, each burning brilliantly. Festoons of ivy and 'dead men's fingers' (a species of woodbine called by this name) are looped gracefully along the sides of the room, and in the centre, stretching from chandelier to chandelier; — the effect not slightly increased by the contrast of the deep green of the rich vegetation with the fine brown bark of the pine logs, and of the white canvas above, striped and interlaced with the rafters. Below, a dense pack of soldiers in the Avengers'[1]

[1] So called in memory of Colonel Ellsworth, who was killed at Alexandria.

uniform sat crouching upon the pole seats, beneath which was a carpet of evergreen sprays;—all silent, uncovered, respectful. As the service opened, you could have heard a pin fall. There was nothing here to make a noise. Pew-doors, psalm-books, rustling silks, or groined arches, reverberating the slightest sound of hand or footfall, there were none. Only the click of that wooden latch and a gliding figure, like a stealthy vidette, creeping in among the common mass, indicated the late comer. The song went up from the deep voices of men,—do you know the effect?— and before our service closed, tears rolled down from the faces of hardy warriors. To be brief, every evening of the week, this house is now filled with men brought together, four times out of seven for religious objects. When they can have no preaching, the soldiers themselves meet for prayer.

I stole in one evening lately, when they were at these devotions. Prayer after prayer successively was offered in earnest, humblest tones, before rising from their knees; those not worshippers were intent on the scene. Officers were present and took part in the service, and seldom have I seen such manifest tokens that God is about to appear in power. No opposition is shown. The whole regiment look upon the house now as a matter of pride; they encourage all the meetings.

The house is attractive to visitors, and when not used for religious purposes is occupied for lyceum debates, musical concerts, and the like. It is easy to imagine how much these two Christian laborers enjoy the success of their work. One of them said to me, " We have been paid for all our labor a thousand times over."

VIII. THE BLIND SOLDIER.

Among the men at the New England Rooms, in New York, (says a visitor to that place,) is one from Michigan. He was shot in the head at Malvern Hill, and the optic nerve was carried away, so that he has become stone-blind. He is now well, in his general health, but will never see again. He is one of the happiest men in the land. He is a person of cheerful, but open and decided piety. "Happy as the day is long," has its literal and expressive meaning as applied to him. It is delightful to listen to him as he speaks of what he did for the old flag while he could see, and still more to observe how he strives to be useful still since his injury, in such ways as he can. He feels his way from couch to couch, drops, as he moves along, fitting words of sympathy and counsel, cheers up the despondent, and makes the heart glad. Those connected with the rooms assure me, (says this visitor,) that the tone of his happy speech, and pious resignation, impress all who have an opportunity to see and hear him.

IX. THE SILENT PRAYER.

An officer reports, that a little drummer-boy was on board one of the transport ships which conveyed his regiment to Fortress Monroe. At the close of the first day, just at evening, the little fellow, overcome by the fatigues of the day, laid himself down upon the deck, and fell asleep. The night was chilly and the dews were falling. The colonel came along and shook him by the shoulder, and told him he would take cold if he continued to lie there, and advised him to go below and go to his rest for the night. As he was getting up, his Bible fell out of his pocket upon the deck. He picked it up and replaced it. Some kind hand, perhaps a mother or a Sunday-school teacher had given him that Bible.

He went below, and prepared himself for his bed. When ready, he kneeled down, and, though many loud-talking men were standing about, put his hands together in the attitude of prayer, and poured out his heart silently to God. He heeded not the noise around him. In a moment all was hushed. The company, as if overawed by the conduct of the boy, reverently stood silent until he had finished his prayer. It was one of the scenes of earth on which angels pause to look down with interest.

X. FOOTE'S FAREWELL TO HIS SAILORS.

This gallant officer, who had long been suffering from the effect of a wound, was obliged at length to seek a temporary release from his command. The parting from his men and the introduction to them of his successor took place on board the Benton, the flag-ship of the Mississippi flotilla, in May, 1862. The remarks which he made on that occasion (we profess to give only the general tenor of them) present him to us as a man of the sternest loyalty, and yet able, by his courtesy and Christian mildness, to bind to himself, as "with hooks of steel," the hearts of those who shared the perils and honors of his naval achievements. He said, —

"Officers and men : It has now become my painful duty to inform you that I am about to leave you, though I trust only for a short time. Commodore Davis, who is here before you, has been appointed my successor, and is the man whom I proposed to the government as the one above all others best fitted to relieve me of my charge. He has talent, and scientific as well as naval ability, and, as he has borne hitherto an unsullied name, will, I doubt not, maintain it in future."

Turning then to Mr. Davis, and pointing to the officers around him, he said, "These gallant officers, — men of the East, West, North, South, and of foreign climes, — who now stand before you, are men on whom you can depend in any emergency. I have tried them, one and all, and know what I say; and although they may never receive the reward due to their gallant and manly bearing, we have, at least, the proud satisfaction of knowing that we have done our duty. The improvising of a squadron like this without means at all adequate to the work has been our greatest labor; it has cost more effort than our signal victories when we have met the enemy face to face. Providence has seen fit to afflict me in this hour of our triumph, just as the great work begins to be crowned with success. But I trust I may regain my failing strength in body and mind, and be enabled to rejoin you. The painful duty is now over. I wish I was able to introduce you singly to each officer; but (affected to tears as he spoke) I am too weak."

He attempted to perform that courtesy, but could not proceed. Captain Phelps relieved him by mentioning the officers by name to Commodore Davis. Pointing then to the seamen, the flag-officer continued: "These men, too, you can depend upon in any emergency. If they have any fault, they are but too anxious to go into a fight; they will never surrender to the enemy. Unless you hold them back, they will be ahead of you in reaching the post of danger. They can run faster than I can, you see," casting his eyes to his wounded foot. "Officers and men, one and all, farewell."

At the close of these remarks, the brave old commodore was assisted on board of the steam-packet De Soto, bound for Cincinnati, the officers and crew of the Benton gazing with tender sympathy toward him, as if he had been to each one of them his best and nearest friend. Some minutes were occupied in starting, and the commodore was placed in a chair on the upper deck of the De Soto. As he looked at the Benton, says an eye-witness, and saw the many familiar faces that fixed their kind eyes upon him so earnestly, his trembling hand frequently sought his quivering lip, and it was evident that he was struggling hard to control his feelings. But nature prevailed, and the brave officer covered his wan face with a fan which he held, to protect himself against the heat, and wept like a child. As the steamer left the flag-ship, three loud, long, and ringing cheers were given by the crew. The commodore stood up on his crutches as the De Soto moved up the broad Mississippi, and with tremulous voice said, "God bless you all! Heaven knows how hard it is for me to leave you! Better and braver men than you never trod a deck. I would much rather stay with you and die with you than go away. But my duty to my country compels me to yield to stronger, though I hope not more willing, hands. God bless you, my brave men, — God bless you all!"

There was hardly one on the deck whose eyes were not filled with tears while the commodore spoke, and old tars that had braved the frozen horrors of the Northern seas and the plagues of the tropics, that had doubled the Horn again and again, and sailed under the equator, and touched at every prominent land-point on the globe, stood in the hot sun, with hotter tears upon their cheeks, melted into tenderness at the thought of parting from their brave old commander, whom they had learned to love so well.

At Hickman, Madison, Cairo, and other places, the citizens crowded down to the wharves to cheer the gallant commodore on his way.[1]

XI. THE SOLDIER'S GREATEST FEAR.

A scene with which every hamlet and neighborhood in the land are now sadly familiar summoned us to the old church. A coffin covered with the stars and stripes, in front of the pulpit, contained all that remained on earth of one whom we had known and loved. He was a young man whose noble traits of character had drawn to him many hearts. Only two years before, he had stood in this very aisle, making a public profession of the religion of Jesus.

A Christian can best afford to be a fearless soldier, for he can look danger and death in the face. William, the subject of this notice, did so. He had been in many battles. He always stood his ground like a true hero. But there was one thing of which this youth, whom the last conqueror only had vanquished, *was* afraid. He was afraid he should disgrace his Christian profession by yielding to temptation in an unhappy moment. The burden of his requests as he wrote to his parents, was, "Pray for me;

---

[1] It was not the will of Providence that this brave and good man should fulfil the hope expressed by him, of rejoining the companions in arms to whom he addressed this farewell. He repaired to Washington, and for more than a year, by his advice and coöperation, rendered invaluable aid to the naval department, with the affairs of which he was so thoroughly conversant. But he was needed for more active service, and at the earliest moment of apparent convalescence, was appointed commander of the fleet engaged in the attack on Fort Sumter and Charleston. The most important results were hoped for from his unquestioned skill and bravery. He had reached New York on his way to the South, when suddenly he was taken ill there, and died on the 26th of June, 1863.

Hardly any one has appeared on the stage of action during the war more distinguished for the highest qualities of the patriot, hero, and Christian, than Admiral Foote.

my temptations are many. Pray for me that I may overcome."

But William's days were numbered. He was attacked by a fatal disease, and borne as far as Rhode Island, where his father, who belonged to Massachusetts, was summoned to come to him. He hastened to the expected place of interview. Here, as the father looked round on a company of sick and wounded soldiers, he inquired, with searching gaze, " Where is William ? "

" That is my name," answered a feeble voice.

Who shall attempt to describe that last fond meeting between father and son ? At length the father found voice to say, " I see, my son, how it is as to the body ; but how as to the temptations about which you wrote to us ? Have you been able to overcome ? "

" Oh, yes, father, I have not put the intoxicating cup to my lips once ; I have fallen into no open sin since I left home."

As he sleeps beneath the flag he loved and defended, we seem to hear a voice from heaven, saying, " Blessed are the dead who die in the Lord ; for they rest from their labors, and their works do follow them." "To him that overcometh will I grant to sit with me in my throne, even as I also overcame, and am set down with my Father in his throne."

XII. SORROW IN THE HOMESTEAD.

I was called last week, (writes one of the army chaplains, Rev. Mr. Bass,) to bury a young man aged about twenty-one years, George Van Schaick, son of Rev. Mr. Van Schaick, of Unadilla, N. Y. He was a noble youth. In the tent, in the camp, in his duties, or recreations, he demeaned himself as a Christian. He was a friend to his chaplain, and many were the pleasant hours we have spent together in friendly conversation and social worship. He helped to sustain and give character to the nightly meetings at the chaplain's tent. Though he shrank from no duty, he was modest and unassuming in his manners. I loved him, delighted to see his open, cheerful countenance, and to hear his voice in prayer and praise in our solemn assemblies. He was sick but one short week. I sat at his bedside, day after day, to hear his words of confiding trust in the wisdom and mercy of his God. Death to him had no sting; the grave had lost its power. It is true his thoughts turned often to the old homestead, to his aged parents, his sisters, and brothers, and friends; but Jesus, the love of the Saviour, and the consolations of his rich grace, were chief in his thoughts and on his tongue. The day before his death, he expressed a wish that I should write to his father for him. "Tell him," said he, "I have not forgotten his counsels and prayers, and my own dedication to God. Tell him I feel prepared for any event;—if I live, I will glorify God on earth, and if I die, I will praise him in heaven." So the pastor's son breathed his last amid sorrowing friends, on Friday, at four o'clock, A. M., with faith and joy steadfast to the end.

But the domain of "tearful" war extends beyond the camp and the battle-field. Heaven gained in this instance a happy spirit, but there was sorrow in the homestead. The pain and anguish of these days are felt by survivors, as well as by those who suffer in hospitals, or yield up their lives amid the shock of arms. Thousands of bereaved households, at this moment, know the meaning of the poet's words:—

> "Not on the tented field,
>   O terror-fronted War!
> Not on the battle-field,
>   All thy bleeding victims are.

" But in the lowly homes
　　Where sorrow broods like death,
　　And fast the mother's sobs
　　Rise with each quick-drawn breath, —

" As sick with pining pain
　　She moves from room to room,
　　As each familiar sight
　　Pierces her soul like doom: —

" A coat upon the wall, —
　　Some book he loved to read, —
　　O cruel, cruel War!
　　Here, too, thy victims bleed.

" To see that fair young form
　　Crushed by the war-horse tread,
　　The dear and bleeding form
　　Stretched by the piled-up dead—

" That dimmed eye, fainting close—
　　And she may not be nigh!
　　'Tis mothers die — O God!
　　'Tis but we mothers die."

XIII. LAST INTERVIEW OF THE HEROES.

While at Gettysburg, (says a visitor to that place,) I learned the following incident from the lips of Professor Stoever. At the close of the bloody battles of the second and third of July, while thousands of the soldiers were lying wounded side by side, and before even the officers could seek out and speak to their bleeding and dying friends, the command came to pursue the flying Confederates. Major General Howard, at the head of the Eleventh Army Corps (who has been called the Havelock of the American army), hastened to the bedside of Captain Griffeth of his staff, between whom and the general a strong personal attachment existed, to take his last farewell. He closed the door, and after a brief interchange of sympathies, the general took his New Testament and read to him the fourteenth chapter of John. The consolatory words have been often heard at the bed of the dying, giving strength to the soul for the last conflict: "Let not your heart be troubled: ye believe in God, believe also in me. In my Father's house are many mansions: if it were not so, I would have told you; I go to prepare a place for you. And if I go and prepare a place for you, I will come again, and receive you unto myself; that where I am, there ye may be also."

The general then knelt in prayer, and commended his wounded friend to the compassionate God and Father of all those who trust in Him, and, rising from his knees, clasped him in one long, fond, weeping embrace. Thus the heroes parted. One went to pursue the Rebels against his government. The other died, in a few days, in perfect peace, cordially acquiescing in God's will, and firmly relying on the merits of his Saviour.

XIV. JESUS WILL TAKE ME HOME.

When Colonel Herman Canfield was wounded at the battle of Pittsburg Landing, knowing that his wound would be fatal, he expressed a wish to his young brother-in-law that he might be taken to his home and family. But as the battle raged, the enemy pressed upon them, so that they were in momentary fear of being made prisoners. The surgeon, chaplain, and others who were looking after the wounded, were taken and borne away. Strange as it may appear, the two relatives were left unmolested. Alone and in such a condition, the moment was one of anxiety and of trial to them both. His brother-in-law was not able, without aid, to convey him to a place of safety; and he expressed a fear that he should not be able to comply with his request. To this apprehension, the colonel calmly replied, "Never mind, Charley, Jesus will take me home."

Oh! what childlike trust, what Christian faith, is there expressed! Having lived near to God, and long trusted in his sure promises, he had no doubts now. He knew that the Lord of hosts was present on the battle-field as well as in the peaceful home. As he lay there, with his life-blood ebbing from a ghastly wound in his lungs, he testified of the goodness of God, and showed with what fearlessness a Christian may yield his soul to him who gave it.

At last assistance arrived, and the wounded man was borne on a stretcher through low, marshy defiles, and over rough, pathless woodland, toward the Tennessee. At night they encamped upon its bank. It was the last night he passed upon earth; a dark and fearful one it was to his companions. A storm raged about them. The very elements seemed pouring forth their sad requiems for the dying and the dead. During the vivid flashes of lightning, they had glimpses of the agonized features of their loved commander. And many were their anxious inquiries; but he assured them that though his physical sufferings were great, his soul was at peace with God, and he knew he soon would be at rest. Doubtless, he caught glimpses of that brighter world where darkness and death cannot enter because God is the light and life thereof. What that brave soldier and true Christian suffered during that night of agony, none but God can know. He did not murmur at his fate, and thought not his life too great a sacrifice for the cause in which he fell.

The following day he was removed to a hospital ship, where his wounds were carefully dressed. But he gradually grew weaker until evening; when, leaving tender messages for his loved wife and children, he calmly committed his soul to God, and Jesus took him home.

XV. THE STORY OF NOLAN.

The Rev. Dr. Marks, after one of the battles on the Peninsula, in which some of our men were captured, gave himself up as a prisoner to the rebels, that he might not be separated from those over whom he watched as a religious guide. On one occasion, he went to the Brackett House, on the battle-field, where were four hundred and fifty of our wounded men. The flag of the country was printed on one of the publications which he was distributing; and he mentions that he often saw those mutilated men lift it to their lips, and kiss the emblem of our nationality, undeterred by the presence and taunts of the enemy.

There was one remarkable man in that group of sufferers whose story, as recounted by this gentleman, deserves to be told from one age to another. His name was Nolan. His right leg had been cut off by a cannon-shot, and he was lying in the midst of fifty or sixty men in one of the rooms.

As I came up to him, I saw that his face was beaming with smiles, and, from his appearance, I could not have supposed for a moment that there was a single pang of pain in that body. I asked him how he had endured his suffering. He said, "I was three days and three nights out on the battle-field, and all that time heard the whisperings of angels, and I only could look up to the stars and think every one of them sang to me. The question of my own personal safety, as a believer in Christ, was settled six years ago; and now I want that all my friends should feel as I do." And then there would burst forth from his lips that sweet song,—

"Jesus, my God, I know his name,
His name is all my trust;
Nor will he put my soul to shame,
Nor let my hope be lost."

And this man, even in the midnight hour, would be singing, and comforting those poor men around him. Subsequently he was carried to Richmond, a prisoner. I followed my charge to that city. And as I was one day passing through the great hall of the prison, where some four hundred men were lying, in their wounds and agony, covering every inch of the floor, as I stepped over one lacerated limb and another, and looked down into their burning eyes, I heard that song again, sweeter and sweeter, and more and more distinct. At length I found my way to the singer, and it was the same man, still singing, —

"Jesus, my God, I know his name."

And so he comforted the hundreds of men about him, to whom he could not go, and silenced their murmurs and stilled their groans, by this hymn.

Afterward it was thought by the physician that he must die, and it was told to Nolan.

I said to him, "It is very probable that to-day you will be called to appear before God, and stand with the great Father before the divine throne."

"Blessed be God!" he said. "I shall be detailed from the battle-field to go up and be with Jesus forever; detailed to dwell in the world of light and glory; detailed to be wounded and to bleed and to die no more. But," he continued, "doctor, I am not going to die to-day. I feel that I shall live to go away from this place."

And through that hour of great danger the man did live by the joy of his soul, and afterward was carried to Fortress Monroe. I heard from a soldier afterward, that there he was still singing as before, and that subsequently he was removed thence to Washington, and there died, and went up unto the bosom of his Saviour.

XVI. THE DYING HAND ON THE BIBLE.

On the same battle-field, (says this devoted chaplain,) I remember that as I went to a spot where many of our wounded soldiers were lying, I came to the side of a man who was just dying. I folded his hands together, and told him to look up to the Lamb of God that taketh away the sin of the world, and before I had done praying he was gone. I stooped down and lifted up a Bible that he held in his hand, when he died, that I might find the name of the man who had departed, and might bear to his friends the testimony that his hand, as he relinquished his hold on life, was resting on the Word of God.

A soldier by his side said, "Sir, do not take the Bible away. The print is plainer than my own, and I wish to read it. My friend here and myself read the Bible together through the long hours of the night. We prayed together, and now he has only gone a step before me into the good kingdom. I shall soon be there. I want to read it until my eyes become too dim to see any more." I said to him that I did not wish to take away the Bible. I found that this man was likewise sustained by a sense of the Saviour's presence. He felt that it was nothing — yes, nothing — to die, supported as he was by the peace and joy of conscious reconciliation to God.

XVII. SUDDENLY AT REST.

One of the Second Regiment of the Rhode Island Volunteers, while he was resting for a moment during a lull in the battle of Bull Run, was seen to take a Testament from his pocket. He was in the act of reading it as a ball struck him, and he fell dead. He was a man of established character as a Christian. His life testified that he was mindful of the charge, "Watch, for ye know not what hour your Lord doth come." He was called away at the moment his eye rested on the promise made to those who "fight a good fight, who have kept the faith." In a moment, in the twinkling of an eye, he was at rest in heaven. He was one of those for whom the Master had in reserve some better thing.

XVIII. SUCH ARE MINISTERING SPIRITS.

Perhaps in no sphere of effort relating to the War have more self-denial and true benevolence been manifested than in the hospital labors performed by Christian women, who have devoted themselves in all parts of the land to the care of our wounded, sick, and dying soldiers. A volume should be written to preserve the remembrance of such services. The following sketch, in the Chicago New Covenant, illustrates the spirit of this class of laborers.

I cannot, says the writer, close this letter from Cairo without a passing word in regard to one whose name is mentioned by thousands of our soldiers with gratitude and blessing. Miss Mary Safford is a resident of this town, whose life, since the beginning of the war, has been devoted to the amelioration of the soldier's lot and his comfort in the hospital. She is a young lady, *petite* in figure, unpretending, but highly cultivated, by no means officious, and so wholly unconscious of her excellences and the great work that she is achieving that I fear this public allusion to her may pain her modest nature. Her sweet, young face, full of benevolence, her pleasant voice and winning manner, install her in every one's heart directly; and the more one sees of her, the more they admire her great soul and her noble nature. Not a day elapses but she is found in the hospitals, unless indeed she is absent on an errand of mercy up the Tennessee, or to the hospitals in Kentucky.

Every sick and wounded soldier in Cairo knows and loves her, and, as she enters the ward, every pale face brightens at her approach. As she passes along, she inquires of each one how he has passed the night, if he is well supplied with books or tracts, and if there is anything she can do for him. All tell her their story frankly,— the man old enough to be her father, and the boy of fifteen, who should be out of the army and at home with his mother.

For one, she must write a letter to his friends at home; she must sit down and read at the cot of another; must procure, if the doctor will allow it, this or that article of food for a third; must soothe and encourage a fourth, who desponds and is ready to give up his hold on life; must pray for a fifth, who is afraid to die, and wrestle with him till light shines through the dark valley;— and so on, varied as may be the personal or spiritual wants of the sufferers.

Doctors, nurses, medical directors, and army officers, are all her true friends; and so judicious and trustworthy is she, that the Chicago Sanitary Commission have given her *carte blanche* to draw on their stores at Cairo for anything she may need in her errands of mercy. She is performing a noble work, and that too in the most quiet and unconscious manner.

XIX. THE FIRST SABBATH IN CAMP.

The soldiers sent to Ship Island, at the mouth of the Mississippi, were chiefly from New England. They constituted the nucleus of the force, which, after a few months, bombarded the forts at the entrance of that river, and captured the city of New Orleans.

On the first Sunday after the landing of the troops, the ordinary military labor was intermitted, and the day observed, as far as possible, in a religious manner. The Ninth Connecticut Regiment, under Colonel Cahil, consisted largely of Catholics, and mass was celebrated in the camp on the forenoon of this first Sabbath. The service was attended by many of the sailors and marines from the fort, and from vessels in the harbor.

In the afternoon, the Twenty-sixth Regiment gathered *en masse* in front of their quarters, when Colonel Jones, taking a sand hillock for a pulpit, performed divine service. After the reading of selections of Scripture, a choir, selected from the rank and file of the regiment, sang a hymn, and the band played an appropriate piece. Colonel Jones, in the absence of the chaplain, Rev. Mr. Babbage, then rose and addressed the men. He said he had never approached a duty when he felt so embarrassed as then. He regretted that he must take the place of one so much more worthy than himself. They had been accustomed to observe the Sabbath at home; they needed its salutary influences there, and he knew of no better means for securing them than such a service. He warned them of their dangers, urged upon them their duties, and assured them that if they obeyed the truth, without regarding the channel through which it might come to them, they would be benefited and saved by it.

As an accompaniment to the solemn service, and reminding us, says the narrator, that we are in a state of war, the gunboat "New London," across the sound, was engaging the enemy, and the booming of cannon was mingled with the notes of prayer and praise. It seemed a fitting inauguration of the great enterprise. The scene was impressive. The speaker spoke to the hearts of the listeners. The allusion to those distant homes in New England brought tears to eyes not accustomed to weep.

CHAPTER III.

COURAGE PROMOTED BY TRUST IN GOD.

I. A MESSAGE FROM THE BIBLE.

IN the course of the first year of the present war, the rebels made an attack upon one of our regiments doing picket duty on the Maryland side of the Potomac. There were three houses standing upon the Virginia shore which afforded shelter to the enemy, and it became necessary to have them removed. The colonel tried the effect of shelling them, but, owing to the short range of his guns and the great distance, could not demolish them. The only thing accomplished by this was driving the enemy out of them to the shelter of the woods beyond.

The colonel then asked for volunteers to cross the river and burn the buildings. Only two men came forward, one a private, the other an orderly sergeant. The colonel gave the command to the sergeant, and told him to select as many men as he needed and go. Selecting three men from his own company to manage the boat and assist him, the brave fellows departed on their perilous mission. Ere they reached the middle of the stream, they were greeted with a shower of bullets. Volley followed volley, each passing over their heads without touching a man. As they neared the shore, the house immediately in front of them, which was a large brick one, offered them shelter for landing; and it was not many minutes after ere the smoke issuing from the roof showed their work was accomplished there. The next house was soon in flames also; but the third stood some distance from the river; to get to it they must cross a ploughed field directly under the fire of the musketry. Here, as in crossing the river, they were made the target for the enemy's bullets. Strange to say, this "forlorn hope" returned uninjured, and were received with enthusiastic cheers from their brave comrades.

The young sergeant, upon being complimented upon his courage, and interrogated as to the source of it, replied, "It is not in me; give God the glory. When I started, I committed my beloved wife and child to his fatherly care, should I never return. I breathed a prayer for myself and the little band with me. I went further. I entreated that we might all return in safety; and as I stepped from that boat, these words of the ninety-first Psalm came forcibly to my mind: 'A thousand shall fall at thy side, and ten thousand at thy right hand; but it shall not come nigh thee. Only with thine eyes shalt thou behold and see the reward of the wicked. Because thou hast made the Lord, which is my refuge, even the Most High, thy habitation, there shall no evil befall thee, neither shall any plague come nigh thy dwelling.' I received it as an answer to my prayer; and though we could hear the bullets whizzing by, almost touching us, I felt no more fear of them than if they had been hailstones."

II. A WORD SPOKEN IN SEASON.

It is related that a colonel in the army went to Governor Buckingham, of the State of Connecticut, and asked him to appoint a godly man, who cared for the souls of men, as chaplain for his regiment. He said he had observed that soldiers who were Christians were more reliable than those who were not; that in the day of battle they were more courageous. The governor told him he would see to it that he had the services of such a chaplain. After this promise the governor said, "Colonel, you manifest a great interest in the religious welfare of your soldiers. This is commendable; but have you no concern for the salvation of your own soul?" This question, so unexpectedly put to him, gave a new turn to his thoughts. He was led to see his own neglect of religion, and his inconsistency, as he had never seen them before, and to feel that the gospel might have claims on himself as well as on others. On returning to his command, he sought the counsel of a Christian friend, and at length came to a settled faith in the Redeemer.

Not long after this result, occurred the bloody battle of Roanoke,[1] and Colonel Russel, the officer referred to, was among the dead. He fell at the head of the brave troops whom he had been anxious to make braver by planting the fear of God in their hearts. He himself acknowledged to an acquaintance that those few, faithful words of the governor were the means of arousing his conscience, and leading him to seek in earnest God's favor. The timely admonition, as we have reason to believe, was the Spirit's instrumentality for preparing him for his sudden departure.

III. MARCH OF THE NEW YORK SEVENTH TO WASHINGTON.

A member of the New York Seventh Regiment informs us how they spent the first Sabbath, on their memorable journey to Washington. This regiment was the first that left the city or State of New York, in response to the summons of the President, after the fall of Fort Sumter.

---
[1] Which was fought under General Burnside, February 8, 1862.

The march occupied several days. The railroad, on the direct route between Philadelphia and Baltimore, had been destroyed by the rebels. Our men were obliged to go by the way of Annapolis, and to rebuild those portions of the road as they proceeded, where the rails had been torn up, in order to prevent the arrival of succor in time to save the Capital.

On the Sabbath, at sunrise, says our informant, the reveille beat, and blankets, guns, knapsacks, — everything was stowed away, and arrangements made to have service at half-past ten o'clock. An order was hardly necessary for this purpose, for all seemed to vie with each other to keep holy the Sabbath-day. Soon after breakfast, some three hundred had gathered on the saloon-deck, and were singing hymns appropriate to the occasion, such as "Guide me, O thou great Jehovah," "When I can read my title clear," and "On Jordan's stormy banks I stand." At half-past ten the services commenced, conducted by the chaplain, Rev. Dr. Weston. Nearly every member had brought with him a prayer-book or a Testament, and all who were near enough to follow the exercise had them in use at this time. It is but truth to say that the Sabbath was passed as every Sabbath should be, — in honoring God.

Just as we left Annapolis, most of the boys, at a temporary halt, took out their Testaments and read a chapter; and I saw a number go aside to offer a prayer that God would be with us on our eventful journey. I myself was among the number. When I returned, I opened my Bible casually at the forty-sixth Psalm, which the boys of Company A requested me to read aloud. It was certainly very appropriate.

Under the circumstances in which we were placed, such passages as these seemed to be written truly for our use and learning: — "God is our refuge and strength; a very present help in trouble. Therefore will not we fear, though the earth be removed, and though the mountains be carried into the midst of the sea. The Lord of Hosts is with us; the God of Jacob is our refuge. Be still, and know that I am God; I will be exalted among the heathen, I will be exalted in the earth; the Lord of Hosts is with us; the God of Jacob is our refuge."

Such is the spirit in which many of the volunteers have gone forth to defend their country. The men who march by prayer are not the men to retreat in the day of battle, through cowardice, or a feeble sense of their responsibility, as the champions of law and liberty.

IV. THE DYING SOLDIER'S PRAYER FOR THE PRESIDENT.

In the summer of 1862, a private named Scott, who belonged to the Third Vermont Regiment, was court-martialled for sleeping on his post, near Chain Bridge, on the upper Potomac. He was convicted and sentenced to be shot. The decision was affirmed by the general, and the day fixed for his execution. The culprit, who had more than ordinary strength of character, did not beg for pardon or complain, but was willing to meet his fate.

The appointed day drew near. The necessity of war required an example, and this case was thought to be an aggravated one. But the circumstances reached the ears of the President, and he was disposed to show mercy. He signed a pardon, and sent it to the camp, in the belief that he had done all that was necessary. Soon the last day itself arrived. Having heard nothing, the President began to fear lest the pardon had not reached its destination. The telegraph was put in requisition, but no answer was received. There was not a moment to lose. "Bring up my carriage," he ordered. The carriage came; the important state papers were laid aside, and, beneath the hot, broiling sun and over dusty roads, he rode to the camp, distant about ten miles, and ascertained for himself that the matter was safe. The pardon was not made known to the soldier, till he had already kneeled down upon his coffin, and the executioners with loaded muskets were awaiting the order to fire. None except a few officers knew that he was to be reprieved.

The President may have forgotten the occurrence, but the grateful soldier did not forget it. At the battle of Lee's Mills, near Yorktown, on the 16th of April, a division of the Vermont troops was ordered to cross a stream and attack a strong work of the insurgents on the other side. As the Third Vermont charged upon the rifle-pits here, they were met by a deadly volley from the rebels. The first man who fell was William Scott of company K, whose life the President's clemency had spared. Six bullets pierced his body. His comrades caught him up, from the ground, and as his life-blood ebbed away, he exclaimed. "Bear witness, I have proved myself not a coward, and am not afraid to die;" and, then, amid the groans of the dying, and the shouts of the enemy, with his last breath, he raised to heaven a prayer for the President.

He was interred in the presence of his regiment, in a little grove, about two miles in the rear of the rebel fort. The grave was dug in the centre of a group of holly and vines, with cherry-trees then in blossom on the outer circle. In turning up the earth, a skull and other bones, and several metal buttons were found, showing that this identical spot had been used in the Revolutionary War, for the burial of those who fell in like manner as martyrs for their country. The chaplain related the history of young Scott to the boys, as they stood with uncovered heads around the grave. Of the President's noble conduct he spoke in fitting terms of admiration.

The military offence of the brave soldier, was not without its mitigation. It was found that he had been on duty two nights in succession; had served voluntarily the second night for a sick comrade, and on the third had been overcome by sleep. Shortly before he enlisted, he had avowed himself a disciple of Christ, in Groton, his native town, and, according to good testimony, had lived a consistent life while in camp. It was his possession of the "hope which is as an anchor to the soul, sure and steadfast," that made him so willing to suffer the penalty of the law, and vanquished his fears of death at the last moment.[1]

V. A SCENE IN THE LOG CHURCH.

A scene which Mr. Alvord mentions as having taken place in the log-church[2] belongs to this class of our illustrations.

On a certain evening (he says), when we had met there for worship, I was surprised to see the colonel of the regiment enter, and seat himself among the boys on the rude benches. He buried his face in both his hands. The soldiers rose one after another, and spoke of their happy experience in the new life. They declared their purpose to serve God, and requested prayers that others would remember them, that they might not falter, but be strengthened for every trial of faith and courage before them. Erelong, the colonel, to my astonishment, sprang to his feet,— his figure tall, soldier-like, imposing. He

---

[1] I have added this statement respecting his religious character from an authentic source.
[2] See page 49.

folded his arms upon his broad chest, and began very deliberately to say to the soldiers, "I am here to-night where, as your military commander, I should be; and I am here especially to say to you two things to which I want you to listen. The first is, if I fall in the battle we are about to fight, I want you to remember me, fellow-soldiers, not as a gallant military officer, but as a humble, Christian man." It seems he had been a member of one of the churches in New York, but after joining the army had not made himself known as a decided follower of Christ. "I want you," said he (dwelling on the same thought), "if I should fall,[1] to remember me as a humble Christian. Do not talk of me as a gallant commander, but think of me and speak of me as having died a soldier of the cross. And then," he continued, "fellow-soldiers, there is another thing I want to testify to, and that is, that my men, whom I see here around me in this meeting, are the men whom I have never known to flinch in battle. My eye falls upon the bravest of my regiment to-night."

A rustle was heard through the cabin and a murmur from the boys, as he said this; for their hearts were strengthened by such testimony. And then, after a few more words, he said, "Let us pray;" and he poured out his soul to God for himself, for his fellow-officers, for his regiment, for his country, for the battle to come, and closed with a hearty "Amen!" to which response was made by all in the house.

[1] They were then on the eve of the battle of Fredericksburg in Virginia.

VI. PRAYER IN TIME OF BATTLE.

It is a common saying of the officers (adds Mr. Alvord), that as a class, the men who stand firmest when the battle rages are the Christian men. Many is the time I have talked with them about such scenes, and they have told me that their souls have stood firm in that hour of strife, and that they have been perfectly calm. I have had Christian generals tell me this. I have heard General Howard often say, that in the midst of the most terrific portion of the battle, when his heart for a moment quailed, he would pause and lift up his soul to God, and receive strength. "And," said he, "I have gone often through battles without a particle of fear. I have thought God sent me to defend my country. I believed it was a Christian duty to stand in the foremost of the fight, and why should I be afraid?"

General Howard, who makes this declaration concerning himself, has shared in nearly all the severest fighting in Virginia and Pennsylvania since the beginning of the war, and bears in his scarred frame marks of his valor, and of hair-breadth escapes from death. No one can surpass him in skill and daring; but his highest title is that of a Christian, which he has maintained without reproach or question in the camp, as well as elsewhere.

The voice of such a man deserves to be heard and regarded, when, as in the following order, he protests against a too common vice in the army. "I have noticed," he says, "with extreme pain, the use of profane oaths and language among the officers and men of my command. I need not remind any thinking man of the vulgarity and meanness of the practice, nor speak of it as a positive violation of God's law, but will simply appeal to the good sense and better feelings of the members of my command, and urge them, by all they hold dear, to abstain from insulting Him whose protection they need."

VII. HE WAS ONLY A PRIVATE.

But he was faithful in that sphere: — and every example is instructive, noble, according to the elevation of the aim that we strive to reach, the use made by us of the opportunities at our command, the manner in which the impulses of conscience control a man, and make him earnest in his adherence to what is right. The case of Andrew B——, therefore, stands high on the record of faithful witnesses. We admire the character of the obscure soldier so much the more, because it was formed against adverse influences and sets forth so clearly the power of that grace of God, which he is ever ready to give to us to help us in our duties and struggles.

The subject of this sketch[1] was born in Brooklyn, New York. His parents were not Christians. His own honest words tell what he was at the beginning.

"When quite a child," he says, "I went to a Sunday school, but soon quit going, and became a bad boy. Tumbling round the streets with other bad boys, I began to curse and swear and drink. I went to meeting now and then, but only to see what I could see. I did not like to hear the preaching; it always made me feel so restless and unhappy." After a time, his father moved down the bay, and "went to oystering," where Andrew's habits, in some respects, became worse than ever. If he heard preaching, it would alarm him; and on one occasion he was so distressed that he resolved to

[1] It has been compiled from Mr. Alvord's Journal.

forsake his sins and serve the Lord; but his good resolutions soon vanished, and again he plunged into sin.

At length, one Sabbath evening, he was walking with a company of young persons to a place of frolic, when, on passing a church, one of them said, "Come, let us go in." They did so, and, as he states, "we had not been there fifteen minutes before my convictions returned stronger than before." Near the close of the service, he was in great distress. "It seemed to me,"—still using his own expressions,—"that, if I did not give my heart to God *then*, I was lost! There was a dreadful struggle in my feelings; at length I gave up, and yielded all my heart to the Lord. From that time, I felt happy, and commenced a new life, working all I could for my Saviour."

He returned after a time to Brooklyn, where he "still tried to do his duty." When the Rebellion broke out, he was among the first to hear the call of his country, and he enlisted for three years. He has suffered much, and been in many battles, but, as he says, "I am not tired of serving my country, and the Lord is still with me."

This young soldier, thus made a trophy of divine grace, with very little education, or previous religious advantages, is here in the field, an ornament to his profession, and an example to all who know him. Without having risen to any rank, being still "a private," he is indeed a soldier of the cross, true to the Captain of his salvation.

In the regiment, which has now no chaplain, he maintains a regular weekly prayer-meeting, in addition to occasional meetings. On the muster-roll are several professors of religion, yet no other one in the whole regiment takes any active part; but Andrew is not discouraged. He reads and talks and sings and prays. Few attended at first, but more came, erelong, especially of the officers. There is an attempt at ridicule, sometimes, but he is proof against it. "When they make a noise," he says, "I feel ready to sink; but I throw myself right into the arms of Jesus, and I begin to rise and rise till I am lifted above the tumult. The blessed Spirit comes and breathes courage into my heart, and soon the boys are quiet and crowd around me, and I have a glorious meeting."

At the battle of Fredericksburg, Andrew, with his comrades was in the hottest of the fire. The night before, as they lay on the bank of the Rappahannock, in expectation of the carnage of the morrow he summoned them to prayer. His voice, remarkable for sweetness and melody, was heard singing his usual call to the meeting for worship. Twenty-five or thirty of the men gathered around him. He talked to them "of the salvation which sinners need. It might be their last time. The battle was at hand, with its certainty of death to so many. As to himself, if such was God's will, he was willing to go; and he then exhorted them all to be prepared for the issue, whether life or death. "They stood round me in the darkness," says he, "and listened. I felt the presence of the Spirit, and spoke to them twenty minutes. No one made fun of me that night." After singing

"Jesus, lover of my soul,
Let me to thy bosom fly,"

he prayed, and his fellow-soldiers returned solemnly to their quarters.

After the battle (he escaped unhurt), they lay on the field all night, close to the enemy, and also during all the next day. Some were wounded, whom he assisted in any way that he could. It was an awful place. Death was on every side. On the next night, they fell back a little, to the outskirts of the city; and again Andrew had his meeting. He invited a few into a small house, read his

Bible, sung, and, under such afflictive circumstances, tenderly addressed those around him. He says, "I was afraid I should not have another opportunity, and I tried to be faithful. I could not close with prayer as we were called upon to 'fall in,' and I had to stop the meeting suddenly." Thus, this dear youth, the hero of battle-fields, is also the Christian hero!

A few evenings ago, in the still twilight of the Sabbath, I heard his voice within the precincts of his regiment singing, and then in a few earnest words dwelling on the love of God.

He has his meetings, not only in camp, but on long marches. "Right out here in this lot, I had one," said he, "when we were marching on." He is also one of the most faithful in the distribution of religious tracts; he comes often to my tent for supplies, and before leaving always wants a season of prayer. Asking him one day how he found a place where he could pray in secret, he replied, "I go down into the woods, and especially if I am to have a meeting. After that the cross is easy. I enjoy the work and expect a blessing." He complains of not having time to go around among his companions privately as much as he could wish, as he must be often on picket and fatigue duty, and always ready to fall into the ranks. "It seems to me," he says, "as if I could draw them to Christ if I could only get near to them."

Andrew modestly speaks of "a number of conversions." "One sergeant begins to talk with me as if he had a change of heart." "I am sure there is more attention among the officers than there was. Eight or ten attended my meeting last Sabbath. One of the lieutenants, at the close of the service, came and took my hand, saying he felt that every word I said was true, and told me to go on with the meeting. Oh, how that encouraged me!"

Let it not be thought that he is less courageous because he fears God, or fails in his duty as a soldier because he is so active in religious things. The very opposite is true, as what has been related shows. The testimony of the officers is, "He is ready, cheerful under any order; his lion heart in battle seems ignorant of fear." And why should it not be so, when he lives so as to be ready for this world or the world hereafter? Surely the time cometh when such a private, though unhonored here, though lowly-born, shall outrank princes.

VIII. RELICS FROM THE BATTLE-FIELD.

In the office of Dr. T., of Cambridge, Mass. (says a visitor to that place), we were recently shown some very suggestive relics from the army of the Southwest. This Christian surgeon had been in the hospital at Memphis, Tennessee. He first laid on the table a skeleton foot and the ankle-bones, the latter of which were shattered to splinters by a Minie ball. It seemed scarcely possible that a single bullet could so break in pieces nearly the entire length of bone from the knee to the foot. Yet the heroic soldier lived, and endured all the suffering without a murmur. By the side of these fragments Dr. T. laid the fractured heel-joint of another victim of the demon of war, with the remark that the case shed light on the question of needless amputation. The effort to save the limb cost the man his life. When Dr. T. inquired of the dying soldier what message he had to send to his family and friends, he replied promptly, "Tell them I am ready to go home to them, home to God or back to the war." These were his last words. His sense of accountability, his faith in the unseen and eternal, destroyed every fear except that of failing to know and perform his duty.

Another, whose hip was shattered, when asked a similar question, replied, "Tell them I die as I have lived, triumphing in Christ."

Such are some of the relics and the dying utterances from the plain of conflict for the Republic and its enslaved millions. What a history it will have can be fully known only when the record in heaven shall be revealed.

IX. WORDS OF THE MARTYR STEPHEN.

At the battle of Shiloh (relates one who took part in it), a young man of our regiment was wounded by a rifle-bullet in the breast, as we were forming in line of battle, and before we had fired upon the enemy. We carried him back to a tent in the rear of our position. The surgeon examined his wound and whispered to me that it was mortal. The soldier overheard what the surgeon said, and replied, " Do not be anxious for me; I am not afraid to die. Understand me; I am not afraid to die. I went into battle repeating to myself what Stephen the first Christian martyr said, 'Lord Jesus, receive my spirit.' I believe he heard my prayer, and beyond that I have no anxiety."

He was in such pain that he could not bear to be moved any further, and, as the enemy were driving our troops back at that time, and bullets were whizzing through the tent, even while we were dressing his wound, we were obliged, after doing what we could for him, to leave him on the spot and hurry away. Shells and cannon-balls were raining around us as we made our escape.

We never expected to see our comrade again in this life. But, to our surprise, he was brought into camp, after having lain forty-eight hours on the battle-field. The rebels occupied that part of the ground nearly all the time after we left him, and the Lord put it into their hearts to be very kind to this young man. They brought him water when the canteen that we left for him was empty, and, as he said, "they treated me as a brother."

He lived two days after he was brought into camp. His sufferings were very great. But he never complained. He always looked up with a smile when I went into the tent. His trust was in Jesus; and the Saviour was with him, helping him to bear the pain, and driving away from him the fear of death. It was a sad and yet a beautiful sight, to see the young soldier dying so peacefully in our hospital tent in the woods of Tennessee.

> "Sweet be the death of those
> Who for their country die,
> Sleep on her bosom for repose,
> And triumph where they lie."

X. THE SOLDIER-BOY'S LAST HYMN.

In the battle of Fort Donelson there was a lad, fifteen years old only, who had enlisted as a drummer. He was remarkable for a tender conscience, for earnestness of spirit. He had been accustomed to take an active part in the meetings for prayer in the camp, and had inspired all who knew him with the utmost confidence in his intelligence and sincerity as a Christian disciple. In this fearful battle he was wounded, having one of his arms shot off close to the shoulder. An eye-witness reports that when last seen, this child, as we may almost call him, was sitting, leaning against a tree, and, as the tide of life was ebbing, from the loss of blood, his countenance was radiant with joy, while he sang the hymn,—

> "Nearer, my God, to Thee,
> Nearer to Thee,

> E'en though it be a cross
> That raiseth me;
> Still all my song shall be, —
> Nearer, my God, to Thee,
> Nearer to Thee."

XI. THE TRACT — "COME TO JESUS."

A young soldier, having received a package of tracts, wrote a letter of the following purport to the donor as a testimony to the value of such publications.

"I have been in the service," he says, "nineteen months. When I first volunteered for my country, I was wild and reckless; but I bless God I was not left long in that condition. I had not been in the army over two months, when I was called to risk my life in the battle of Peach Mountain, but, happily I was not without a friend in that trying hour. I had a brother with me in the same company, who, I believe, was a true Christian. When we were led up in line of battle against the enemy, this brother was by my side, and whispered these words into my ear: 'I shall fall in this battle, but I fall for my country, and God will take care of my soul.' This was a true presentiment. The third round was not fired before I held him in my arms, shot through the breast, but apparently in no pain.

"I shall never forget the words he spoke to me at that moment. His first thought was not for himself, but his country, dearer to him than life. 'Oh,' he exclaimed, 'are we beaten?' I told him, No. 'Leave me,' he says; 'go to your post and fight. It is a good cause, and I am willing to die for it.' He took me by the hand, and said, 'Hear my last words, brother: Be a praying man, and you need not then fear death, whether it comes at home or in battle.'

"He requested me to take all the things out of his pocket,

and among them was a tract headed 'Come to Jesus.' As he saw me looking at it, he asked me what it was. I told him. 'Yes,' said he, 'that is the tract that has made me what I am. I owe to it this peace, and all my hopes. Brother,' he continued, 'keep it, read it, and pray God to bless it to you, and to forgive you.'

"I have done as he bade me. The blessing followed, and I share, I trust, the peace which supported him. I believe God has done for me all that can be done for man in this world. I have now a hope of seeing that slain brother again in heaven."

XII. THE MODEL OF A CHAPLAIN.

A soldier on board of a steamer on the Mississippi was asked respecting the character of the chaplain in his regiment. His eyes gleamed with enthusiasm and delight at the mention of his name.

"Why," said he, "over at Frederickstown, as our lines were beginning to give way, and many thought the day was lost, our chaplain stepped right forward from the ranks, between us and the enemy's lines, knelt down upon the ground and lifted up his voice in most earnest prayer to God for divine help in the hour of need. I never was so impressed by any human act in my life. An inspiration as from God seemed to seize us all. We rallied at the instant, charged, drove the enemy before us, and gained the important victory of Frederickstown, which perhaps has saved to us the State of Mississippi."

It was an outburst of genuine Christian heroism; for this same chaplain is at the same time unsurpassed for his devotion to the line of his more strictly official duties.

Another soldier says of him, "He is one of the best

men in the world. He has a temperance-meeting and a Sabbath school one evening in the week, and has a prayer-meeting twice a week, and other meetings besides, as he is able to hold them; and then he labors personally among the men, especially giving us good books to read." He continued, "You would hardly believe if I should tell you the change that has come over our company. We had not when we enlisted, as far as I know, a single Christian man among them. It would not be easy to find a rougher set of fellows any where than were most of us; but now they have nearly all pledged themselves to abstain from profane swearing, from gambling, from intemperance, and other vices; and a good many have been converted to Christ. He comforts the sick and dying. I saw him with one of our comrades before he died, watching with him, and praying with him; and when he died, he closed his eyes, and prepared his body with his own hands for the grave."

The Rev. Mr. Savage,[1] who reports the case of this chaplain, found the body of a personal friend among the slain, on the battle-field of Shiloh or Pittsburg Landing. He was a Congregational clergyman, in the first years of his manhood, who enlisted from motives of pure Christian patriotism. He was faithful, also, to the great Captain of our salvation.

I had furnished him at different times with publications, which he had faithfully distributed in camp. He fell early in the battle of Sunday, and died, as the chaplain of the regiment testifies, "with a sweet, serene smile resting upon his finely-wrought features, — a smile that left its impress on the cold clay."

Among the wounded on the same field he found another

---

[1] Who has earned for himself so excellent a name as a Christian laborer in our armies at the West.

personal friend, a Baptist minister, who was a lieutenant. He had been shot through the thigh, shattering the bone so that it could not be set, and also through the arm. He lay for hours, after he was wounded, within the rebel lines, with his wounds undressed, unable to get even a drink of water; a part of the time the balls and shells falling thick around him. Yet he told me, as he lay there, he enjoyed some of the sweetest experiences of his life. He several times found himself unconsciously singing that sweet hymn:

> "When I can read my title clear,
> To mansions in the skies,
> I bid farewell to every fear,
> And wipe my weeping eyes."

Such men, too, are examples of those whose fear of God and dependence on him have given them courage to face the enemy, and encounter death in obedience to the call of duty.[1]

XIII. WORSHIP ON THE FLATBOAT.

Commodore Foote, the praying commodore, as he has been truthfully called, acted often as his own chaplain. The following sketch of the services on his flatboat, on a certain Sunday, was given in a letter from the Mississippi fleet. It affords another proof of the anxiety of this noble man for the spiritual welfare of those who served under him, and of his conviction that he would have better soldiers in them if he could lead them to honor God and trust in Him.[2]

The sailors, clad in their clean, plain blue uniforms, congregated on the forward port side. We look around us,

---

[1] See Report of the American Tract Society for 1863, page 72.

[2] For other notices of this lamented officer, the reader is referred to pp. 35 and 64 of this volume.

and a scene presents itself very different from the ordinary employment of warlike men. Here, in line on the starboard, we see the marines drawn up in line, or at ease, with their muskets and fixed bayonets resting on their left shoulder. In the foreground is the capstan, covered with the "Union Jack,"— its blue field and white stars adorning the patriotic pulpit. Around it stand Flag-officer Foote, Lieutenant Phelps, Colonel Buford and other officers. As the flag-officer approaches, he is saluted by all hands, who stand with uncovered heads. The gay, glittering, showy uniforms of the officers are in striking contrast with the plain garb of the seamen and marines. The flag-officer, in a few brief and eloquent remarks, reminds us that this is the Sabbath, — the day set apart for rest and the worship of the Most High. It is the first religious service, we are told, held on this flag-ship, because, on the last Sabbath we could not perform it, owing to an engagement with the enemy which could not be avoided.

In the course of his address, he urged us to bear in mind our duty to be prepared to meet our Maker, and hoped that all, officers and men, would refrain from intemperance, profanity, every immoral practice, and be ready to give their account to God, let the summons come when and as it might.

He also offered up a prayer from the Episcopal service. The services were impressive and interesting. While Flag-officer Foote was praying "Our Father, who art in Heaven," the report and zip, zip, zip, of shot or shell from the enemy's guns could be distinctly heard by all present. The flag-officer was calm and unmoved, however; he went forward eloquently and feelingly with the service until all was concluded in due form.

XIV. GARMENTS ROLLED IN BLOOD.

In this paragraph, a striking figure, an impersonation, if I may so call it, rises before us, which represents to us the barbarity of war on the one hand, and the ameliorating spirit of Christ's gospel on the other.

In a regiment at Fort Donelson, which was engaged in a battle of three days at that point, was a chaplain, of whom one of the soldiers gives an excellent testimony. "He was with us," he says, "day after day; and as soon as a man fell wounded, he would take him up in his arms, and carry him out where the surgeon could take care of him; and the last day I saw him, his clothes, from head to feet, were literally dripping with the blood of dead and wounded men that he had carried off from the battle when at Fort Donelson. His health was impaired, and he went home, but came back again in a few weeks, and reached Pittsburg Landing on the day of the battle, and there again went with his regiment into that battle, and performed similar labors. He was again at the battle of Cross Lane, where he was taken prisoner, and remained a prisoner for some days because he was unwilling to leave his wounded men. The last I saw of him was at Memphis, where he embarked for Vicksburg, and he was again in those battles, and has been there, in like manner, a spiritual comforter, an angel of mercy and relief to the wounded and dying."

XV. THE CABIN A BETHEL.

The following circumstance is related of a company of volunteers, whom Captain Washington, of Dubuque, Iowa, forwarded to the lower Mississippi.

They were on board of the Steamer Canada, on the way

to St. Louis. It was Saturday evening, and most of the passengers in the cabin were engaged in conversation, or passing away their time with cards or dice, while some of the more rude were uttering the ribald jest or ungentlemanly oath. Amid this scene, one of the youthful soldiers seated himself at a table, and engaged in reading his Bible. Another and still another took their places around this temporary altar, until nearly all of that little band, about twenty in number, were occupied in the same manner. An aged man then rose, and took his position in the centre of the group thus formed. He had a pious and venerable air, for his hoary locks proclaimed that many a winter had passed over his head. There those boys, the sons of farmers, in such a presence, with that patriarchal man as their leader, lifted up their voices and hearts in prayer to the Ruler of nations, and the God of battles, presenting a spectacle which no thoughtful person could regard without interest and hopeful anticipations of the future. The creaking machinery of the boat, the dirge-like music of the wind, was loud; yet, above the clatter, above all the tumult, we know that the voices of those boys were heard in heaven, and that their prayers will be answered. Their Bibles, precious gifts of love, are sacred to them, and by their hallowed influence will strengthen them, and shield them from greater dangers than those from which cuirass and glittering mail are worn to protect the warrior.

Parents and friends at home, fear not for such brave sons, who, relying on Heaven, are not ashamed nor afraid to praise God, and in his name to do battle for the rights and truths symbolized by the Star-spangled Banner.

XVI. STRENGTH OF THE RULING PASSION.

In one of the wards of a field hospital at Gettysburg, a young soldier of the Massachusetts Second, who had been shot through the lungs, lingered a fortnight after the battle. He was cheerful as a believer in Christ, and unoppressed by the fear of death.

It was difficult for him to breathe, but he never complained. All was done for him that kindness and skill could suggest. A soldier-loving chaplain spent many hours ministering to his temporal and spiritual wants, holding up Jesus to the eye of his faith, and remaining with him during that memorable night when he yielded up his life for his country, and his spirit to Him who redeemed it. His languid eye kindled as often as he heard the name of Jesus, and his countenance reflected the peace with which he rested there.

He expressed a wish that he "could pray again with his mother;" and wondered that no one came from home to visit him. At length, greatly to his relief, a dear brother arrived, whom he was longing to see. During most of the time, he manifested the sweetest composure and Christian tenderness. At other times, his mind wandered. Vivid recollections of the battle-field came over him, and in his delirium he enacted a pantomime of the deadly strife.

The ruling idea of the soldier's life seemed to take possession of his imagination, and there was witnessed an imitation of the battle, most vivid and life-like.

He went through the whole manual of loading and firing; the flashing of his dying eye and the nervous vigor of his trembling hands gave fearful interest to the supposed encounter with the foe.

Being assured that the enemy was gone, he became

calmer, and recognizing his brother and the chaplain, he seized their hands and showered loving kisses with his cold lips upon them. His physical and mental powers now sank almost beyond recall.

On being told that he was dying, he said, half-conscious, chanting in measured cadence, "I've — got — to die — I've got to die."

This he repeated many times; and then in cadence still more thrilling, "I'm — willing — to die. I'm — willing — to die. — Here — I — go, — I — go. I — am — going — here — there. I'm — prepared — better — prepared" — than some of his fellow-soldiers, (he meant), at the point of death like himself, who had been thoughtless and irreligious. With these broken words — "better — prepared — better — prep" — his lips refused further utterance.

The little group then bowed around the soldier's dying couch, and prayer in his behalf was breathed into the ear of the ascended Redeemer. Again we spoke to him of Jesus; and at the mention of that loved name, his pallid features glowed with seraphic radiance, and his spirit soon passed away.[1]

[1] From Mr. Alvord, in the *Tract Journal*.

CHAPTER IV.

CHEERFUL SUBMISSION TO HARDSHIPS AND SUFFERINGS.

I. HEROISM IN THE HOSPITAL.

NOTHING so reconciles men to the endurance of privations and suffering as the consciousness of a good cause and a conviction of the value of the objects for which their sacrifices are made. A chaplain in one of the Massachusetts regiments, Rev. Mr. Clark, of Swampscot, who was sent home in charge of a great number of wounded and sick soldiers, stated it as a remarkable fact that in all his intercourse with soldiers wounded in battle, he had not found one who expressed or seemed to feel the least regret for what he had suffered in his country's cause.

"Oh, how brave," writes a lady who has labored for months in the hospitals of Kentucky, — "how brave and patient those men are! In all the sufferings I have seen, I have never heard the first regret at the giving up of home and health, and life itself, for the country. When I have tried to find out, the spirit of the answer has almost invariably been, 'What I have done, I would do again, even if it brought me here.'"

William Lowell Putnam, of Boston, a young officer of social rank and education, lost his life in the battle of Ball's Bluff. With a presentiment, it would seem, of his approaching death, he wrote a letter home, in which he said, "You know, mother, that it is easy to die in such a cause; and, after all, death is but one step onward in life."

After his fall, with a self-denial worthy of Sir Philip Sidney at Zutphen, he would not even accept the service of a surgeon, knowing that he was beyond human skill or cure, and feeling that there were others around him who might need it more than he.

In a hospital, crowded with the wounded from the bloody field of Antietam, was a mutilated soldier, Charles Warren, from Massachusetts, one of whose limbs required amputation. There was little hope of saving him, but as no other resource was left, it was thought advisable to make the attempt. The wound was such that the operation could not be otherwise than painful in the extreme. A clergyman, Rev. Mr. Sloane, who had been useful to the young man in spiritual things, felt that he could not bear the sight of the inevitable suffering, and was about to leave the room. "But what was our surprise," he says, as they placed him on the table beneath the surgeon's knife, "to hear him singing in a clear and cheerful voice, the familiar words: —

'There'll be no more sorrow there;
In heaven above, where all is love,
There'll be no more sorrow there.'

"I stayed, assured that Charley was calm, trusting in God. The limb was taken off, and he remained in a drowsy state for twenty-four hours, and then gently passed away. We buried him in a quiet spot, with appropriate services, and, as we left the grave, felt that we could think of him as in that heaven of which he so cheerfully sang."

An agent of the Christian Commission says of others wounded in the same battle, "The patience and fortitude with which they endure their privations and sufferings are truly marvellous. Owing to painful wounds and uncomfortable positions, many of them spend sleepless nights, but they suffer in silence. You seldom hear any audible expression from them. I found occasion several times to chide them for not making known their condition when they had an opportunity to do so."

"Not long ago," said Mr. Gough, at a public meeting in Boston, "I was in a hospital, and saw a young man, twenty-six years of age, pale and emaciated, with his shattered arm resting upon an oil-silk pillow, and there he had been many long and weary weeks, waiting for sufficient strength for an amputation. I knelt by his side and said, 'Will you answer me one question?'

"'Yes, sir,' was his reply.

"'Suppose you were well, at home, in good health, and knew all this would come to you, if you enlisted, would you enlist?'

"'Yes, sir,' he answered, in a whisper; 'I would in a minute! What is my arm or my life compared with the safety of the country?'"

That is patriotism, and an army composed of such men has claims upon us that we cannot resist.

II. A FUNERAL IN THE FOREST.

A visitor to the Peninsula just after one of the battles there, in the month of July, 1862, writes as follows:—

One of the poor sufferers, shot through the lungs, seemed near his end. He was breathing heavily, his lips were pale, his eyes glistening with the lustre which betokens approaching death. I stopped and spoke to him of Christ. "I can trust in him," he faintly replied; and the smile upon his pallid countenance showed that his faith was resting upon the Rock of ages. Never did I feel the value of the Christian hope to the dying as then. I remembered that others, too, like him, must seal their loyalty with their blood; and, oh! how earnestly should those who love the soldier pray that they all may be prepared to die as calmly as did this youthful martyr to the cause of his country!

As I came in sight of the camp, a military wagon and a guard of soldiers were bearing one of their comrades to his last resting-place. It was a mournful sight. The deceased was a fine young man, from Nantucket, highly esteemed and brave, but his last battle was fought. I turned and followed the little procession. The sun had set, and twilight was fading into night. They entered a narrow glen, which led into a dark forest, and, stopping at a small open space, silently lowered the soldier into his grave. No chaplain was present (the regiment had none), nor were mothers or sisters there to drop the tears of affection over the loved form. How dreary, I thought to myself, to be buried thus without mourners. But, as the grave was filled slowly and noiselessly with the soft mould, I could hear the hard breathing and the suppressed sob, though it was so dark I could not see the faces of those present. Ah! I was mistaken. The bereaved ones on that ocean isle may be assured that mourners were there, — sincere, true mourners, — for the soldier has a heart of tenderness. Comrades in war are brothers; and, ere the grave was full, there was the audible expression of a brother's grief. Then all was hushed, heads were uncovered, and the lieutenant-colonel slowly, solemnly, repeated the Lord's Prayer. I never heard it when it so impressed me as then.

As I turned away, I addressed the officer in words of sympathy, telling him who I was, and why I was there. He was surprised at seeing me.

"Yes," said he, in response to my remarks; "these are indeed dark days for us."

The sad tone in which he uttered this, the deepening

twilight, the sight of the shattered ranks around us, produced a feeling of sadness in me not unmixed with awe; and I am sure no friend of our brother soldiers could have stood at the lonely grave, and not been a mourner, as I was there.

"Lonely grave," should we say? Those graves, hidden as they may be in the shades of the forest, or remote from the homes of those whose bodies rest in them, shall not be forgotten,— shall not be unvisited. Memory shall watch over them. Fathers shall point them out to their sons; they shall speak forth their mute lessons of self-sacrifice and patriotism in the ear of generations yet unborn.

> "How sleep the brave who sink to rest,
> By all their country's wishes blest!
> When Spring, with dewy fingers cold,
> Returns to deck their hallowed mould,
> She there shall dress a sweeter sod
> Than Fancy's feet have ever trod.
>
> By fairy hands their knell is rung,
> By forms unseen their dirge is sung:
> There Honor comes, a pilgrim gray,
> To bless the turf that wraps their clay,
> And Freedom shall awhile repair
> To dwell a weeping hermit there!"

III. WIPING THE TEARS FROM THEIR EYES.

Few men have had means so ample for learning the spirit of our soldiers as the Rev. Mr. Savage, agent of the American Tract Society, in the Western Department.

While I have conversed (he says) with thousands of our wounded from the battle-fields of Lexington and Pea Ridge and Fort Donelson and Shiloh and Corinth and Iuka, sometimes on the field, sometimes on transports, sometimes in hospitals, I have never found the first wounded man yet that has uttered a single word of complaint, or expressed a regret at having enlisted. It is most wonderful to me. I have seen them armless and legless, pierced through every part of the body, and upon the surgeon's bench, undergoing amputation. I have seen them dying, and heard them speak of wife and children and loved ones at home; but I have never heard a word of complaint or regret at having enlisted in the army.

I made a recent visit to the wounded at Vicksburg, at Arkansas Post. I found there cases of the deepest interest, one of which I will mention. There was a noble young man lying upon his cot on the hospital steamer, who, by the bursting of a shell directly in front of him, had had an arm cut off by a fragment, and another fragment had struck the right arm, and shattered it so that it had to be amputated. There he lay upon his cot, with both arms gone, and knowing that such must be his condition for life; but yet with a cheerful, happy countenance, and without a word of complaint. I ministered to his wants; and, as I put the food into his mouth, which he had no hands to convey thither, he would say, " Well, now, how good that is! How kind of you! The Lord will bless you for it. I don't see why you are so kind to me;" — as if any one could be too kind to a man who had suffered such a loss in defence of his country!

When I spoke to him of his religious feelings, he said, "When I had my arm shattered, I was no professed Christian; but as I lay upon that battle-field at Hurdman's Post, I felt, as I never felt before, the importance of immediately making preparations for another world; and I cried mightily to God that he would have mercy upon me, and I believe Jesus heard my prayer, and granted me forgiveness, and that I did there consecrate myself, on that battle-field, to his service." And his soul seemed to be resting peacefully upon Jesus amid all his great sufferings. One thing touched me exceedingly. As he spoke of his feelings, the tears coursed down his cheeks and lay upon them. He had no hands with which even to wipe away the tears from his own cheeks. And as I took a handkerchief and tenderly performed this office, that beautiful passage from the Book of Revelation occurred to me with a force it never had before: "And God shall wipe away all tears from their eyes."

IV. THE SOLDIER'S FAREWELL.

After the battle of Williamsburg, a soldier mortally wounded was lying on the field at night, dying. So severe were his sufferings that one of his comrades, who was also wounded, dragged himself near to him so as to be able to converse with him, and, if possible, speak a word of comfort to him.

The dying man looked up to him and said, "It is of no use, William, — I must die. I had hoped when I died to be surrounded with the friends of life's early morning; but here, far from them, with the cold, damp ground for my bed, I must go. And now, William, if you survive the war, I have a message for you to carry home. I have a wife, two lovely children, and an aged mother. When I came away, my dear wife gave me this, her picture. Open it; I want to look at it once more before I go, and if you will read this, her last letter to me concerning herself and the children, it will seem as though she was speaking to me."

He then drew from his side-pocket a little pocket Bible. "This," said he, "is the last gift of my poor aged mother. Oh, how mother will mourn when she hears I have fallen!

When I was coming away, she came to the door, and trembling with emotion and grief, put this little volume in my hand. She could not utter a word, but I knew what she wanted; and tell her, William, that I have read it constantly. And tell her, too, that through it I was led to pray, and, as she already knows, found acceptance in Christ. Tell her it kept me from vice, and the evil influences of the camp; that it cheered me and consoled me, and brought me down to my death in peace.

"And now, good-by, my dear absent wife and children! I commit you to God. Good-by, aged mother!—good-by, William,—an everlasting farewell to long marches, lonely rounds as sentinel, hardships, dangers of the field, and bloody battles. I am going to the home of which I read yesterday,—where 'the former things are passed away'—to die no more.

And he closed his eyes, and, stepping into the chariot of love, he ascended the skies; and, amidst the acclamations of the shining hosts on the other shore, he reached his home.

V. TRUE TO THE FLAG.

The sea-fight between the rebel, iron-plated Virginia, formerly the Merrimac, and the Cumberland and Congress, aided at the last and critical moment by the Monitor, took place in Hampton Roads, the eighth and ninth of March, 1862. The wooden vessels were no match for the iron-clad. The Cumberland was sunk, and went down, leaving nothing visible but her pennant still flying from the topmast above the waves. The Merrimac then turned to the Congress, and a contest between them, almost hopeless from the outset, was kept up for nearly an hour. The steamer raked the doomed vessel fore and aft with her broadsides, swept away nearly all the gunners, with a shot killed her commander, Lieutenant Joseph Smith, set her repeatedly on fire, and then, having driven her aground, compelled her to hoist the white flag and surrender. But the Monitor, which came up so suddenly on the morning of the second day, turned the scales of victory, drove back and disabled the Merrimac, and saved to us Fortress Monroe and our fleet in those waters.

The father of the brave commander of the Congress, who lost his life on that fatal Saturday, is Commodore Joseph Smith, of Washington. It appears that the elder Smith had exerted himself specially to finish the work on the Monitor, and hasten her departure to the scene of action. The son, too, had written repeatedly to the naval authorities at Washington, expressing his fears for the consequences of an attack from the Merrimac, and urging plans for guarding against it. The father knew the spirit of his son, and that the only issue of a battle for him was death or victory. When he saw, therefore, by the first despatch from Fortress Monroe that the Congress had raised the white flag, he only remarked quietly, "Joe is dead!" No Roman father ever paid a nobler or more emphatic tribute of confidence to a gallant son than is contained in the words so uttered, nor ever gave that son to his country with more cheerful and entire devotion. The sad assurance was well founded. The flag was not struck until his son had fallen.[1]

[1] This incident is from the *Boston Daily Advertiser.*

VI. "IS THAT MOTHER?"

Among the many brave, uncomplaining fellows who were brought up to the hospital from the battle of Fredericksburg was a bright-eyed, intelligent youth, sixteen years old, who belonged to a Northern regiment. He appeared more affectionate and tender, more refined and thoughtful, than many of his comrades, and attracted a good deal of attention from the attendants and visitors. Manifestly the pet of some household which he had left, perhaps, in spite of entreaty and tears, he expressed an anxious longing for the arrival of his mother, who was expected, having been informed that he was mortally wounded, and failing fast. Ere she arrived, however, he died.

But before the end, almost his last act of consciousness was the thought that she had really come; for, as a lady sat by his pillow and wiped the death-sweat from his brow, just as his sight was failing, he rallied a little, like an expiring taper in its socket, looked up longingly and joyfully, and in tones that drew tears from every eye, whispered audibly, "Is that mother?" Then, drawing her toward him with all his feeble power, he nestled his head in her arms, like a sleeping infant, and thus died, with the sweet word "mother" on his quivering lips.

VII. LITTLE EDDIE, THE DRUMMER.

The narrative which follows is so touching, and displays so many of the best feelings of the human heart, that it would be wrong to leave it out of these pages. It is from the pen of a correspondent of the "Chicago Tribune." It has been extensively copied, and may be familiar to some of our readers:—

A few days before our regiment received orders to join General Lyon, on his march to Wilson's Creek, the drummer of our company was taken sick and conveyed to the hospital, and on the evening preceding the day that we were to march, a negro was arrested within the lines of the camp, and brought before our captain, who asked him what business he had within the lines. He replied, "I know a drummer that would like to enlist in your company, and I have come to tell you of it." He was immediately requested to inform the drummer that if he would enlist for our short term of service, he would be allowed extra pay; and to do this, he must be upon the ground early in the morning. The negro was then passed beyond the guard.

On the following morning, there appeared before the captain's quarters, during the beating of the reveille, a good-looking, middle-aged woman, dressed in deep mourning, leading by the hand a sharp, sprightly-looking boy, apparently about twelve or thirteen years old. Her story was soon told. She was from East Tennessee, where her husband had been killed by the rebels, and all their property destroyed. She had come to St. Louis in search of her sister, but not finding her, and being destitute of money, she thought if she could procure a situation for her boy as a drummer, for the short time that we had to remain in the service, she could find employment for herself, and perhaps find her sister by the time we were discharged.

During the rehearsal of her story, the little fellow kept his eyes intently fixed upon the countenance of the captain, who was about to express a determination not to take so small a boy, when he spoke out, saying, "Don't be afraid, captain; I can drum." This was spoken with so much confidence that the captain immediately observed, with a smile, "Well, well, sergeant, bring the drum, and order our fifer to come forward." In a few minutes the drum was produced, and our fifer made his appearance, — a tall, round-shouldered, good-natured fellow from the Dubuque mines, who stood, when erect, something over six feet in height.

Upon being introduced to his new comrade, he stooped downward, with his hands resting upon his knees that were thrown forward into an acute angle, and after peering into the little fellow's face a moment, he observed, "My little man, can you drum?"

"Yes, sir," he replied, "I drummed for Captain Hill, in Tennessee."

Our fifer immediately commenced straightening himself upward until all the angles in his person had disappeared, when he placed his fife to his mouth, and played the "Flowers of Edinburgh," one of the most difficult tunes to follow with the drum that could have been selected, but nobly did the little fellow follow him, showing him to be a master of the drum. When the music ceased our captain turned to the mother and observed, "Madam, I will take your boy. What is his name?"

"Edward Lee," she replied; then, placing her hand upon the captain's arm, she continued, "captain, if he is not killed" — here her maternal feelings overcame her utterance, and she bent down over her boy, and kissed him upon the forehead. As she arose, she observed, "Captain, you will bring him back with you, won't you?"

"Yes, yes," he replied; "we will be certain to bring him back with us. We shall be discharged in six weeks."

In an hour after, our company led the Iowa First out of camp, our drum and fife playing "The girl I left behind me." Eddie, as we called him, soon became a great favorite with all the men in the company. When any of the boys had returned from a horticultural excursion, Eddie's share of the peaches and melons was first apportioned out. During our heavy and fatiguing march from Rolla to Springfield, it was often amusing to see our long-legged fifer wading through the mud with our little drummer mounted upon his back, and always in that position when fording streams.

The night after the fight at Wilson's Creek, where Lyon fell, I was detailed for guard duty. The hours passed slowly away, when at length the morning light began to streak along the eastern sky, making surrounding objects more plainly visible. Presently I heard a drum beat up the morning call. At first, I thought it came from the camp of the enemy across the creek; but, as I listened, I found that it came up from the deep ravine; for a few minutes it was silent, and then, as it became more light, I heard it again. I listened; the sound of the drum was familiar to me; I knew that it was

> Our drummer-boy from Tennessee,
> Beating for help the reveille.

I was about to desert my post to go to his assistance, when I discovered the officer of the guard approaching with two men. We all listened to the sound, and were satisfied that it was Eddie's drum. I asked permission to go to his assistance. The officer hesitated, saying that the orders were to march in twenty minutes. I promised to be back in that time, when he consented. I immediately started down the hill through the thick undergrowth, and upon reaching the valley I followed the sound of the drum, and soon found him seated upon the ground, his back leaning against the trunk of a fallen tree, while his drum hung upon a bush in front of him, reaching nearly to the ground. As soon as he discovered me, he dropped his drumsticks and exclaimed, "Oh, corporal, I am so glad to see you!

Give me a drink of water," reaching out his hand for my canteen, which was empty.

I immediately turned to bring him some water from the brook that I could hear rippling through the bushes near by, when thinking I was about to leave him, he commenced crying, saying, "Don't leave me, corporal; I can't walk." I was soon back with the water, when I discovered that both of his feet had been shot away by a cannon-ball. After satisfying his thirst, he looked up into my face and said, "You don't think I will die, corporal, do you? This man said I would not; he said the surgeon could cure my feet."

I now discovered a man lying in the grass near him dead. By his dress, I recognized him as belonging to the enemy. It appeared that he had been shot through the bowels, and had fallen near where Eddie lay. Knowing that he himself could not live, and seeing the condition of the boy, he crawled to him, took off his buckskin suspenders, and corded the little fellow's legs below the knee, and then lay down and died. While the child was telling me these particulars, I heard the tramp of cavalry coming down the ravine, and in a moment a scout of the enemy was upon us, and I was taken a prisoner. I requested the officer to take Eddie up in front of him; he did so, carrying him with great tenderness and care. When we reached the camp of the enemy, the little fellow was dead.

VIII. WHAT A PHYSICIAN SAW.

A physician, in the naval service on our Western waters, describes in a familiar letter some of his experience as a witness of the sad effects of war.

You remember (he says to his correspondent) the sad

loss of the "Cincinnati," the latter part of May. We were in full sight of Vicksburg at the time, and could distinctly see the firing, but could not see the ship. After a while there was silence, and intense anxiety. This might have been eleven o'clock. About twelve o'clock, word was brought that "The Cincinnati is sunk." Then our hearts sank. In the afternoon, the wounded were brought in. I will give you the story of one of them. He was a handsome, finely-developed young man of twenty-three or twenty-five years. His wound was of the left leg, shot off just above the knee, but left hanging by a few shreds of mus cle

In this condition he swam ashore, refusing to be assisted. He was brought aboard pale, haggard, bloodless. Not a murmur, not a groan was heard, but such a weary, weary aspect! Presently he said, "Can you put me to sleep? I am in great pain."

"Yes, yes; we will put you to sleep right away."

His eyes were large, clear, blue eyes, full of an unutterable soul. They continued their wonderful silent eloquence, — noiseless, alternate light and shade, — till the chloroform closed them.

Another patient was brought in, also severely wounded, making the same request, "Can you put me to sleep?" So I left the first, before the amputation was begun, to give relief to the second. After a little while I had him very quiet, for he was of a different temperament from the first, and more clamorous. Then I said to the sister, "Watch him for a few moments. If he stops breathing, call me; I must see the other man." I went. The operation was completed. Soon the dressings were applied, and we laid him on a bed. After the other amputation I went to him again. He was awake, and again in pain.

"I want to go to sleep; will you put me to sleep?"

Oh, poor pale face! I see it now. Even the tongue was white. I almost wept. Could I hope? But I could not hesitate what to do. That meek inquiry, "Will you put me to sleep?"—brave, yet bordering on the plaintive, having the slightest touch of piteousness, yet so quiet and so grand! He was teaching me the sublimity of unmurmuring suffering.

"Yes, yes; we will put you to sleep."

His eyes opened and closed so wearily, so wearily! They were wonderful eyes, clear as two perfect stars, and over them was the fine, smooth brow and wavy hair, abundant and beautiful.

"Will you give me some water?"

He drank and lay still again. Presently a little stimulant was brought in. He swallowed it indifferently.

"Will that help me sleep?"

"Yes; you will sleep now."

Previously a small anodyne powder had been given him. Then he was quiet for a little while.

I had a hope for him, but with it an awful sense that it rested on no foundation. Very soon, he grew restless,—a restlessness hard for words to picture,—peculiar, and such as I, poor yearling doctor, had already learned to dread. The restlessness became extreme. I left him for a while; then I returned. Will he be asleep?

He is quiet now, and oh! beautiful eyes,—beautiful no longer. It was the soul that gave them beauty. Then the soul must be very beautiful! Everything is calm now. Is he asleep? Yes, thank God, asleep now, and an angel will waken him one day.

IX. THE HOSPITAL TREE NEAR FAIR OAKS.

There is a large tree near the battle-ground of Fair Oaks,[1] the top of which was used as an observatory during the fight, which stands as a memento of untold, and perhaps never to be told, suffering and sorrow. Many of the wounded and dying were laid beneath the branches of this tree after the battle, in order to receive surgical help, or to breathe their last there more quietly. What heart-rending scenes, (wrote a Massachusetts chaplain,) did I witness in that place, so full of saddened memories to me and to others. Brave, uncomplaining men were brought thither out of the woodland, the crimson tide of whose life was ebbing away in the arms of those who carried them. Almost all who died, died like heroes, with scarcely a groan. Those wounded, but not mortally, — how nobly they bore the necessary probings, and needed amputations!

Two instances of this heroic fortitude deserve to be specially mentioned. One of them is that of William C. Bentley, of the Second Rhode Island Regiment, both of whose legs were broken by a bomb-shell, and whose wrist and breast were mangled, and who yet was as calm as though he suffered no pain. He refused any opiate or stimulant that might dim his consciousness. He asked only that we should pray for him, that he might be patient and submissive, and dictated a letter to be sent to his mother. Then, and not till then, opiates were given to him, and he fell gently asleep, and for the last time.

The other case was that of Francis Sweetser, of Company E, of the Sixteenth Massachusetts Regiment, who witnessed in death, as he had uniformly done in life, a good confession of Christ.

[1] One of the Peninsular battles under McClellan, June 21, 1862.

"Thank God," he said, "that I am permitted to die for my country. Thank God more yet that I am prepared to go;"—and then, after a moment's thought, he modestly added, "at least, I hope I am."

When he died, he was in the act of prayer, and in that position his limbs grew rigid, and so remained after the spirit had left his body. We shall miss him at the regiment meetings for prayer, and at our Sabbath worship. We shall miss him at the temperance meetings,—nay, everywhere, and always, when any good is to be done for the soldiers, among whom he held an honored, though humble, place.

X. THE WOUNDED AT FORT WAGNER.

This fortress is on Morris Island, in the harbor of Charleston, S. C. It was stormed by our forces on the eighteenth of July last, in two successive attacks, ineffectual, but among the fiercest struggles of the war. In the first charge, the advance was led by the Fifty-fourth Massachusetts, composed, with the exception of the officers, of colored men, one-third of whom were originally slaves, and the others recruits from the Free States. They were under the command of Colonel Robert G. Shaw, who had sought this position to show his faith in the loyalty and courage of a despised race, and his regard for the rights of a common brotherhood. His confidence was not misplaced. After the fire of the rebels had begun to thin their ranks, the men still pressed forward through a storm of shot and shell, with shouts as they advanced. At the distance of a hundred yards from the fort, the battalion wavered for a moment. But the colonel, springing to the front, and waving his sword, shouted, "Forward, once more!" and then, with another cheer and shout, they rushed through the ditch, gained the parapet, and fought hand to hand with the enemy. Colonel Shaw was among the first to scale the walls. He was in the act of directing and cheering his men, when he was shot dead, and fell into the fort. His body was found with twenty of his soldiers lying dead around him, two of them on his own body. The regiment went into action with six hundred and fifty men, and came out with a loss of two hundred and eighty, — more than a third of the whole number. Eight only, of the twenty-three officers, were uninjured.

Amid all this carnage and confusion, the color-bearer, though he was severely wounded, and obliged to make his escape by creeping on his knees, held his staff erect, and brought off the flag without allowing its folds to touch the ground.

But the saddest scene is yet to be related. The Sunday which followed was a day of distress and mourning in Beaufort. The arrival of the "Cosmopolitan," with the wounded from Morris Island, with intelligence that our brave troops had been repulsed there, cast a gloom over the community, such as had not been felt since the affair at Pocataligo, and the death of the noble Mitchell.

As the vessel neared the wharf, with its freight of suffering, a silent, mournful concourse gathered around the landing, eager to lend a helping hand in removing the wounded to the hospital. As those who were able to walk filed off the boat, and wended their slow way through the crowd, the scene was truly pathetic. The emotional nature of the negro broke forth in sobs and moans of compassion, while the sympathy and commiseration of the white man was shown only in the pale face and trembling lips. The wounded of the Fifty-fourth Massachusetts came off from the boat first; and, as these sad evidences of the bravery and patriotism of the colored man passed through the lines of

spectators, every heart was melted with tenderness and pity
We will vouch for it, says an eye-witness, that no word of
scorn or contempt for negro soldiers will ever be heard
from any who beheld that spectacle. In that moment, our
volunteers saw suffering comrades in the black men, and
the tender hand and strong shoulder were extended as
readily to them as to their more favored compatriots. All
day and far into the night did the sad procession pass
toward the hospital, and every man and woman at the post
who could do anything to alleviate the sufferings of our
brave fellows was soon busily at work.

The cheerful resignation with which the soldiers, white
and black, bore the terrible mutilations, and the sufferings
inevitable in moving them, was worthy of all praise. As
we looked upon some youthful form, lying upon a stretcher,
with a cloth covering a torn and shattered limb, and watched
the struggle to bear up with fortitude and patience, we
bowed in spirit to a hero as great as any whose fame has
employed the pen of the historian, or the muse of the poet.

On the second and third days after the fight, I passed,
says a correspondent, through nearly all the wards of the
hospital. The wounds of many of them had not been
dressed, and were very painful. Some of them lay there
with mangled legs or arms, or both; others, with amputated limbs.

"Well, boys," I said to them, "is not this something you
did not count upon?"

"Oh, no, no," was the answer. "We expected to take
what might come. Thank God, we had made up our
minds to live or die."

"But if out of it, and at home once more, how many
would enlist again."

With brightened eyes, and, in some instances, with
uplifted stumps of arms or hands, they cried out, "Oh, yes,

yes! We will never give up till the last brother breaks his chains. If all our people may get their freedom, we are ready to die."

No one can pass among these sufferers, so patient, so cheerful, and listen to the expressions of their conviction that they are soldiers for Jesus, to help on his war of freedom for the oppressed,[1] without being inspired with the deepest abhorrence of slavery, and praying anew and with greater earnestness that God would hasten the day of its overthrow.

The body of Colonel Shaw was denied the rites of sepulture. It was thrown into a pit and buried beneath heaps of his faithful soldiers. This was meant as an insult and ignominy, but shall be counted an honor, and shall give added potency to the voice which speaks from his grave.

> "They never fail who die
> In a great cause; the block may soak their gore;
> Their heads may sodden in the sun; their limbs
> Be strung to the city gates and castle walls,
> But still their spirit walks abroad. Though years
> Elapse and others share as dark a doom,
> They but augment the deep and living thoughts
> Which overpower all others, and conduct
> The world at last to freedom."

XI. THE AFRICAN STANDARD-BEARER.

The conduct of this hero, to whom allusion has been made, deserves a more distinct notice. The soldier who carried the colors of the Fifty-fourth, having been disabled, William H. Carney, a sergeant of Company G, caught them

---

[1] So far as they have this spirit, the motto on one of their banners — *In hoc signo vinces*, By this sign (that of the cross), thou shalt conquer — was well chosen.

up, rushed forward, and was the first man to plant the "Stars and Stripes" on Fort Wagner. The ranks, as he himself said afterwards, were full as they ascended the wall, but "melted away" before the enemy's fire "almost instantly." He was wounded in the head and thigh, but fell only upon his knees. Having raised the flag on the parapet, he lay down on the outer slope, in order to be sheltered as much as possible. There he remained for more than half an hour, till the second brigade arrived and renewed the conflict. During all this time, he kept the colors flying; and when the retreat for such as were left became necessary, he followed on his knees, pressing his wound with one hand, and holding up the emblem of liberty with the other. When he entered the hospital, nearly exhausted from loss of blood, his companions, both black and white, rose from the straw on which they were lying and cheered him and the colors till they could cheer no longer.

"Boys," he replied, "I have but done my duty. The old flag never touched the ground."[1]

This gallant soldier was born in Norfolk, Virginia, in 1840. He belonged to a family, originally slaves, who became free by the conditions of their master's will, at the time of his decease. In his early years, he received by stealth[2] some knowledge of the rudiments of learning from a minister in that city. The father and mother, with their children wandered from place to place till they found a home at length in New Bedford, Mass.

We have reason to ascribe William's bravery and fortitude, his patriotism and zeal for liberty, to a Christian source. In a letter written by himself, he states that he

---

[1] An official letter states these particulars.
[2] Readers of the next generation may need to be informed that it was a penal offence in our Southern States, at this period, to teach slaves to read.

embraced the gospel in his fifteenth year, before he left Norfolk; that after he removed to New Bedford, he became a member of the church under the care of Rev. Mr. Jackson, now chaplain of the Fifty-fourth, and that he was hoping to prepare himself for the ministry, until the way was opened for his striking a blow with his own arm for the government and for liberty. "When the country" (to quote his own words) "called for all persons, I felt I could best serve my God by serving my country and my oppressed brothers. The sequel was, I enlisted for the war."

XII. A SINGULAR DEATH.

I was conversing not long since with a returned volunteer.

"I was in the hospital," said he, "for a long time, as attendant on the wounded, and assisted in taking off limbs and dressing all sorts of wounds; but the hardest thing I ever did was to take my thumb off a man's leg."

"Ah!" said I; "how was that?" He then related the following case:—

A young man had been placed under our care who had a severe wound in the thigh. The ball passed completely through, and amputation was necessary. The limb was cut up close to the body, the arteries taken up, and he seemed to be doing well. Subsequently, one of the small arteries sloughed off. An incision was made, and it was again taken up.

"It is well it was not the main artery," said the surgeon, as he performed the operation. "He might have bled to death before it could have been taken up."

But the patient Charley, as we always spoke of him, got on finely for a time, and was a favorite with us all.

I was passing through the ward one night, about midnight, when suddenly, as I was passing Charley's bed, he spoke to me: —

"H——, my leg is bleeding again."

I threw back the bedclothes, and the blood spirted in the air. The main artery had sloughed off.

Fortunately, I knew just what to do; and in an instant I had pressed my thumb on the place and stopped the bleeding. It was so close to the body that there was barely room for my thumb, but I succeeded in keeping it there, and arousing one of the convalescents, sent him for the surgeon, who came in on a run.

"I am so thankful, ——," said he, as he saw me, "that you were up and knew what to do, for otherwise he must have bled to death before I could have got here."

But on examination of the case, he looked exceedingly serious, and sent for other surgeons. All came who were within reach, and a consultation was held over the poor fellow. One conclusion was reached by all. There was no place to work save the spot where my thumb was placed; they could not work under my thumb, and, if I moved it, he would bleed to death before the artery could be taken up. There was no way to save his life.

Poor Charley! He was very calm when they told him, and he requested that his brother, who was in the same hospital, might be called up. He came and sat down by the bedside, and for three hours I stood, and by the pressure of my thumb kept up the life of Charley, while the brothers had their last conversation on earth. It was a strange place for me to be in, to feel that I held the life of a fellow-mortal in my hands, as it were, and stranger yet, to feel that an act of mine must cause that life to depart. Loving the poor fellow as I did, it was a hard thought; but there was no alternative. The last words were spoken.

Charley had arranged all his business affairs, and sent tender messages to absent ones, who little dreamed how near their loved one stood to the grave. The tears filled my eyes more than once as I listened to those parting words. All were sad, and he turned to me: —

"Now H——, I guess you had better take off your thumb."

"Oh, Charley! how can I?" said I.

"But it must be done, you know," he replied, cheerfully. "I thank you very much for your kindness, and now, good-by."

He turned away his head, I raised my thumb, once more the life-current gushed forth, and in three minutes poor Charley was dead.

XIII. THE LAST DUTY TO HIS COUNTRY.

Death has enough that is sorrowful and gloomy even when it enters the quiet and comfortable home, where loving friends and kindred surround the bedside. But to die away from those we love, among strangers, and in circumstances unattended by so many outward alleviations, — and yet to die peacefully, joyfully, requires a strong faith, and shows a resignation to the will of God which is surely one of the fruits of the Spirit. Many a brave man, since the war began, has met this last enemy of the Christian with as much heroism as he met the enemy of his country in battle.

One of the delegates of the Christian Commission reports an instance of this nature which should be recorded among the examples of the power of the gospel in the last dread hour.

Among those wounded at Fredericksburg, on Saturday, May third, who were early brought across the river from the field of carnage, covered with blood, was a young man from Newburyport, Mass. He had been among the most faithful in attendance at our weekly prayer-meeting. I saw at once that his wound was mortal. His injury was such that he could not see. I grasped him by the hand and spoke to him. He knew me by my voice.

"Oh!" said he, "I am mortally wounded, and soon must die."

"Do you feel willing to die?" I asked.

"Yes; I have done the last duty for my God and my country. Life is dear, but I know that all is right. I have a dear mother and sister at home, whom I love. I would like to die with them in the quiet of home; but I cannot, and am willing to die here."

It must be enough, one would think, to scatter the doubts of the most unbelieving, to stand at the side of such a dying soldier. To see how calmly, with what assurance of hope, the young Christian breathes out his life in the arms of the Saviour, shows at once the power of the consolations which support him, and the reality of the faith from which they spring.

CHAPTER V.

EFFORTS FOR THE SPIRITUAL WELFARE OF THE SOLDIERS.

I. PRAYER IN A CHURCHYARD.

SCATTERED over the battle-fields and camping-grounds of the present war, are consecrated spots, Bethels, every one of them sacred to some soul who there held sweet communion with God. A laborer in the work of the Christian Commission gives the following account of a prayer-meeting which was organized and held for a time, in the churchyard of a village, near Fredericksburg, in Virginia:—

Prayer-meetings (he says) had been held previously every evening, and many souls, I trust, converted to God. In the Seventh Michigan, especially, a glorious work commenced erelong, and I trust that it has been carried on by the Holy Spirit of God, and that eternity will reveal glorious results which God wrought for the souls of these earnest, truth-seeking men. Before leaving them, I assisted in organizing a prayer-meeting of their own. Nine or ten, sometimes more, faithful young men, retired every evening after roll-call to their little retreat, and there they prayed together, and talked together to strengthen each other in faith and love. That retreat was the village churchyard. Around a broad, flat, old-fashioned tombstone, as an altar, this faithful little band met, and God met with them and blessed them.

I have often thought what a solemn spot that is which has been the scene of so much devotion, and what solemn moments those were which those disciples spent in prayer, in that habitation of the dead. Around them lay the lifeless remains of those who, in years gone by, had lived and moved and thought and filled their places among men. Near by was a long row of graves which contained the remains of Union soldiers who had fallen at the first battle of Fredericksburg. Not long since they, too, were living men, soldiers, like these worshippers. Perhaps some of them were praying soldiers, perhaps some of them died without having learned how to pray.

These faithful, Christian young men did not forget their prayer-meeting when the fortunes of war called them away from this chosen spot. They still met as often as the evening came. On one of the evenings during the battle of Gettysburg, when the hour arrived for the meeting, some of the wonted attendants were present, but it was found that some of the most devoted had that day fallen as sacrifices on the altar of their country. They had fallen, but they fell with their armor on, bright and polished. They died exemplifying the power of that faith which had sustained and supported them during the weeks they had lived as Christians.

II. REGIMENTAL CHURCHES.

A gratifying feature which religious effort in behalf of the soldiers assumed during the progress of the war, was the formation, in some of the regiments, of temporary churches. These churches (wrote one of the promoters of this measure) are designed to embrace those who are already professors of religion, as well as new converts. In these they find a spiritual home, in which they can receive the benefits of church care and fellowship. As in the camp, the tent is the soldier's substitute for his ordinary dwelling, so this church is the soul's tabernacle, in the absence of his regular and permanent sanctuary.

A church in the camp! What a novelty! With it is connected the prayer-meeting, the Bible-class, the singing of God's praise, the preaching of the Word, the rite of baptism, the communion of the saints, and all those sacred services which bless communities at home. We hail the movement as a happy device of Christian enterprise. Faithful, efficient chaplains are needed; but, in the hands of such men, an institution like this must be a great blessing to those whom it is designed to benefit.

A minister of the gospel sits beside me (writes Mr. Alvord, in one of his letters), who has just related to me a scene that took place last Sunday under his own eye.

A young man who had been converted in their meetings was received to the camp church. The chaplain had been preaching to at least eight hundred of the regiment, and, at the close of the service, this young man was asked to give some account of his experience and hopes. He rose to his feet, and was stepping forward to a place where he could be heard. At that moment, most unexpectedly, a group of soldiers joined him, and all pressed forward together to the stand. They were Christian men, and they wished in this way to uphold their comrade, and show themselves on the side of Christ. The candidate was then admitted into the church in due form, while the regiment looked on, and showed by their earnest attention how deeply the scene had interested them.

"The major," said the chaplain, "though he did not profess to be a pious man, grasped me by the arm, after the service, saying with deep feeling, 'Never did I witness so impressive a scene as that!'"

The chaplain of the Sixth Pennsylvania Regiment refers to a similar organization, under date of October 23d, 1861.

Yesterday (he writes) was the happiest Sabbath I have known in camp. We have just established a regimental church, which we call the Army-Union Christian Association. I enclose a copy of our creed and articles. At eleven o'clock, A. M., the regiment was assembled for public worship. In the presence of all, twenty-five of the men stepped out of the ranks to the front, and made public profession of their faith in Christ. To-day, several others have come to me and expressed their wish to join us on the next occasion. Two were baptized, on the same day, and thus, for the first time, declared themselves publicly on the Lord's side. The others are members of churches at home. This association does not make it necessary for them to separate from those churches. It stands only in the place of the church at home, during their service in the army.

We have deeply interesting meetings for prayer every evening, except Wednesday, when some of us come together for practice in singing. To-night, several new voices were heard in prayer, for the first time since the individuals left home. One poor sinner was melted to tears, and sobbed out a prayer to Jesus to wash away his sins and make him a new creature. I believe that God is pouring out a blessing upon us, and trust he may bring many of this regiment to himself.

III. THE LAST SOUL-CHEERING WORD.

I went into another ward (writes one of the tract-distributors), where I was told a volunteer from one of the Maine regiments was lying dangerously ill from a gunshot wound in the thigh. There the poor sufferer lay, pale, emaciated, fast sinking. It needed but one look to see that he could not long survive. I inquired his name. "Wm. J——," was the only answer that he had strength to make audible. I had several of the little books in my hand which have been prepared for the soldiers, and I placed these by his pillow. He reached out his feeble hand, and looking them over picked out one with the title "Welcome to Jesus," printed in gold on a purple cover, and whispered to me to place that on the window-sill before him, upright, so that he could see those words without turning his head. I did so.

The surgeon came to dress his wounds. The patient, evidently near his end, and almost without breath for speaking, held out his hand to thank me, and I left him. That night he died. The last comforting message he had was, as I have reason to believe, the soul-cheering one, "Welcome to Jesus." But what a message was that! Thanks, many thanks, to the liberal people who sustain me and my associates in furnishing such means for comforting the departing soul in such an hour.

IV. ALL ONE IN CHRIST JESUS.

We are indebted to Professor M. L. Stoever, of Gettysburg College, a faithful workman in the hospitals of that place, for various instructive incidents, which his labors there have brought to his notice. We have from him the following fact, showing how in the estimation of the true Christian, the value of the soul is paramount to everything else; how it leads him to forget the distinctions of creed, and to lay aside the most cherished prejudices in his desire to save the unconverted.

On the Sabbath succeeding the battle (said this intelligent witness) my attention was directed to the destitution at the

Catholic church, which was used as a hospital. On entering the building, filled with the wounded and dying, I was met by a Catholic woman, whom I very well knew to be a good woman, but a rigid Catholic. As soon as she saw me, she said to me, —

"Do come and speak to this man. The surgeon says he will not live, and he is unconverted."

I followed her to the place where he was lying, within the chancel and near the altar. She introduced me as a Protestant, and as one connected with the college, and then left me to minister to him the comforts of religion.

After briefly and earnestly presenting to him the only way opened for his return to God, I knelt by his side and offered prayer, the first Protestant prayer, doubtless, ever offered in that Catholic church, and that too at the request of a member of the church. The man died a day or two after that, most peacefully, trusting in Christ, cheerfully acquiescing in God's will, and with the hope of eternal happiness beyond the grave. He was the son of a pious mother, and had been reared under religious influences. Although he had never made a profession of religion, his early instructions had prepared his mind to lay hold of the cross and to embrace the Saviour.

In Christ Jesus all Christians are one.

V. WORSHIP IN CAMP.

Rev. A. H. Quint, chaplain in the Second Massachusetts Regiment, attached at that time to the Army of the Potomac, thus graphically describes the meetings for preaching and prayer among the soldiers: —

The Sabbath service is held at half-past four o'clock, P. M., under the lengthening shadows. The drum and fife play "church call;" the companies are formed as for parade. Each marches to the sound of music, to its place, till the regiment forms three sides of a square, leaving, perhaps, fifteen feet each side of the preacher. Just within the square are the field and staff officers, and the band, which plays a voluntary. At a word of command, the singers leave the ranks and stand near the band. In the service, the men stand until the time for sermon, when, at the word "Rest," all are seated, but still in order. The sermon closing, all instantly rise, uncovered, for prayer and benediction. These ended, "Attention! Company A, left face, march!" and, to the music of the band, the men march to their tents. There is no lack of attention, and never a disrespectful look.

Sabbath evening, at half-past seven o'clock, is our prayer-meeting, lately established. It is held, now, on an open space, near the tents of our band. Each time, it has been a dark evening. A few candles cast a dim light. The flame of near or distant camp-fires shines fitfully on the bronzed faces of hardy men, bringing into deeper shadow the sombre blue of their uniform. They stand closely,— a hundred of them. A familiar revival hymn, perhaps "Behold, behold, the Lamb of God," or "We're going home, to die no more," attracts others, for music is a great charm in camp. A prayer, reading of Scripture, a short address from the chaplain, singing, and then all are invited to speak, or pray, or sing. One comes forward quietly into the little vacant space, and in a low voice testifies to the grace of God. Then another; and one prays, or singing breaks forth; or one, in whose heart the springs have been long choked up, bears witness that the fountain is once more gushing, and mourns over his sins. Here and there are visible tears rolling down some rough cheek; "it seems so like home," or "it makes us feel human," or "it reminds one of a praying father."

The hour passes. Tired? No; though no cushioned seats have rested them,— they have all been standing the whole period. But they have rested on the grace of God; and they look forward with yearning hearts to the Wednesday evening prayer-meeting. Wednesday evening I chose for its beloved associations with the "Young People's Meeting" at home.

VI. A REGIMENTAL REVIVAL.

The following narrative was written by the Rev. Dr. Marks, chaplain of the Sixty-third Pennsylvania Volunteers.

It must ever be a source of relief and hope to thousands of Christian parents, whose sons have gone into the army without any avowed interest in religion, and have been slain in battle, or have died in hospitals, that their lost ones had an opportunity to witness such scenes as this narrative describes; and that the symbol of the divine presence rested so visibly here and there on the tents in which they sojourned. We need not put away from us the consolation of thinking that many of those who have been thus cut off may have been reached by the silent operation of such influences, and fitted for their end, though they may not have left the recorded proof of their acceptance of the terms of mercy.

The Sixty-third Regiment of Pennsylvania Volunteers entered the service of the government on the 25th of August, 1861, at Pittsburg. We reached Washington about the first of September, and very soon entered General Heintzelman's division, and were stationed on the Mt. Vernon road, about three miles from Alexandria.

The first Sabbath after the chaplain arrived in camp, he noticed unusual solemnity, and on that day gave away more than three hundred Testaments to those who called at his tent. On the next Sabbath, he gave away, in the same manner, more than three hundred of your hymn-books; and, from that time, has distributed every week from five hundred to a thousand religious papers, small books, and tracts. These were uniformly read, and deep and permanent religious impressions were produced.

We were for three months without any shelter or tent for religious worship; but uniformly had two services on the Sabbath day, and one or more prayer-meetings during the week.

In the month of December, the heart of the chaplain was cheered by more than one soldier coming to him, confessing his sins, and asking prayers. Others came to the chaplain earnestly desiring religious instruction, and professing some interest in the question of their salvation.

About the last of January, through the kindness of some Christian friends in Pittsburg, I was enabled to purchase a tent for worship. This we immediately pitched, and on a rainy night, and the mud fabulously deep in camp, we met in the new tent, and, without fire and almost without light, stood up and dedicated it to God.

The following Sabbath was one of marked solemnity. Many of the soldiers were deeply moved. The chaplain announced, during the service, that he would that day take measures to organize a church in the regiment, and invited all Christians to unite with the new association, and thus aid to advance the cause of the gospel in the army. Many gave their names that day, and rejoiced greatly in the privilege of "standing up for Jesus." The evening was marked by still greater solemnity, and many requested the privilege of enrolling themselves with the people of God.

On Monday morning, I commenced going from tent to tent, talking to the soldiers and officers in each, and praying in several. I found that the Lord had gone before me, and that it was wholly his work. Many had been deeply impressed by recent letters from home. There had been excited in Western Pennsylvania a great interest for the moral and spiritual welfare of the army. The papers abounded with appalling details descriptive of the crimes, vices, and impiety of the troops upon the Potomac. These accounts, when read, excited the deepest concern in many hearts, and led to letters of entreaty, warning, and earnest appeal. No doubt these letters were often wet with tears, and sent with many prayers.

During the week, the religious solemnity increased. We held meetings every morning, and again visited from tent to tent. I was nowhere repulsed, but in many places received kindly, and often with gratitude. Often, the mess of a tent would confess their sins, and promise to each other a better life. While I was talking with one of these companies of soldiers, one of the mess, with tears in his eyes, lifted from under a pile of books and clothes a pack of cards, and put them, with the approbation of all, into the fire.

During this week, I was, for many hours each day, conversing and praying with those who came to seek advice and help. We celebrated the Lord's Supper on the morning of the third of February. The day was most beautiful and balmy; never had there been such quiet and stillness in camp. It was like a Sabbath in one of the most orderly of our villages. We had a most delightful prayer-meeting at nine o'clock, and commenced more public services at half-past ten.

First, after singing and prayer, I read the Articles of Faith which were the basis of union, then administered baptism to six young men, and read the names of those who desired to associate themselves as a church in the army. There were one hundred and fifty-nine names, among which forty-six were the names of those who had been recently converted, and confessed Christ for the first time.

There were, likewise, thirteen persons who placed themselves under the care and teaching of the church as catechumens or inquirers. Several of these, I have no doubt, will soon be confirmed in the love of God.

In the afternoon, I preached at the hospital, during which there was a most precious prayer-meeting held in the tent, and many spoke, and with the deepest emotion told of the new joys they felt. Sabbath night I preached on the words, "My Spirit shall not always strive with man." Five or six remained after preaching for religious conversation and prayer. Thus ended the most memorable day in the life of many, and one that must have a most important influence on our future in time and eternity.

VII. PREACHING BY MOONLIGHT.

The Rev. Mr. Alvord, who has written so much, as well as travelled so much, for the soldiers, illustrates the varied nature of his Christian mission by the following vivid sketch. I can hardly doubt that "the guides" will hereafter point out the spot to which he refers as one of the memorable places,— the place where, in the war of the Rebellion, the soldier's friend preached by moonlight. In a letter to a correspondent, Mr. Alvord says, —

Last evening was beautifully moonlight, and I had a scene which you would have delighted to witness. On the hillside yonder lies a cloud of canvas, and the chaplain proposed that I should go up and have preaching. "Of course," I said; and soon the church-call from the bugle brought me a crowd of two or three hundred. There they stood, forming a circle a number of rods in diameter, and two or three feet deep. The moon swam through the heavens above, the great blue dome resting on surrounding hills and distant water. Far over the Potomac, the sun in going down had left behind a gorgeous aurora, — his day-robes thrown off at bedtime. Near and below us were the transports dotting the water or hanging along the rude wharves, and all the bustle of the day was sinking into a hum broken only by some neighing horse, or sweet bugle strains from afar, and nearer, by the in-tent talk of multitudes.

In such a church, with such galleries, we broke forth with "Come, Holy Spirit," and then the chaplain's strong voice was heard in prayer. Again, "Live on the battle-field" rolled out in the night air. It was a kind of inspiration. All eyes were now upon me. I could not see the eyes of any one. A ring of grim warriors in great-coats, each face seemingly alike, (shadowy cartoons), centred eye and ear and heart upon my lips. It was easy to preach, and I trust with a blessing. Again the song rose more loudly than before, and with a short benediction the strange assembly dispersed. The majority wheeled into squads and marched to quarters. Others, especially officers, came around to thank me for the service. I retired, feeling that the word of the Lord is fitted to all people and all places, and that we may in the morning sow our seed, and in the evening hold not our hand.

VIII. A SOUL BROUGHT TO JESUS.

A correspondent of the "Boston Recorder," over the initials "J. J. M.," writes as follows: —

In one of my visits to the Court House Hospital, in Gettysburg, I noticed lying in the hall, among many others, an individual of a large and powerful frame. There was something in his countenance that fixed my attention at once, and awakened a special sympathy in his behalf. He had the look of a man who had never known fear, nor asked for help,— he could suffer without a groan and die without a complaint.

In answer to my inquiries, I learned that he was from Wisconsin, and of the Sixth Regiment; he had been wounded on the first of July, and the fatal ball had entered the right breast and passed out near the spine.

He did not ask me, as many others, if I thought he might recover; but said, in answer to an inquiry in regard to his religious hopes, —

"Sir, I am anxious to do everything I can for my soul. I have received no religious education. Can you teach me, and tell me what I must do to be saved?"

I knelt on the floor by his side and endeavored to explain to him the first principles of Christian faith. He told me that during the days and nights that he had been lying wounded and alone, he had been thinking most of the time of his sins against God; much of the time he had despaired of forgiveness. And he wished to know if there was any way in which God could forgive them, for he felt that he himself could do nothing.

I sought to unfold to him the way of life, and to lead him to the Lamb of God. I was rejoiced that he comprehended every truth, and appeared to rest upon the blessed promise, "I will be merciful to your unrighteousness, and your sins and your iniquities will I remember no more."[1] Before I left him, he said to me, "Sir, I want you to baptize me; I believe in Jesus Christ as my Saviour, and I wish to confess him before I die."

I found on proper examination that he did not rely on

[1] Hebrews viii. 12.

baptism to save him, but merely wished to obey the divine command, and I hoped, as an humble and penitent sinner, he was entitled to the ordinance.

But in order that he might rest, and have time to think on the subject, I left him, and returned again in an hour. He was expecting me, and earnestly requested me not to forget what I had promised.

I brought one of the surgeons with me and a friendly soldier, and, kneeling by the side of the wounded man, I invoked the presence of the great Sufferer and endeavored to lift the anxious one into the bosom of eternal mercy. I then baptized "Levi Steadman" in the name of the blessed Trinity.

When the ceremony was ended, he said, "I thank you, I thank you; now I will rest."

On the following morning, I came to his bed, but he was asleep, and for many hours, being called away, I was not able to see him; but when I again came to him, he was sensible, and, while suffering the greatest pain, was evidently peaceful.

"Do you still trust in Jesus," I said to him.

"Oh, yes," he replied; "I lean on him; I hope in him alone; pray for me that God may forgive me, and not forsake me in death."

I was again absent for more than a day, visiting the field hospitals, and when I returned, I hastened to the Court House; but when I came to the bed of Steadman, he was not there.

"Where," I said to the man, "is Steadman?"

"He died half an hour ago," was the answer.

"And how did he die?" I asked.

"He was sensible and peaceful to the end, and prayed much that God would not judge him for his sins, but would show him mercy, for the sake of Jesus."

May we not hope that the repenting soldier, like the dying thief, was received that day into the paradise of God?

IX. A MOTHER'S THANK-OFFERING.

The following letter furnishes an indirect, but expressive and deserved testimony to the value of the labors of the Christian Commission in sending pious men to our armies and hospitals, to attend to the wants of the soldiers, supply them with religious books, preach to them, pray with them and for them, and, with the blessing of God, lead them to a saving knowledge of his truth and the way of eternal life. It was written by Mrs. Isabella G. Duffield, a sister of the late Dr. Bethune, of New York, and a grand-daughter of Isabella Graham, of whose piety and benevolence so many traditions still linger in the memory of our own and of a former generation. It becomes others, surely, who have sons and brothers in the army, in like manner, to remember by their prayers and gifts those who go forth to alleviate the sufferings of our soldiers, and to save them from the shoals and quicksands on which they are so liable to be wrecked, for time and eternity.

The letter is addressed to the President of the Commission.

DETROIT, September 30th, 1863.

GEORGE H. STUART, Esq.

DEAR SIR:— Having, with great thankfulness to God, heard by telegraph that my youngest son, Adjutant H. M. Duffield, is not wounded, but quite well at Chattanooga, I send you twenty dollars, as a thank-offering from a mother for the preservation of her son at the battle of Chickamauga.[1] May the blessing of our Father in heaven go with it!

I think of the Christian Commission and the Sanitary Commission as twin brothers going forward to their glorious work. Oh, my friend, what a field is open to Christians now, and how ought they to improve it in trying to rescue those who are "led captive by the Devil at his will!" God bless you, and the dear precious Christian Commission! Surely the blessing of those who are ready to perish will rest upon you. Ah! little do you know how much comfort you give to anxious mothers, when they hear of your locations. "My boy is there," is her thought; and then she bows the knee and prays that your labors may be blessed to him and others.

Surely, it is like going out into the highways and hedges, when you look after the spiritual wants of soldiers. You encourage Christian soldiers, while you awaken the impenitent. Oh, how noble to be near the sick-bed and cheer him with your blessed words!

> "When the groan his faint heart giveth
> Seems the last sigh of despair."

Oh, how I have wept and prayed for our beloved country! Two sons (one colonel, and the youngest the adjutant) I gave. The colonel is wounded so that he cannot go back, and the dear young adjutant has been in this battle. But I put him under the shadow of God's wing, and he has kept him safe. I am anxious, but still I say,

> "If new sorrow should befall,
> If my noble boy should fall,
> If the bright head I have blest
> On the cold earth finds its rest,

---

[1] In Tennessee, where the battle was fought between General Rosecrans and the Rebel Bragg.

> Still, with all the mother's heart
> Torn and quivering with the smart,
> I yield him 'neath Thy chastening rod,
> To my country and my God."

You will never know the good you have done till "God shall wipe away all tears from every eye," and you see how many gems shall sparkle in your crown which have been gathered from our army.

How much good your Commission has done! God bless you all! In haste,

Your sister in Christ.

X. A NEW THING IN THE ARMY.

In one of my circuits, (says a follower of Him who "went about doing good,") I made a singular discovery. In the Vermont Twelfth, the lieutenant of the guard stepped from the ranks (they were then on duty), and took "Banners"[1] for all his company. He expressed his hearty and repeated thanks for them. Having directed me to the chaplain, whom I wished to see, he added, "And I have just paroled fifty men for Sabbath school service." He then pointed to some unfinished barracks outside of the camp, and said, "You'll find the scholars there."

I turned my steps thither. The new Bucktail Regiment lay partly between this and the barracks, and on the way I gave some of my stores to them. Reaching the place, I found what I have never seen before in this army or any other. I found what I think was never seen before in any army on earth,—a regularly organized Sabbath school,—organized, as I afterwards learned, before the brave Vermonters left their native mountains. There they were, in squads or classes, each with a teacher at its head, intent on their lessons.

[1] The title of a periodical for soldiers.

XI. THE LORD'S SUPPER IN CAMP.

A clergyman, who, among other labors which he performed on a temporary visit to the army, took part in the administration of the Lord's Supper, sets before us the following scene:—

I enjoyed this privilege (he says) in the camp of the Seventieth Indiana Regiment, whose chaplain, the Rev. A. C. Allen, was a room-mate with me at college many years ago. The colonel of the regiment was B. Harrison, a grandson of President Harrison, a pious man and an elder in the church. He, with a captain, who holds the same religious office at home, and a pious surgeon, in whom I found a former pupil of mine, acted as officiating elders.

The preparatory service was held on Saturday night, in the open air, before the chaplain's tent. Hundreds of officers and soldiers were present. On Sabbath morning, the dress parade and inspection were held before breakfast, so as not to interfere with the religious service. At nine, A. M., the bugle sounded, and the people came flocking to the front of the colonel's tent, each bringing his chair, stool or box, on which to sit. The prayer, the hymn, the text and the sermon, all pointed to a common theme,— Calvary and its victim. None were unaffected, and many were moved to tears, when, with bowed heads, the communicants gathered together to partake of the broken bread and poured-out wine. We all felt that Jesus was at the head of the table, and that he was there to dispense rich blessings to his humble, grateful guests. The closing act was an exhortation, earnest and direct to those who had renewed the vows of their espousal, and the soldiers then retired with strength for days to come,—days of temptation fierce and strong to all,—days of trial and suffering to many.

There was an evening service, at which the object was to incite Christians to set the standard of their piety high, to show themselves worthy followers of Him who, among the other ends of his work on earth, has taught us how to live as well as to die, who "was holy, harmless, undefiled." In the army, especially, men need all the strength that a due observance of the Lord's Supper can afford. Helped by such means, and compelled as they are to be watchful, or forfeit all, no doubt some among them develop a more robust, symmetrical character in the army than they would ever have reached amid the more quiet scenes of life at home.

XII. THE FIRST SABBATH AT BEAUFORT.

Our forces took possession of this town on the tenth of November, 1861. The flag of the nation, which had been hauled down and dishonored in the capture of Sumter, had just been raised once more, at Hilton Head, on the soil of South Carolina, with shouts of triumph and salvos of artillery.

The Roundheads,[1] and the Michigan Eighth were sent to this outpost of the chief military station. The first Sabbath came;—and shall its wonted rest, the teachings and prayers of the sanctuary, be denied to those wanderers from a distant home? No; there were pious officers there, and ministers of Christ, who were careful to mark the day as the day which God has hallowed, and to turn its opportunities to account for the benefit of the soldier.

We were strolling leisurely through the streets, on that Sabbath (writes a correspondent from the place), when suddenly the glorious notes of "Old Hundred" burst on our ears. The extreme quiet of the town, the gentle sigh-

[1] See the account of them on page 27.

ing of the moss-grown oaks, the full, deep tones of the organ, and the powerful voices of the singers, as they joined in the hymn, combined to awaken feelings which it is not easy to describe. We followed the sounds, and were led to the Baptist church, and there a scene met our eyes, for which, in our ignorance of any such gathering, we were not at all prepared. The glittering muzzles protruding from the windows, and the stack of drums without, proclaimed the nature of the exercises. Nor, on entering the sacred place, was the sight less novel or unexpected. Over the pulpit, from which treason had so long been preached, hung in graceful folds the regimental colors of the Pennsylvania "Roundheads." Ministers of the gospel were in the desk. A sermon was preached, and the other parts of worship performed in connection with the sermon. A prayer for our common country and its lawful rulers was offered once more, and for the first time there since the beginning of the rebellion. After the benediction the Roundheads and the men of the Michigan Eighth gave three patriotic cheers, and then taking down their arms, marched quietly back to their tents.

XIII. A LEAF FROM HIS JOURNAL.

A correspondent from the army who went, with a friend, among the soldiers to distribute medical stores, and Bibles, tracts, and other religious books, found a general eagerness among them to receive such donations. A single leaf from his journal may be copied here.

Wending our way down a deep gully beyond the fort, we passed up and around Fort Marcy, and approached a regimental hospital. Here the sick boys of the Vermont Second took gratefully both our tracts and the comforts for invalids. I said to one of them, "Do you not want to go home?"

"Yes," said he, "but not till we conquer the rebels."

There were tents in a wooded region on our right, from which the men, as soon as they heard of our errand, came up and begged for books.

"How glad I am for this," said one of them, as he pressed a Testament upon his bosom between his two hands. Half a mile further, we came upon the Pennsylvania First Cavalry. We stopped and handed a tract to a soldier by the road-side. He thanked us, and flourishing the prize over his head, shouted to his comrades, of whom twenty or more came rushing to the spot. The supplying of these brought to us ten times their number, and in five minutes they were twenty deep on either side of our wagon, shouting, "Give me one," "Give me one," "Give me a Testament," and a perfect palisade of extended arms and grasping hands environed us. We urged them to stand back; for it seemed as if wagon and horse would break down under their weight. They did so instantly; but the clamor only rose from a wider circle, "Give me a book! Give me a book!"

One of them held up a pack of cards in his hand, and challenged an exchange.

"Give me a Testament," he said, "and I'll give up the cards!"

The Testament was given, and he then threw the cards beneath our horse's feet. And so we worked, both of us, dealing out our supply of books to the eager, hungering crowd, as fast as our hands could pass them to those who received them. I could think of nothing but the assault of starving men, and these men like a pack of hungry wolves from the forest, that had broken loose upon us. I noticed among them one poor fellow, who, shot through the lungs, seemed near his end; his lips were pale, and his every feature marked him as a victim of the grave. I stooped down and spoke to him of Christ.

"I can trust in Him," he faintly replied.

The smile on his pallid countenance showed that he was resting on the hope "which is sure and steadfast."

"Dear youth, happy even in such distress," I said to myself. Christian friends of the soldiers should pray that all who die may die as calmly, and remember that what we do for them must be done quickly.

The next regiment to which we came had a chaplain, but the men said, "We never see him!" He is one of a class that ought never to have been here. Many of the chaplains are noble, faithful men, who honor their profession, and make themselves indispensable to the army. But some, I must say, have no fitness for their work, and some are a disgrace to the office.

XIV. GIFT OF THE PRAYER-BOOKS.

It was a gift which illustrates the Preacher's word:[1]—

"In the morning sow thy seed, and in the evening withhold not thine hand: for thou knowest not whether shall prosper, either this or that, or whether they both shall be alike good."

"Are you going to take your book with you to the battle-field?" This question Edward R. Graton, of Company C, a native of Clappville, Mass., addressed to one of his companions, the day before the fight at Newbern, N. C.

"I don't know," the other replied.

"I shall take mine," said he, and at the word he placed it carefully in the left breast pocket of his blouse.

[1] Ecclesiastes xi. 6.

These prayer-books, (says the Rev. Mr. James, chaplain of one of the New England Regiments,)[1] had been given to them by a friend at home the day they started for the war. A copy was given also to another soldier of the company, but he threw it away at Camp Hicks, in Annapolis.

Among the first who were brought back wounded from the field was Graton, — shot with a ball through his side. It had passed in at his left breast, and out at his back, making a severe and dangerous wound. It would have proved mortal at the instant, had it not passed directly through his prayer-book, a distance of an inch and a quarter. This obstacle deadened the force of the bullet, and gave it another direction. The book lies before me as I write, (says the chaplain,) pierced on its side; and very near the middle of the cover is seen the blood of the owner, staining it through at least two hundred pages.

This prayer-book, worn in his bosom, which turned aside thus the shaft of death, lengthened out his probation a whole precious month. During this time, there was an opportunity for many interviews with him. He often expressed fully and freely his trust in the Lord Jesus, as the sinner's friend and Saviour, and when he died, died peaceful and happy in his sheltering arms.

This little book will be dear to his friends, and especially to his mother. I have engaged to give it to her in person, (says Mr. James,) after our return home.

XV. FORTUNES OF A BIBLE.

The battle had been raging fearfully for many hours on the bloody field of Antietam, with alternate victory and defeat. In one continued shower the leaden hail poured

---

[1] Connected with General Burnside's expedition to Newbern and Roanoke.

thick and fast into the ranks of our brave soldiers, leaving thousands of them dead or wounded.

Where the contest had been fiercest, a soldier, severely wounded, was lying upon the ground, unable to move. The dead and dying were all around him, but the voice of one among them seemed to rise above the rest, indicating by its tone the most intense anguish. The wounded man looked around him this way and that as far as he was able, to see if he could distinguish whose voice it was, but in vain. He then called to know who it was, and the reply came in an agonized voice: "It is I. Oh, I'm dying, I'm dying." His unseen comrade tried to comfort him as well as he could, and suggested that he might be better in a short time; but the poor fellow replied, "Oh no; I'm dying, I'm dying."

Then rallying all his remaining strength, he threw a book in the direction of his new-found friend, and asked him to take care of it. At that moment a rebel soldier came along, and gave this friend a drink from his canteen; and emboldened by his kindness, the Union soldier asked him to show the same favor to the dying comrade, who was writhing in his agony a few feet from him. Very soon the Southerner returned, saying that it was too late, the man was already dead. He then asked the Southerner if he would hand him the book that had been thrown to him, and he kindly complied with this request. It proved to be a pocket Bible, handsomely bound, with the name of "W. S. Pollard, Thirteenth Regiment Massachusetts Volunteers," engraved in gilt upon the cover.

The wounded soldier was soon taken with others of his comrades to a place of safety, and he carried with him to his hospital bed the dying gift so affectionately presented to him. He knew nothing of the donor except his name, and whether or not the precious truths contained in his

Bible were the solace of his dying moments will be known perhaps only in eternity; but it was evidently his last earthly thought and care to place the sacred volume where it would be cared for and blessed to others. Doubtless some kind friend, perhaps a mother or a sister, had presented it to him, and with thoughtful care, had made an oil-silk cover, which, though carried through marches and into battle, had preserved it pure and unsullied.

The soldier into whose possession the Bible came in such a peculiar manner was a Pennsylvanian, and was induced somewhat reluctantly to dispose of it to a pious fellow-soldier in the hospital, who was from Massachusetts. This soldier has since returned, and it was at his house that the writer saw the Bible, and learned its interesting history. The blessed promises contained in this book may have comforted and cheered the poor soldier who first owned it through many a weary hour in the camp and on the march. Having passed unharmed through the smoke and peril of battle, and been rescued from among the dead and dying on the field of blood, may it yet be the means of leading many a precious soul into the paths of peace.[1]

XVI. AN ANSWER TO PRAYER.

I was passing the camp of a Rhode Island Regiment, near Falmouth, when a soldier came up and said to me abruptly, "Do you belong to the Christian Commission?"

"I do," I replied.

"Then I saw some of your men at Stoneman's Station, and received some papers from them."

[1] From "S. E. D.," in the *American Messenger*. The writer appends to the article this notice:—"Mr. Pollard's relatives may obtain this Bible by addressing Mr. S. H. Lincoln, Plainfield, Mass."

This was all the introduction, and he then went on to relate to me some passages of his life.

"I came out here," said he, "as rough and bad as any of the men. But I had left a praying mother at home. While in camp at Poolesville, I heard that she was dead. After that, her image was never out of my thoughts. It seemed as if her form appeared to me as in a mirror, and always as wrestling for her wayward son. Go where I might, I felt as if I saw her in her place of prayer, kneeling and putting up her petitions to God, and not even the roar of the battle could drown the soft tones of her voice."

He was in the fight at Fair Oaks, and when it ceased, sat down exhausted upon a log by the road-side, and then, to use his own words, he "thought over the matter." Heaps of dead men lay on every side of him. They had fallen, but he was still unharmed. The melting words of his mother's prayer came back to his mind with new power. He thought of his own condition, and of her happy home, so far removed from the strife and agony of war.

A pious soldier of his company noticed that he was very thoughtful, and inquired the reason. To this friend he opened his mind freely, and told him how he felt. They sought occasions for private conference, communed together and prayed, and strength was given him to make "the last resolve;" and the soldier who had been so "rough and bad" became a soldier in the army of the meek and lowly Jesus. The sainted mother had not prayed in vain. A battle had just been fought, a victory won, which was spreading joy throughout the nation; but here, too, was a triumph, — a different triumph, — such as causes the angels of God in heaven to rejoice.

I have seldom found a happier man than I found in this young soldier. He was happy in the service of his Master, and happy in the service of his country. Nearly all the company were irreligious and profane, but he was firm against ridicule and opposition. He and his friend did what they could to hold up the cross, and save their comrades. He told me that they went often into the woods to pray, and enjoyed happy seasons there, even when they were the only two.

XVII. A SABBATH WITH THE CONTRABANDS.

I had attended a meeting of chaplains at Bealton Station, on Saturday, and on Sabbath morning went out from the tent of the Christian Commission, and met a company of contrabands at the depot, with whom I had, on the previous evening, had some conversation.

There were probably one hundred and fifty of them. Some of them were men of families, and had left their wives and children in slavery, and were every hour praying for the advance of our army, in order that our troops might have an opportunity to reach them and conduct them to freedom. Several of these men were most devout and earnest Christians. Every evening, they held a prayer-meeting in the midst of their tents, in which there were shed many tears at the mention of their families. The scene would often strike those from our orderly and severely quiet churches as wild and boisterous; but these children of nature cannot pray in set forms, nor always act with measured propriety. Loud are their cries for pardon, many are the trembling and convulsive movements of the body.

"You have had a stormy time of it to-night, uncle."

"Yes, massa; the living child when it is born cries, the dead say nothing."

[1] From the correspondence of Rev. Dr. Marks, in the Army of the Potomac.

I listened on Saturday night, at their camp-fire, to the stories of these children of oppression, and admired more than ever their forgiving temper. In some cases, however, it was evident the iron had often entered into the soul, and they had many times in the past said, "It is better to die than to live."

To these men I preached on Sabbath morning at six o'clock, first asking permission of the superintendent. This was most freely granted; he at the same time bore the highest testimony to the sobriety, honesty, and piety of these contrabands; and said, in contrast with this, that some months ago he had under his care one hundred Irishmen, and every day he had quarrels among them, fights, and drunkenness, and often his life was threatened and in danger; but here he had no trouble. These men were satisfied with their rations, thankful for employment, and quiet and gentle.

They gathered around me, and I preached to them on the tenderness and pity of our Lord, and that in their trials and sorrow they might have the assurance of his help and aid. I likewise reminded them of the patience and long-suffering of the Son of God, and said they, in imitation of his example, should forgive those who had inflicted on them stripes, torn from them their children,. and in other ways made their lives so bitter to them. They listened with the greatest interest, and some with tears exclaimed, "Yes, blessed Jesus, we will forgive, for we are great sinners."[1]

A few days after this, I was walking in the streets of Alexandria, and heard some one running behind me, and crying aloud, "Massa, massa preacher!"

I looked around and saw a young black man who with

---

[1] That petition in the Lord's Prayer — "Forgive us our debts as we forgive our debtors" — could not have a more beautiful illustration.

a beaming face addressed me as an old friend, and said, "Massa, I can never forget you; you preached for us last Sabbath morning at Bealton. We all thanked you, and talked afterward of what you said."

The whole appearance of his face was that of one who had met a life-long friend. The incident gave me much food for reflection. What a noble and grateful race have we been long despising and trampling under our feet!

XVIII. THE POWER OF SYMPATHY.

The human heart is won to the truth much oftener by sympathy and example than by argument.

As Miss A—— passed through the wards of the soldier's hospital on B—— Street, dispensing words of comfort and encouragement to the patients, a middle-aged man, stern by nature, at times morose, complained to her of a night of extreme pain. She expressed to him her sympathy in the kindest manner, and added, "I hope you felt, though absent from loved ones, that you had the presence of a loving Saviour with you."

He replied harshly, "Miss A——, you spoke to me on that subject once before; I wish to say to you, never mention it to me again. If I want to be religious, I will send for a minister, and get his advice."

In a sorrowful tone she bade him good-morning, and turned away.

One morning after this, as she passed his cot and he was sleeping, she laid some fresh flowers on his pillow and noiselessly withdrew. As the fever left him, he was disposed to sleep much, and she could repeat the act again and again without his notice. Day after day, his eyes were greeted with these fragrant messengers, without his having seen the hand that brought them to him. He became at length impatient to know to whom he was indebted for the grateful favor. He inquired of some of those around him who could be in the hospital that cared so much for him. Perhaps secrecy had been enjoined; at all events he obtained no information.

After several days, when he had become decidedly stronger, he awoke one morning, and, instead of the accustomed bouquet, he found a neat copy of the New Testament on his pillow. At the sight of this, he inquired, "Is Miss A—— in the hospital? I know it must be she; will you please to send for her?"

On her coming to him, he took her hands between his, and, with a voice choked with emotion, exclaimed, "Can you forgive my rude, ungentlemanly conduct toward you? How could you, after such treatment, be so kind?"

"I only want you to know how kind Jesus is, and how he loves you," was her gentle reply.

Months passed away, and I heard again of the same man as being in one of our suburban hospitals. He was still an invalid, but so much better that he was acting as a nurse, and, in strange contrast with what he had been formerly, was taking a deep interest in the religious welfare of the inmates. Happening to speak of his being in the hospital on B—— street, he was asked if he ever saw a lady, Miss A——, who attended on the sick."

"Miss A——?" he replied. "Certainly I saw her, and have cause to remember her. She was the angel of the hospital, and the means of leading me to a knowledge of the Saviour."[1]

[1] See the kindred article on page 66.

XIX. A RELIGIOUS SERVICE FOR THE VETERANS.

After breakfast at the Commission tent, I started (says Dr. Marks) in company with a brother in the ministry, from Long Island, and two others, for White Sulphur Springs, around which were the encampments of the Third corps.

We found the Fortieth New York Regiment, of which an excellent brother, Rev. Mr. Gilder, is chaplain, drawn up to hear addresses from us. This regiment has passed through all the severe battles of the Army of the Potomac, and has had at different times united to it the Hundredth New York, the Eighty-seventh and the Thirty-seventh New York. It is now one of the most powerful in the service; though it has lost more than twelve hundred men, by disease and battle.

We had with these veterans a most interesting service. The pleasure with which we looked upon the scene was increased by the presence of all the officers. No congregation in the army, that I have had the privilege to address, ever enlisted my interest like these — none more awake, none more easily touched. We stand with reverence before these men, for they have been in deaths oft, and perilled all that is dear to man for their country.

After the services, we went through the camp streets, and conversed with many whom we had known in the Peninsula.

We found in this regiment many truly pious men, who had suffered apparently no spiritual loss in consequence of long absence from home and the sanctuary.

At three o'clock, P. M., we went to the camp of the Fourth Maine, of which the Rev. Mr. Chase is chaplain, and found assembled the officers and men of the Fourth,

Third, and Seventeenth Maine, for public worship. One of the streets in camp was selected as the place for preaching. The men sat down on blankets, gun-cloths, and leaves on the ground. A man of any thought or emotion must stand with the deepest reverence in the presence of such veterans.

The remnant of these regiments are the strong dauntless men who have endured every sacrifice, braved every peril, and met death a hundred times. These are the men who, for more than two years, have borne all that to human imagination is most terrible, in trial, suffering, sickness, privation, and wounds. And yet all has been patiently and uncomplainingly endured.

The face beaten by so many storms is bronzed and stern, reminding one of the appearance of the Roman soldiers as seen on the monuments of antiquity. But one has only to speak to these men to find there is a heart that still feels, and to be convinced that the pulses of piety still beat.

I preached to this most interesting assemblage of men, and reminded them of scenes in the Peninsula; of the long marches, the storms, and the terrific battles through which they had passed; how many of their companions had fallen, and how deep should be their gratitude to Heaven that they were alive. After I had finished, the other brethren followed and added much to the impression and interest of the hour. After the service was ended, we went through the throng conversing with many.

After night, we went to the camp of the Sixty-third Pennsylvania, and held a meeting with that and the soldiers of surrounding regiments. It was a spectacle never to be forgotten. The solemn grandeur of the heavens, the silent stars looking down upon us, the multitude of upturned faces, lighted by the camp-fires, the burst of holy song borne afar off and reëchoed in murmurs from the valleys, the subdued silence of prayer, the profound and reverent attention paid to the sermon, the greetings of hundreds of old friends, and the revival of memories of marches, battles, and hospitals, made this night-scene and worship of the greatest interest.

I was greatly rejoiced, in subsequent conversations, to find that many whom I had feared were dead had recovered from their wounds and were now in the regiment or had returned to their homes. And I gathered from the conversations of the day, and from the feeling manifested, that there never was a time in the history of the army when the men more desired religious instruction or were so eager to listen to the gospel.[1]

[1] This communication is under date of October, 1863.

CHAPTER VI.

HAPPY DEATHS OF BRAVE MEN.

I. DEATH OF GENERAL MITCHELL.

This distinguished officer died at Beaufort, S. C., on the evening of Thursday, October thirtieth, 1862, shortly after his assumption of the command of that district. He had already performed some of the most brilliant exploits of the war, and great hopes rested on him for the future. His death was justly regarded as one of the greatest losses that the country has sustained. His name will shine with lustre in American history, as long as the memory of patriotism, valor, and genius shall abide among men. A gentleman who watched at his bedside has given the following description of his last hours.

The general, as I stood near him, reached out his hand, and taking mine, looked up in my face, and said, "It is a blessed thing to have a Christian's hope in a time like this." After an hour, perhaps, he beckoned to me, and feebly shaking my hand, said, "You must not stay longer; go now, and come to me in the morning."

Major Birch, who had been untiring in his attentions, entered, almost convulsed with grief. He had just taken down the last will and wishes of his beloved commander. He conducted the Rev. Mr. Strickland to the bedside of the general, and beckoned me to follow. I did not hear all the words of the general, as the Rev. Mr. Strickland stooped to speak to him; but I did hear him say, "Kneel down," and then add the request that he would offer a short prayer. How still he lay while that prayer was addressed to the throne of the God of Battles! At its conclusion, as we rose from our knees, his eyes rested on me, and his hand was extended again. "You can do me no good," said he faintly; "do not stay." His mind seemed perfectly clear and calm, but he was failing constantly.

Oh, it is a tearful sight to us all to see a father thus dying at the same hour with his two sons, and they not know it, — not permitted to treasure up his last words, his last look; that all these must be given to strangers. But they are too sick yet to bear the blow; it would shatter them; therefore they must be kept in ignorance till a coming hour.

At seven o'clock, P. M., of the same day, the writer adds, —

General Mitchell has breathed his last. He is gone from us. Our hopes that were placed on him must be placed higher, higher. With Victor Hugo, we must learn to say, "It is not generals or soldiers, but God, who must give us the victory, in this war of the powers of darkness!"

General Mitchell had entire possession of his faculties till within an hour or two of his departure, when his reason seemed to wander. His last intelligent expression was, "I am ready to go." His last intelligent look was directed to the Rev. Mr. Strickland and when he could speak no longer, seeing that friend approach, he pointed with his hand twice toward heaven, and the next moment his soul took its flight thither.[1]

He died after an illness of four days only. His remains rest in the shadow of the Episcopal church in Beaufort, S. C., near those of his aid-de-camp, Captain Williams, who died two days before him.

[1] I have added a few words to this letter from a supplementary report.

II. THE CHILD'S PRAYER THAT OF THE MAN.

It was the evening after a great battle. All day long the din of strife had echoed far, and thickly strewn lay the shattered forms of those so lately erect and exultant in the flush and strength of manhood. Among the many who bowed to the conqueror Death that night, was a youth in the first freshness of mature life. The strong limbs lay listless, and the dark hair was matted with gore, on the pale, broad forehead. His eyes were closed. As one who ministered to the sufferer bent over him, he at first thought him dead; but the white lips moved, and slowly in weak tones he repeated,

> "Now I lay me down to sleep,
> I pray the Lord my soul to keep;
> If I should die before I wake,
> I pray the Lord my soul to take;
> And this I ask for Jesus' sake."

As he finished, he opened his eyes, and, meeting the pitying gaze of a brother soldier, he exclaimed, "My mother taught me that when I was a little boy, and I have said it every night since I can remember. Before the morning dawns, I believe that God will take my soul for 'Jesus' sake;' but before I die, I want to send a message to my mother."

He was carried to a temporary hospital, and a letter was written to his mother, which he dictated, full of Christian faith and filial love. He was calm and peaceful. Just as the sun arose, his spirit went home. His last articulate words were, —

> "I pray the Lord my soul to take;
> And this I ask for Jesus' sake."

So died William B—— of the Massachusetts Volunteers. The prayer of childhood was the prayer of manhood. He learned it at his mother's knee in his far distant Northern home, and he whispered it in dying, when his young life ebbed away on a Southern battle-field.

III. SO THE YOUNG SOLDIER DIED.

"Bring me my knapsack," said a young soldier, who lay sick in one of the hospitals at Washington, and was evidently near his end, — "bring me my knapsack."

"Why do you want your knapsack?" inquired the head lady of the band of nurses.

"I want my knapsack," said the young man again and yet more earnestly.

His knapsack was brought to him, and, as he took it, his eye gleamed with pleasure, and a smile passed over his countenance as he brought out from it, one after another, its hoarded treasures.

"There," said he, "that is a Bible from my mother. And this — Washington's farewell address — is the gift of my father. And this "—— His voice failed.

The nurse looked down to see what it was, and there was the face of a beautiful maiden.

"Now," said the dying young soldier, "I want you to put all these under my pillow."

She did as she was requested, and the poor sufferer, overcome by the strength of his feelings and the progress of disease, laid himself down to die, with the precious tokens under his head. He directed the mementos to be sent to his parents when he should be no more. Calm and joyful was he as he rapidly breathed his life away. For him it was only passing from night to endless day, from death to immortality. So the young soldier died.

IV. THE LAST MESSAGE.

A young soldier, while dying very happily in the Douglas Hospital, in the District of Columbia, broke out in singing the following stanza: —

> "Great Jehovah, we adore thee,
> God the Father, God the Son,
> God the Spirit, joined in glory
> On the same eternal throne:
> Endless praises
> To Jehovah, three in one."

The chaplain then asked him if he had any message to send to his friends.

"Yes," said he. "Tell my father that I have tried to pray as we used to pray at home. Tell him that Christ is now all my hope, all my trust, that he is precious to my soul. Tell him that I am not afraid to die, — all is calm. Tell him that I believe Christ will take me to himself, and to my dear sister who is in heaven."

The voice of the dying boy faltered in the intervals between these precious sentences. When the hymn commencing, "Nearer, my God, to thee," was read to him, at the end of each stanza, he exclaimed with striking energy, "O Lord Jesus, thou art coming nearer to me." Also, at the end of each stanza of the hymn (which was also read to him) commencing, —

> "Just as I am — without one plea,
> But that thy blood was shed for me,
> And that thou bid'st me come to thee,
> O Lamb of God, I come,"

he exclaimed, "I come! O Lamb of God, I come!"

Speaking again of his friends, he said, "Tell my father that I died happy." His last words were, "Heavenly Father, I'm coming to thee!" Then the Christian soldier sweetly and calmly fell "asleep in Jesus."

This scene was witnessed by about twenty fellow-soldiers, and the effect upon the feelings of all was very marked.

A Roman Catholic, who lay near the dying one, said, with tears in his eyes, and with strong emotion, "I never want to die happier than that man did." Another said, "I never prayed until last night; but when I saw that man die so happy, I determined to seek religion too."

V. SURPRISED, BUT READY.

The clock had just struck the midnight hour, when the chaplain was summoned to the cot of a wounded soldier. He had left him only an hour before with confident hopes of his speedy recovery,—hopes which were shared by the surgeon and the wounded man himself. But a sudden change had taken place, and the surgeon had come to say that the man could live but an hour or two at most, and to beg the chaplain to make the fearful announcement to the dying man.

He was soon at his side, but, overpowered by his emotions, was utterly unable to deliver his message. The dying man, however, quickly read the solemn truth in the altered looks of the chaplain, his faltering voice and ambiguous words. He had not before entertained a doubt of his recovery. He was expecting soon to see his mother, and with her kind nursing soon to be well. He was therefore entirely unprepared for the announcement, and at first it was overwhelming.

"I am to die, then; and,—how long?"

As he had before expressed hope in Christ, the chaplain replied, "You have made your peace with God; let death come as soon as it will, he will carry you over the river."

"Yes; but this is so awfully sudden, awfully sudden!"—his lips quivered; he looked up grievingly—"and I shall not see my mother."

"Christ is better than a mother," murmured the chaplain.

"Yes." The word came in a whisper. His eyes were closed; the lips still wore that trembling grief, as if the chastisement were too sore, too hard to be borne; but as the minutes passed, and the soul lifted itself up stronger and more steadily, upon the wings of prayer, the countenance grew calmer, the lips steadier; and when the eyes opened again, there was a light in their depths that could have come only from heaven.

"I thank you for your courage," he said, more feebly, taking the hand of the chaplain; "the bitterness is over now, and I feel willing to die. Tell my mother"—he paused, gave one sob, dry, and full of the last anguish of earth—"tell her how I longed to see her; but if God will permit me, I will be near her. Tell her to comfort all who loved me, to say that I thought of them all. Tell my father that I am glad he gave his consent, and that other fathers will mourn for other sons. Tell my minister, by word or letter, that I thought of him, and that I thank him for all his counsels. Tell him I find that Christ will not desert the passing soul, and that I wish him to give my testimony to the living, that nothing is of real worth but the religion of Jesus. And now, will you pray with me?"

With swelling emotion and tender tones, the chaplain besought God's grace and presence; then, restraining his sobs, he bowed down and pressed upon the beautiful brow, already chilled with the breath of the coming angel, twice, thrice, a fervent kiss. They might have been as tokens from the father and mother, as well as himself. So thought perhaps the dying soldier, for a heavenly smile touched his face with new beauty, as he said, "Thank you; I won't trouble you any longer. You are wearied out; go to your rest."

"The Lord God be with you," was the firm response. "Amen," trembled from the fast whitening lips.

Another hour passed. The chaplain still moved uneasily around his room. There were hurried sounds overhead, and footsteps on the stairs. He opened his door, and encountered the surgeon, who whispered one little word, "Gone." Christ's soldier had found the Captain of his salvation.

VI. LOOKING UP.

As the Rev. Mr. Chidlaw was leaving the side of a dying soldier, in one of the Western hospitals, he heard the uncomplaining sufferer say, "It is a blessed thing to die looking up."

"And what does my brother behold, looking up?"

"Christ and heaven," was the prompt and joyous response.

VII. NOT DUMB, THOUGH SPEECHLESS.

In one of the hospitals near Alexandria lay a youthful soldier gasping his last breath. He could not speak; but by signs he made his comrade, who was a kind-hearted though unlettered son of Erin, understand that he wanted the chaplain. Rev. Mr. B—— was soon by his bedside.

"What is it, my poor boy?" he said kindly.

The dying youth feebly pointed to his mother's signature

in a letter lying beside his pillow, then more feebly to the dark locks which shaded his pale brow.

The chaplain was quick to catch his meaning. "Send a lock of hair to your mother, James?" The eager nod answered him.

"Any message, dear boy? Can you whisper a word of farewell?"

No, he could not; his breath was nearly spent. But a slight movement of his finger, first pointing to his heart, and then upward, was full of significance to the intent eye of the soldier's friend.

"Yes, Jamie, I understand, — your soul is resting on Jesus, you are going to your heavenly home. I shall write to your mother, and she will bless God amid her tears."

A loving, grateful smile beamed upon the chaplain, and Jamie was no more.

VIII. THE DOCTOR'S YOUTHFUL PATIENT.

An army correspondent of the Philadelphia "Presbyterian" gives the following incident as related by a medical friend, in the cabin of a Mississippi transport steamer, to a group of listening soldiers:—

In the town of L——, where I reside and practise my profession, a company was raised for the —— Iowa Regiment. Among the volunteers was a boy about sixteen years of age, and known as Billy W——. His home was a den of iniquity and vice. His parents were the vilest of the vile. I know of no moral, and of but few human, laws that they did not habitually violate. So far as I know, Billy never attended a Sabbath school. I do not believe he ever attended church half a dozen times in his life; and as to religious knowledge, I regarded him as little better than a heathen. Before the company left us, every member of it was furnished with a copy of the New Testament. Billy received his, joined his regiment, went to the seat of war, and for months we heard nothing from him. In the bloody and terrible conflict of Shiloh, in the month of April last, Billy, the drummer-boy, was dangerously wounded. He was put upon a cot, placed upon a government transport, and brought down to Cairo, with other wounded soldiers. Here a kind Providence seemed to watch over the boy. His youth, his manly fortitude, and his interesting appearance, enlisted the sympathies of strangers, and, instead of being sent to the hospital, he was taken upon his cot to the cars and carried to Dixon, whence he was sent directly to his home at L——. On his way from Pittsburg Landing he contracted a disease which would, I think, of itself have soon terminated his brief life. Immediately upon his arrival home, I was called to visit him professionally. The news of his arrival had drawn to the house three or four of our pious women, who went to minister to his wants. I saw at once that he must soon die, and said to him,—

"Billy, I will do all I can for you. I will give you medicine, but it will, I fear, do you no good. You probably have but a very short time to live."

He received the announcement with a composure which astonished us all. It was evidently not the result of stupidity or indifference. A pleasant smile was upon his countenance, and there was something about him which those of us who had known him before his enlistment failed to comprehend. After a few moments' silence, he looked up to me, and said, pleasantly,—

"Doctor, I bless God that I am not afraid to die. Jesus is my Saviour. You have been very kind to me, doctor, and now I have one favor to ask. It is the last request I shall ever make of you. Kneel right down here, by my bed, and pray for me."

I was astonished. I never supposed the boy knew what prayer meant, and wondered where he had learned. I was never so perplexed before.

"Billy," I replied, "I cannot do that. I try sometimes to pray for myself, but I have never in my life prayed audibly in public. You must excuse me."

"Doctor, I cannot. You can,—you must pray with me."

"But, Billy, I cannot. I will do this, however. We will get a Bible, and I will read to you a chapter,—some of the words of the Saviour. Then we will all kneel around your bed, and one of these good women will lead us in prayer."

He assented, though with great reluctance. He was evidently not satisfied. The one great desire of his heart seemed to be that *I* should offer the prayer. After a moment's silence he said to me,—

"Turn me upon my side, doctor, if you please, that I may lie with my face toward you as you read."

As gently as I could, I turned him upon his side. A large Bible was then brought and laid before him upon the bed. In an instant he threw his attenuated arms around it, and pressed it to his heart with all his remaining strength. It seemed as if he could not let it go. I remembered that Testament, and I knew then how Billy had come to love his Bible, and how he had learned to pray. God seemed to direct me what to read to this dying boy. I opened at one of those chapters in John's Gospel so full of precious words, and read it, with a faltering voice, I assure you. Billy kept the Bible firmly clasped in his arms, while I was reading. As soon as the chapter was finished, we all knelt around his bed, while one of the women offered one of the most appropriate and touching prayers I ever heard. There were no unmoistened eyes there as we rose from our knees. Then I bade Billy good-by, promising to call and see him in the morning, if he was then alive. Just as I was leaving the room, one of the women present touched me on the shoulder, and said, —

"Doctor, Billy wishes to see you a moment."

I went back. As soon as I was near enough, he caught my hands in his, and said, —

"Doctor, I cannot be denied. You must, — you must pray with me."

I could resist no longer; and so, sinking down on my knees beside him, in faltering accents and as best I could, I commended that poor, dying boy to the Friend of sinners. Perhaps the petition was not rejected. I am not much given to the melting mood, but I am free to say that I wept then as I never wept before. Billy was satisfied. He grasped my hand, and thanked me as I rose from my knees. We then bade each other good-by a second time, and parted to meet no more in this world. Within the next hour he died a most triumphant and happy death, and doubtless now stands before the throne with

> "A crown upon his forehead,
> A harp within his hands."

Such was my friend's story. Comment could add nothing to its point; and, for some moments after its conclusion, the silence was unbroken by a single word from the little group of attentive listeners. Was there one there who did not breathe the prayer, "Let me die the death of the righteous, and let my last end be like his"?[1] I hope not.

[1] Numbers xii. 3.

IX. SURELY I COME QUICKLY.

I have seen (writes the Rev. Mr. Alvord from the army) a Testament pierced with a minie ball which also pierced the owner's heart. Opening the book, I found name and date, and pencilling which seemed to indicate premonition. On one of the fly-leaves he had commenced as follows: —

"With tearful eyes I think I see" —

and then, as if he had recollected the verse, he began again, just below, —

"With tearful eyes I look around;
Life seems a dark and stormy sea;
Yet 'midst the gloom I hear a sound,
A heavenly whisper, — Come to me."

I followed the bullet, and the first passage struck was, "Surely, I come quickly, Amen: even so, come, Lord Jesus." The journey of the messenger from that passage to the life of the poor fellow was very short. The "whisper" of the herald was scarcely heard ere he was in eternity. The mutilated Testament, with its touching record, will be sent home to mourning friends.

X. THE STUDENT'S LAST WISHES.

The chaplain of the Eighty-first Illinois Regiment vouches for the truthfulness of the scene described below.

The Eighty-third Illinois was stationed at Fort Donelson at the time of the last battle there, and is well known for having repulsed an attack of some six thousand of the enemy. A Christian youth, named Adams, belonged to this regiment and was severely wounded in the engagement. He afterwards lay wasting away day by day in the hospital. He had enlisted, while he was a member of college, with a number of others, to fight the battles of freedom. One day when he was extremely weak, he asked the physician how long he would probably live.

"Not long," was the reply; "you are near your end."

"Is it so," he demanded; and was told, "Yes, it is indeed so."

Making then an almost superhuman effort, he raised his body, with the help of his companions, many of whom were standing around his cot, and, stretching forth his emaciated arms, with a voice faint, but firm, he articulated the request, "Now come; give three cheers for the flag of our Union."

His fellow-soldiers gave them with a will and an emphasis such as only our brave boys know how to exhibit, and then awaited his further wishes.

Thus far we have seen in him the traits only of the dying patriot and hero. But he was more than that. The dear fellow added then the request, "Now boys, let one of you kneel down and pray." They dropped on their knees. A Christian comrade led them in prayer. While he was performing the solemn act, the spirit of young Adams, joyful and triumphant, as in a chariot of glory, took its flight home!

Such a mode of dying becomes a soldier who is a Christian as well as a hero.— Such is the power which the religion of Jesus gives to the believer.

XI. THE FAVORITE HYMN.

A workman in Christ's vineyard, who has done much for our sick and wounded soldiers at Washington, writes to a friend as follows: —

The hundred hymn-books you sent me will be very useful, and, I think, will do much good. There is one hymn in the book that I can never forget if I live a thousand years. It is the sixty-third, beginning

> " One sweetly solemn thought."

I had held by the bedside of a dying soldier several prayer-meetings; it was at the Patent Office Hospital, and the soldiers would gather round the bedside of this interesting Christian, and we would pray with him and them, read to them, talk a little, and sing several pieces out of the hymn-book. This sixty-third hymn was his favorite, and he always wanted it sung. We used to sing it to the sweet tune of "Dennis." One evening, just as the sun was setting, we went in, and he wanted us to have the prayer-meeting. In the course of the service, I leaned over and asked him what we should sing. He said, "My hymn." We knew very well what that was, and sung it as far as the conclusion of the third verse, and there we had to stop. He actually went to "wear his starry crown," just as we were singing, at his request, those very words.

Last Sunday, I told the story to a company of soldiers who had just lost a companion, and there was not a tearless eye among the listeners.

We may stand at the grave of such a patriot, and with trustful heart, may say, —

> " One more absent,
> The battle done;
> One more left us,
> Victory won.

One more buried
  Beneath the sod,
One more standing
  Before his God.

Lay him low, lay him low,
  Ere the morning break;
Sorrow not, sorrow not,
  He minds not heart-ache.

He is one, he is one,
  Of that noble band,
Who have fought, who have died,
  For their father-land.

He needs no tears,
  An angel now,
A saintly crown
  Upon his brow.

We should not weep
  That he has gone:
With us 'tis night,
  With him 'tis morn!"

XII. "ASLEEP IN JESUS, BLESSED SLEEP!"

Sergeant John Hanson Thompson was the son of the Rev. Joseph P. Thompson, D.D., of the City of New York. He was a youth of the finest culture, large-hearted, genial in his disposition, who gave himself to his country from motives as pure and lofty as ever actuated patriot or martyr. He was a member of Yale College; but, at the time of the alarm which aroused the country, when General Banks retreated down the Shenandoah valley before the overwhelming force of Stonewall Jackson, in May, 1862, the student laid aside his books and enlisted as a private in the Twenty-second New York Regiment. On the expiration of the three months for which he went out first, he re-enlisted for three years as sergeant in the Hundred and eleventh New York. He served in this capacity until March, 1863, when, worn out by exposure and fatigue, he died at North Mountain, in Virginia, at the age of twenty. During this brief career, he displayed not only the highest qualities of the soldier, but a social and Christian spirit which made him the darling of his regiment. Nothing can exceed the touching interest of the narrative of his death.[1]

In the last letter that the young soldier wrote, after speaking of the arrival of his regiment at North Mountain, he says, —

"A hard march of ten miles, in mud and water; — a hard one for me at least, as I was not fully in strength; but it did me good, I am sure."

His captain and the surgeon had attempted to dissuade him from marching; but he insisted that he would go with his men. The men endeavored to relieve him of his knapsack, but he insisted that a sergeant should set a good example to privates. "I never saw," said one of them, "such courage and energy as the sergeant showed. We all thought he was not equal to the march; but he would not be relieved. He said that he must be a *soldier*, and do all his duty for his country."

He had just been advised that his promotion to a lieutenancy was determined upon by the colonel — "Well," said he to his informant, "if a commission comes to me, of course, I shall not object; but I do not aspire to it." And to another he remarked, that "he had enlisted with a determination to do anything for his country; and he sometimes felt that he could serve it better as he was, than

---

[1] It was not my intention to quote from a book so well known; but the account of this last scene in the *Sergeant's Memorial*, the father's beautiful tribute to his son's memory, must form an exception to the rule.

in some higher office, with more temptations to consult his own ease."

On the day after the weary march to North Mountain, he insisted upon taking his regular turn on picket duty, and for this purpose went out several miles from camp. A snow-storm came up in which he passed the night. The next morning, Monday, he barely dragged himself back to camp, and sank down in his tent, with severe symptoms of typhoid pneumonia. The surgeon was absent, and there was no hospital. But after two days, he was removed in an ambulance to a private house, where he lingered until the night of the following Sabbath.

The kind friends who waited on him there found him "so gentle, patient, and uncomplaining in his spirit, and so delicate and sensitive in his habits, that it was almost impossible to render him any service. And at the same time he was so composed and resolute, so cheerful and hopeful, that it was difficult to realize how sick he was."

A pious captain visited him for the sake of religious conversation, knowing nothing of him personally. "I soon perceived," he says, "that I was talking with one who was no stranger to these things; and found him entirely at peace with God."

Two of his tent-mates watched over him with brotherly fidelity, and one of them reports from written memoranda the closing scene:

"About 11 p. m., the doctor called to see him; his breathing was very irregular. The doctor shook his head, as much as to say the case was hopeless. It seemed that the sergeant for the first time fully realized his danger. He asked the doctor if he could stand under it; the doctor told him he could not. He then asked if it would not be well to telegraph to his father. He was told that the captain had already done so. He expressed his satisfaction, adding, 'I am so glad; father will be sure to come to-morrow.' He then looked me full in the face and grasped my hand and said (calling my given and surname), 'Good-by.' A cold shudder went through my frame, as it was the first time I had ever stood face to face with death. He still held my hand and said, 'Send my love to my dear father and mother, brothers, and sisters. I hope to meet them in heaven.' He made a few requests concerning his personal effects, then prayed to God to forgive him his sins. After two or three short prayers, he asked Tanner to sing. He sang, as well as his voice would permit, a verse commencing, 'Asleep in Jesus, blessed sleep!'

"When he had finished, the Sergeant requested him to repeat it, which he did with more composure. He then asked some one to pray; but neither of us had ever made a prayer, and were silent. He made the request again, but neither of us could say a word. He then prayed again himself. The captain came in soon after and tried to revive him; but he kept gradually sinking until about a quarter past one, when he settled into a composure or ease, and breathed more regular but shorter, until his breath entirely left him at 1.30 A. M., March 16th, 1863."

Servant of God, well done!
  Rest from thy loved employ:
The battle fought, the victory won,
  Enter thy Master's joy.

At midnight came the cry,
  "To meet thy God prepare!"
He woke — and caught his Captain's eye;
  Then, strong in faith and prayer,

His spirit with a bound
  Left its encumbering clay;
His tent, at sunrise, on the ground
  A darkened ruin lay.

> Soldier of Christ, well done!
> Praise be thy new employ;
> And while eternal ages run,
> Rest in thy Saviour's joy.

XIII. THE LOWLY EXALTED.

In September, 1862 (says a missionary in the army), I visited the batttle-field of Antietam. Thousands of poor soldiers were still lying as they fell upon that field of blood. Having occasion to procure water from a farm-yard, I noticed there what seemed to be heaps of tattered garments, but beneath them were the wasted bodies of men who had crawled thither and died. Nor were they the only occupants of the place, for near them were thirteen others, still living but desperately wounded. Having relieved their wants, I heard the sounds of distress elsewhere, — they came from a stable not far off. There I found several other men, whose condition was, if possible, more deplorable still.

The one whom I approached first had his arm torn off by a shell. As I washed the wound, I spoke to him of the Good Physician, who heals forever the wounds that sin and Satan have made in the soul. Turning from him, I began to speak to another, whose face was covered by his hat, but there was no reply. The man next to him saw the mistake, and said, "You are too late there, sir. It is useless to speak to such a sleeper. The man has been dead these three days."

I uncovered his face, and found it, alas! too true. The probationer had gone beyond the reach of any ministry for soul or body which man's power can supply.

We then turned sadly to the other side of the stable, where lay a young man, twenty-three years old. His leg had been shattered by a shell, and roughly amputated on the field. The bandage had become loosened, and the wound had burst open, so as to cause for days the severest suffering. As I stooped over him, and tried to place him in an easier position, I could not help exclaiming, "Poor, poor fellow! yours is indeed a sad lot; alone here, friendless and dying!"

But what was my surprise, when, looking up with a sweet smile, he said, "My case is not so bad, sir, as it might be. The man there (he pointed to the spot), has been dead these three days."

"What!" I exclaimed. "Have you no complaint to utter?"

"Of what should I complain?" he said almost reproachfully. "Why, sir, I am happier than a prince. I would not change my place for his, even here."

"And what makes you so happy?" I asked.

"I have the presence of Christ," he replied. "I love him who showed his love for me by being born in a manger. If I suffer, I remember that he suffered more for me than I suffer now."

I spoke to him of his earlier days, and learned something of his history. He had not fled to the Refuge in the hour of distress for the first time. He had been led to put his trust in the Redeemer in his days of health and prosperity. He could add his confession to that of "the goodly company" of saints and martyrs who testify that God is faithful to those who truly seek his salvation, and imparts to them the supports of his grace more and more fully as earthly props fail and pass away.

"Look here, Adair," I said to my companion, in a tone of exultation. "Come and see a prince upon his throne!"

We had proof before us that the apostle means to allow of no exception when he says, "In everything by prayer and supplication, with thanksgiving, let your requests be made known unto God."[1]

We knelt down at the side of the pain-stricken one, and as our tears flowed, offered up thanksgivings at the remembrance of Him who had loved this poor soldier, and washed him from his sins in his own blood, and made him a king and priest unto God, who could rejoice though his body was wracked with pain, and a scene of such wretchedness lay around him.

XIV. WAITING FOR DAYBREAK.

The sermon at my funeral (said a dying soldier), should be from Solomon's words: — "Until the day break, and the shadows flee away."[2] He chose that text not so much for his own sake, as for others.

When the present struggle (said the preacher[3] on that occasion) shall be over, and it takes its place among the sternest and sublimest convulsions by which the powers of darkness have ever tried to overthrow or hinder the establishment of the kingdom of righteousness and of peace, the costly offerings which praying fathers and mothers have laid upon the altar, the setting up the walls in the blood of the first-born and fairest of our sons, all that has been done and suffered in the awful baptism of fire through which we are passing, — it will not seem, then, to have been too much.

Lieutenant Edgar M. Newcomb was the son of such

[1] Philippians iv. 6.
[2] Solomon's Song ii. 17.
[3] The sermon was preached by Rev. J. O. Means, of Roxbury, Mass., in the Park Street Church, Boston. The writer is indebted to this discourse (printed but not published) for the material of the present sketch. The synopsis is longer than usual, but not every soldier who may have deserved as much has had the lesson of his life so well recorded.

parents, and the offering up of his life for his country was one of the "costly sacrifices," respecting which we hesitate not to pray that if it be possible God may be pleased not to require them at our hands. He was born in 1840, trained in the Grammar and Latin Schools of Boston, entered the college at Cambridge, and was graduated there in 1860. It had been his purpose to preach the gospel, but ill-health compelled him to relinquish that hope. He went abroad and travelled in England and France.

Shortly after his return, the rebellion broke out; and though he had just entered on mercantile pursuits, he recognized at once the voice of God in the call of the government for volunteers, tore himself away from the allurements of gain and the charms of home, and entered the ranks of the army as a common soldier. "He went," says one who knew him, "against all the impulses of a tender and beautiful nature, in crucifixion of his peaceful and loving spirit, from the simple and strong impulses of Christian duty. Putting aside his repugnance to that which might be deemed hardening in the life of camps, a man of womanly purity and refinement, blushing at the suggestion of anything that would pollute his virtue, as quickly as at anything that would stain his honor, — with an instinctive and irrepressible sense of what right demanded, and with a conscientious and eager readiness to do her behests, he sprang forward with alacrity, as a child of his country and of his God."

And what did this shrinking youth become amid the actualities of war? "No braver officer or man," says his captain, "ever stood upon a battle-field than Lieutenant Edgar M. Newcomb." "Sometimes," says another, "he spoke in his letters 'of the hardships of the poor fellows' around him; but he never grumbled about his own fare or condition; and, in fact, this patient, cheerful endurance kept him not only in health, but built up his youthful person into the stalwart, sinewy, muscular form of an athletic man."

He felt, at length, the enthusiasm of a genuine soldier, and looked upon the fame of his regiment (which he did so much to promote) as a part of himself. Speaking of the march to the Rappahannock, on the eve of the fatal crossing[1] he wrote, "Though we were the last regiment of the brigade and division on the march, the latter had no sooner halted than we passed them all except the Sixth Michigan, and formed in line on the bluff overlooking the river. Lieutenant-Colonel Devereux could neither walk or ride; otherwise, we flatter ourselves that we should have been the first. Didn't we feel proud as we moved along past the regiments, which looked on us with a kind of awe, and whispered, "The Nineteenth Massachusetts." The Seventh Michigan took the boats, and filed into them, twenty in a boat, and without a moment's delay poled over the river amid a hail of bullets and the cheers of thousands of soldiers who crowded the bluff. Never in my life did I feel as I did when the first boat grounded on the opposite shore, and its noble crew leaped out and climbed the bank. Alas! the first man who landed fell in the street, mortally wounded. As soon as the boats came back we rushed into them and crossed and ran up the bank. Immediately we deployed as skirmishers, and, climbing the fences, and filing through the back gardens, entered the houses."

The eventful months pass away, and we enter the sanctuary where the youthful soldier of Christ was trained for the conflict which he has now finished. His sword and cap, scarred and riddled with bullets, are laid among the

[1] From Fredericksburg, to attack the rebels on the other side of the river.

flowers on his coffin, and the tattered flags of the Nineteenth Regiment, brought down from the State House, are crossed behind it. The church is filled with mourners who listen to the story of his brief, instructive life.

He had shared in all the fourteen battles and skirmishes of his regiment, and in the desperate forlorn hope of the passage of the Rappahannock, safe and untouched. But in the fight of December thirteenth, after the return to Fredericksburg, he received a mortal wound.

"The ball," says the captain, "struck the brass band of his sword, passed through the left leg and grazed the right. He was wounded while holding the American flag high above his head, having just given up the State colors. The color-sergeants had been shot down one after another, when Edgar sprang forward and picked up both flags, holding one in each hand, and called upon the men to stand by the colors." In this posture, waving the flag and cheering the men, after bullets had passed through his hat and blanket and coat and canteen, he was struck with a shot which tore his limbs in pieces. He lingered for a week in the greatest suffering, and died on Saturday, the thirtieth of December, 1862.

When his time came, he was prepared for it. He had been faithful and active as a Christian in the camp. He frequently preached, and held prayer-meetings, and performed such religious services that some of the pious chaplains supposed that he belonged to their number. In his last hours he earnestly commended the Saviour in whom he trusted to officers, soldiers, and friends who called to see him. "It never seemed before to me so great and noble a thing to die. I had hoped to preach the gospel, but I shall serve my country better in heaven."

He sent messages to the absent ones. "Tell mother I could not die in a holier cause, or more happy."—"It is all light ahead." — "Prepare to meet me in heaven." — "I am only going to a different sphere of labor, and shall be as near you as ever." — "To live is Christ and to die is gain."

He asked that no words of praise should be put on his tomb-stone, but simply, "Lieutenant Edgar M. Newcomb, of the Nineteenth Massachusetts." His last thoughts were not for himself, but the welfare of mankind. The property at his disposal he devised equally to the Societies for Home and for Foreign Missions.

His last letter was written on Saturday morning, and was in his pocket when he fell. The last sentence in that letter was, "C. thinks I owe my present safety to the prayers of my friends. I have often thought the same; and when I consider the temptations of this most trying life, my protection from sin is more marvellous than from wounds and death. Good-by."

Yes, "Until the daybreak and the shadows flee away!"

"How calm and blest
The dead now rest,
Who in the Lord departed;
All their works do follow them,
Yea, they sleep glad-hearted.

"Oh! blessed Rock!
Leave grant thy flock
To see thy Sabbath morning;
Strife and pain will all be past,
When that day is dawning."

CHAPTER VII.

OUR DEPENDENCE ON GOD FOR SUCCESS.

I. THE PRESIDENT'S JOURNEY TO WASHINGTON.

On the eleventh of February, 1861, Mr. Lincoln left Springfield, Illinois, to proceed to Washington to be inaugurated as President of the United States, on the fourth of March following. The first words clothed with anything like official significance, addressed by him to the country after his election, were those which he uttered on this journey to the capital. Those who may read those words in future times can form but a faint idea of the relief and encouragement which they brought to anxious hearts in the hour when clouds of distrust and fear, of civil discord and anarchy so darkened our sky.

It is the part of true statesmanship, as well as of piety, to feel at all times that "Except the Lord build the house, they labor in vain that build it; except the Lord keep the city, the watchman waketh but in vain."[1] The President's avowal of this truth, in terms so unreserved and earnest, as he approached the great work allotted to him, reassured the Christian heart of the nation, and inspired us with hope in the wisdom and success of his administration.

It adds to the suggestive import of his language, under such circumstances, to remember that the President elect was pursuing his way to the seat of government at that

[1] Psalm cxxvii. 1.

very time, through a band of hired assassins, who were watching, as he went from city to city, for an opportunity to slay him.

The train which was to bear him away started at an early hour in the morning; but more than a thousand people had collected at the station to bid adieu to their friend and neighbor. After shaking hands with his more intimate friends, he addressed the crowd as follows:—

"My Friends:—No one not in my position can appreciate the sadness I feel at this parting. To this people I owe all that I am. Here I have lived more than a quarter of a century; here my children were born, and here one of them lies buried. I know not how soon I shall see you all again. A duty devolves upon me which is perhaps greater than that which has devolved upon any other man since the days of Washington. He never would have succeeded except for the aid of divine Providence, upon which he at all times relied. I feel that I cannot succeed without the same divine aid which sustained him, and on the same Almighty Being I place my reliance for support. I hope you, my friends, will all pray that I may receive that divine assistance, without which I cannot succeed, but with which success is certain. I bid you all an affectionate farewell."

Expressions of approbation, tearful greetings, and cries of "We will pray for you," followed the delivery of these remarks. During the speech Mr. Lincoln betrayed much emotion, and the crowd was affected to tears.

At Columbus, Ohio, he remarked in the same strain,—

"I cannot but know, what you all know, that without a public name, perhaps without a reason why I should have such a name, there has fallen upon me a task such as did not rest even upon the Father of his country; and, so feeling, I cannot but hope for the support without which it will be impossible for me to perform that great task. I turn and look to the American people, and to that God who has never forsaken them."

At another point of his progress, Steubenville, in the same State, Mr. Lincoln further said, —

"I fear that the great confidence which seems to exist in my ability is unfounded; indeed, I am sure it is, encompassed as I am by such vast difficulties. I can only say nothing shall be wanting on my part, and I hope to be sustained by the American people and the blessing of God, who alone can prosper my endeavors."

II. THE PRAYER AT FORT SUMTER.

During the Christmas night of December 1860, Major Anderson, commandant at the harbor of Charleston, S. C., with his little garrison of only sixty effective men, passed stealthily from Fort Moultrie to Fort Sumter. This unexpected movement was the spark which electrified the nation. The storm of civil war might not burst at once, but it was seen now to be inevitable. Here was the opening act of the great drama which was to end in the triumph of law, civilization, and liberty, or in the subversion of the republic, and the reign of anarchy, barbarism, and slavery. Major Anderson deeply felt the responsibility and importance of the step he had taken. He gave expression to that feeling by a simple but significant act.

The flag which he had brought from Moultrie was to be thrown to the breeze from Sumter. The ceremony was fixed for twelve o'clock, the noon of December twenty-seventh. The commander assembled his little force and the workmen employed on the fortifications, at the foot of the flag-staff. His own heart led him naturally to God, as now the only efficient helper. He was anxious to bring those with him into sympathy with himself in this critical hour. The chaplain stood forth and stated the object of the service. The flag which they were there to defend as the symbol of the national unity and life was then attached to a cord, and Major Anderson, taking the ends in his hands, knelt down, while the officers and men, with heads uncovered, gathered around him. The chaplain then prayed. He commended the little band, their cause, and the country, to God, the arbiter of nations. His petitions, his tones, bespoke the earnestness of one who felt that if saved it must be because man's extremity is God's opportunity. As the fervent, heaven-winged words of the speaker ceased, and the men responded a hearty "amen," the commander hauled up the flag to the top of the staff. The band saluted it with "Hail Columbia," the accents of supplication gave place to those of enthusiasm, and cheers after cheers broke from the lips of all present.

Just at that moment, a boat arrived from Charleston, and the traitors whom it brought heard in those shouts the vows of men who resolved in their hearts that the old flag should suffer no dishonor while it remained in their hands. History will record how well they kept those vows during the four weary months they were imprisoned there without succor from the government, and the two fearful days in which the starved garrison held out against the concentric fire of so many batteries.

A gifted writer[1] has well represented the spirit of the transaction:—

> "Who doth that flag defy,—
> We challenge as our foe;
> Who will not for it die,
> Out from us he must go!

[1] The late Dr. Bethune, of New York.

So let them understand;
Who that dear flag disclaim
Which won their father's fame,
We brand with endless shame;
God for our native land.

"Our native land! to thee
In one united vow,
To keep thee strong and free
And glorious as now—
We pledge each heart and hand;
By the blood our fathers shed,
By the ashes of our dead,
By the sacred soil we tread,
God for our native land."

III. AN ALTAR IN THE TENT.

The victories of General Burnside have been among the most important of the war. No one has been more enterprising or uniformly successful than he. It is well known that where he pitches a tent, there he erects an altar, and prayer and worship are among the daily occupations. When he was planning his expedition to Newbern and Roanoke, "It was my fortune," says Bishop Clarke, of Rhode Island, "to occupy the same room with him in Washington, and every morning and every evening, we used to kneel down together, and pray for the blessing of God on his solemn work."

That blessing ensures success, and without it all man's efforts may be baffled. That blessing this noble commander seeks, and desires that others should seek for him. There is not a right-thinking man in the land who does not respect him for that trait of character, and feel the more confidence in him, or any one like him, for such reliance on the strength of the Mighty One.

IV. THE PURITAN SPIRIT.

The religious element has always been acknowledged as a great power in military success. The more intelligent that principle is, the more efficient it must be in securing this result. There is every reason, natural as well as rational, why those who hold their lives in their hand should acknowledge the God of battles, and pray for themselves and their country in the midst of danger. The simplest expression of the relations of "praying and fighting" was, perhaps, the blunt order of the Puritan chief: "Put your trust in God and keep your powder dry." Cromwell and his praying Puritans were dangerous men to meet in battle. The "sword of the Lord and of Gideon," was exceeding sharp, tempered as it was with hourly prayers.[1] The Cavaliers affected to despise, but feared the "cant" of the Roundheads, and imitated them as they repeated their Collects for church and King. "O Lord," said one of them, "if I forget Thee, as in the press of battle I may, do not thou forget me."

There is something sublime in the spectacle of Gustavus Adolphus and his vast army, on the eve of the battle of Lutzen, in which he fell, praying on bended knee, and then chanting,—

> "Be of good cheer; your cause belongs
> To Him who can avenge your wrongs;
> Leave it to Him, our Lord."

The king fell, but the battle was gloriously won.

---

[1] "That which chiefly distinguished the army of Cromwell," says Macaulay, "from other armies was the austere morality and the fear of God which pervaded their ranks." Hence, though "often surrounded by difficulties, sometimes contending against threefold odds, they not only never failed to conquer, but never failed to destroy and break in pieces whatever force was opposed to them.

And so, unless we are untrue to our better nature, it must ever be. Before going into battle the foolish, wicked, unmeaning oath is silent. With the bracing of the nerves, there goes up a silent prayer for strength and valor and deliverance. The wounded pray to be saved from death; the dying recall the words of old petitions learned in their childhood, and in these broken accents commit their souls to God.

On the battle-field of Gettysburg, where the *morale* of the Northern troops was put to the severest test, were found, broad-strewn, Bibles and prayer-books. Carried in coat-bosoms or pockets, they came forth in the bitter moment, a solace to the wounded and dying, and a proof that soldiers pray as well as fight.

All honor and thanks to the worthy chaplains who foster this noble spirit, and to the philanthropic men who care for the soldier's interest at home, taking with them, in timely visits on battle-fields, and in crowded hospitals, comforts for the poor suffering mortal bodies, and holy books and words of prayer for the well-being of the immortal souls.[1]

V. A REGIMENT ON THEIR KNEES.

A letter, written from our army while in pursuit of the rebels in Maryland, says, —

The troops march with alacrity, and seem in good spirits. Last evening, I beheld a sight that might well remind one of a scene in Cromwell's camp; — it was that of a whole company attached to a Philadelphia regiment, kneeling

They at length came to regard the day of battle as a day of certain triumph, and marched against the most renowned battalions of Europe with disdainful confidence." Never be ashamed of the Puritan spirit.

[1] Mostly an extract, but at this moment I have lost the reference.

upon the ground with every mark of reverence, at the hour of their worship.

They had just bivouacked for the night after a weary and dusty march. It was in a grove of majestic trees, which resounded with strains of sacred music and the voice of prayer intermingled. The bright beams of a full moon fell upon the forms of the prostrate soldiers through the branches. It seemed at the moment like a symbol of the beaming face of Deity, giving answers of peace to suppliants for his grace and protection. Some entire companies in the army are made up of men who belong to churches.

The impression was unique, and no description can convey it to another.

VI. NATIONAL FAST IN THE ARMY.

A joint committee of both Houses of Congress waited on the President and requested him "to recommend a day of public humiliation, prayer and fasting, to be observed by the people of the United States with religious solemnities, and the offering of fervent supplications to Almighty God for the safety and welfare of these States, his blessing on their armies, and a speedy restoration of peace."

The President, in compliance with this request, appointed the last Thursday in September, 1861, as a day in which we should "recognize the hand of God in this terrible visitation, and in sorrowful remembrance of our own faults and crimes as a nation, and as individuals, humble ourselves before him, and pray for his mercy, — pray that we may be spared further punishment, though most justly deserved; that our arms may be blessed and made 'effectual for the reestablishment of law and order and peace, throughout the wide extent of our country; and that the boon of civil and religious liberty, earned under his guidance, may be restored in all its original excellence."

It may be worth while to record an example of the manner in which this fast was kept in the army, at that critical moment in the prosecution of the war. A correspondent of the "Traveller" thus describes its observance in General Banks's Division, then stationed on the Upper Potomac:—

Yesterday, the fast-day appointed by the President was observed in this Division in a marked method. All drill was omitted of course. Public services were held in a rare manner. In accordance with a general order, all the regiments in the immediate locality assembled in a beautiful field at the entrance of Darnestown village, with full bands, and the artillery and cavalry. The Major-General, Brigadiers, and other high officers, attended in full uniform. A march, varying from a very short distance to a mile and a half, brought all together, when the infantry formed in mass, flanked by artillery and cavalry.

Six chaplains officiated. Assistant Adjutant-General Drake read the General's order. Chaplain Gaylord, of the Twelfth Massachusetts, read the President's Proclamation in a most impressive manner. Chaplain Reed, of the Thirtieth Pennsylvania, offered the opening prayer. Chaplain Sewall, of the Twenty-ninth Pennsylvania, read selections of Scripture, and the hymn,

"My country, 'tis of thee."

Chaplain Phillips, of the Ninth New York, offered prayer. Chaplain Quint, of the Second Massachusetts, read the Army Hymn, and also made the address of the day; and Chaplain Lasher, of the Fifth Connecticut, offered the concluding prayer, and, after the Doxology, pronounced the Benediction.

The grand mass of soldiery, as brigade after brigade took their places in perfect order; the great number of State and National banners floating in the breeze; the respect of the men, with the devoutness of many, and especially the majestic music of the united bands pouring out "America" and "Old Hundred," in which blended a multitude of voices, made it a scene long to be remembered. The author of the "Army Hymn" has never yet heard his own poem sung in all its majesty. He never will till he hears it from thousands upon thousands of men in active service, waiting impatiently for the order to advance to victory, with the sunlight playing upon sabres of dragoons, on the pieces of artillery caps, and on a forest of bayonets.

VII. THE ARMY HYMN.

After the allusion to this noble lyric in the last paragraph, the reader may be pleased to read it again in this connection. The hymn became popular at once; and not least because the earnest moral tone which pervades it found its echo in every patriotic heart.

The author added the last verse but one when the President's Proclamation of Emancipation went into effect, on the first of January, 1863.

O Lord of Hosts! Almighty King!
Behold the sacrifice we bring!
To every arm thy strength impart,
Thy spirit shed through every heart!

Wake in our breasts the living fires,
The holy faith that warmed our sires;
Thy hand hath made our Nation free;
To die for her is serving thee.

Be thou a pillared flame to show
The midnight snare, the silent foe;
And when the battle thunders loud,
Still guide us in its moving cloud.

God of all nations! sovereign Lord!
In thy dread name we draw the sword,
We lift the starry flag on high
That fills with light our stormy sky.

No more its flaming emblems wave,
To bar from hope the trembling slave;
No more its radiant glories shine
To blast with woe one child of thine!

From treason's rent, from murder's stain,
Guard thou its folds till Peace shall reign,
Till fort and field, till shore and sea,
Join our loud anthem, PRAISE TO THEE!

VIII. GENERAL ANDERSON IN THE SUNDAY SCHOOL.

General Anderson, the hero of Fort Sumter, on the invitation of a Christian friend, visited a German Sunday school in Cincinnati, Ohio. The golden words which he spoke to the members of the school on that occasion should be treasured up in the hearts of all the children and youth of the land.

My dear friends and children (said he), I did not expect, when I came here, to be asked to address you. It may be well, perhaps, for me to say a few words. I have been placed, providentially, in a situation which has turned the attention of the country to me and to my little band. But I would not have you misunderstand me or my position.

If I have been led wonderfully through many and great perils, I wish you to ascribe it to the right causes. No unaided power of man, no skill or bravery of our own, could have saved me and my companions. I am not ashamed, my young friends, to declare the truth. I say openly, that no event, no transaction of any interest or importance to our cause, took place while I was in Fort Sumter, without my looking to God in the morning of each day for his blessing on us. I besought him to give me a spirit of wisdom to learn and obey his will. I besought him to give me strength of purpose and energy to perform my duty to him, and to my country. None of the credit, therefore, of what was done belongs to me. It belongs to him who cares for us and who, if we commit our ways to him, will give to us all needful success.

Before I left Fort Sumter, I was admonished that I might be in more danger from my friends than I had been from enemies. Some who wished well to me wrote that I must be on my guard, and not be spoiled by flattery. The advice was well timed; but I trust God has saved me from that danger. I say again, I do not feel that I am to take to myself the least credit for what has been done. It was God who put it into my heart to decide and act as I did.

Therefore, my young friends, I would urge upon all of you to look to God in the transactions of life you may be called on to perform. Each individual has transactions to perform as momentous to him as what I have performed is to me. Each one of you has to gain or lose for himself the true end of his being here and hereafter. The destiny of each one depends, under God, on his own actions. I would have you all put your trust in God. Do that with a humble heart, and you will be blessed in this life and prepared for everlasting blessedness in that which is to come. I can say no more.

IX. PRAY FOR THE PRESIDENT.

It is impossible to read the following words of the chief magistrate of the country and not be convinced that they are prompted by the real feelings of his heart. It is evident that the cares of office have not diminished his sense of the difficulties of his position,[1] or of his need of the guidance and wisdom which "God giveth liberally to them that ask him, and upbraideth not." Pray for the President.

On Saturday, October fourth, 1863, the members of a Synod of the Presbyterian Church, holding their annual session in Washington, went to the executive mansion in that city, and were received by the President. The Moderator stated that the Synod wished, as a body, to pay to him their respects, and offer to him their salutations. Each member, he added, claimed to belong to the kingdom of God, and was loyal to the government.

The President, in reply, spoke as follows:—

"I can only say, in this case, as in so many others, that I am profoundly grateful for the respect given in every variety of form in which it can be given from the religious bodies of the country. I saw, upon taking my position here, I was going to have an administration, if an administration at all, of extraordinary difficulty.

"It was, without exception, a time of the greatest difficulty this country ever saw. I was early brought to a lively reflection that, with nothing in my power whatever, or in that of others, on which I could rely, no undertakings of

---

[1] See page 180.

mine could succeed without direct assistance of the Almighty. I have often wished that I was a more devout man than I am; nevertheless, amid the greatest difficulties of my administration, when I could not see any other resort, I would place my whole reliance on God, knowing all would go well, and that he would decide for the right.

"I thank you, gentlemen, in the name of the religious bodies which you represent, and in the name of our common Father, for this expression of respect. I cannot say more."

The members of the Synod were then severally introduced to the President.

X. FAITH AND WORKS.

An example of self-denying patriotism like the following deserves to be put on lasting record. In July of the present year, the Rev. D. B. Bradley, a self-supporting missionary of the American Missionary Association, of Bangkok, Siam, sent an order to the treasurer of that society, to pay over to the United States three hundred dollars on Dr. Bradley's account. This patriotic missionary writes as follows: —

"I regard the war, on our part, as one of the most righteous that was ever waged, and I see the hand of God in it so distinctly, and his merciful purposes for those millions of our enslaved brethren at the South so gloriously fulfilling, that my whole heart ascends to God in prayer continually for our cause. And while I pray, I feel that I must also contribute what I can from my small resources to the millions of money that will yet be needed to complete the great and glorious work of our government now in hand. Please, therefore, to pay over to the department, as soon as you well can, the sum above named."

Dr. Bradley makes the fact that he has a son who is of age to serve in the army the occasion of this contribution; though the son, not being a resident in this country, would be exempted from military duty.

The Secretary of the Treasury, Mr. Chase, in acknowledging the remittance, says that this "noble expression of love of country in an American missionary," who, out of his personal earnings, "in the far-off kingdom of Siam, sends so considerable an amount to the Treasury" of his struggling country, fills him "with admiration," and inspires him "with confidence that a people whose sons in remote regions exhibit such devotion to their country cannot fail in the speedy suppression of a rebellion the most unprovoked and the most iniquitous recorded in history."

CHAPTER VIII.

INCIDENTS OF THE CAMP AND BATTLE-FIELD.

THE contents of this chapter are miscellaneous. Some of the pieces might have been assigned to the other chapters, but were not at hand in time to be inserted there. Some of the incidents, also, take a wider range as to their import than those of the bulk of the volume.

I. HOW A BODY WAS IDENTIFIED.

The consecration of the National Cemetery at Gettysburg, Pennsylvania, on the nineteenth of November, 1863, brought to that place many relatives of the slain soldiers who were anxious to recover and identify the bodies of sons, brothers, and husbands. Among these was a beautiful lady from Harrisburg, who had been married to one of the Thirteenth Massachusetts Regiment shortly before the battle, but who had heard nothing from him or of him since the first day of the fight. She had gone to Baltimore to ascertain if he had been taken prisoner, and had visited the hospitals there and in other places, hoping to find some acquaintance of her husband who could give her some clew to his fate. All her efforts were unavailing.

On the battle-field, near where the Thirteenth had fought, were twenty "unknown" graves, which, at her request, the committee of the cemetery allowed her to open. The earth was removed and the bodies exposed to view, one after another, but without her discovering the object of her search. At the last moment, as she was about to turn away in despair from the last of the twenty graves, her eye caught sight of a button upon the overcoat of the buried soldier. She knew instantly that the remains of her husband were before her. In a previous battle, this button had been struck by a ball, and indented in a peculiar manner. The officer had promised to leave it with her as a memento of the danger escaped, but in the haste of departure had forgotten to do so; and now there it was, — the only means of enabling her to discover the fate of him to whom she had so lately committed the hopes of her young life.

II. DREAD OF TEMPTATION.

In an address at the Music Hall, in Boston, Mr. Wendell Phillips related the following instance of heroic firmness on the part of a soldier who felt that he had other enemies to fear than those of the battle-field: —

I know a soldier in the Army of the Potomac, who was picked up in the streets of Philadelphia one year ago, a complete wreck, a confirmed inebriate, but who was, by the love of a sister and the charity of a Boston home, placed once more on his feet.

He was at Ball's Bluff, and three times, with unloaded musket, charged upon the enemy. He was one of the six who heroically defended and brought away the body of the fallen leader of that bloody fight. The captain of the company to which he belonged died in his arms, receiving the last words of consolation from his lips. He was afterwards conspicuous in the conflict until the orders were given for each one to seek his own safety. Removing some of his apparel, he plunged into the inhospitable river, and after great exertion landed on the opposite bank, seven miles below the encampment. Nearly exhausted, chilled, half-clad, half-starved, he finally reached the camp.

The captain of the next company to which he belonged kindly said to him, pouring out a glass of wine, "Let me give you this; you will perish without it."

"I thank you, sir," said the soldier, "but I would sooner face all the cannon of the enemy than taste that glass of wine."

III. USE YOUR TALENTS.

"And unto one he gave five talents, to another two, and to another one."[1]

There are many warm hearts and willing hands in the world, anxious, eager to do good; yet because they have not the ability to do precisely what they see others perform in walks of usefulness, they are often discouraged, and sometimes idle. That each person is gifted with power to be useful in some way, let us illustrate by a story which is a true one.

A young lady was heard to say, "I wish I could do something for my country; I would willingly become a nurse in a hospital, but I have not the physical strength. What can I do?"

A friend replied, "You can sing."

"Yes, I can sing, but what of that?"

"Go to one of the hospitals, and sing for the soldiers."

The idea pleased her. She accompanied a friend who was long used to such visits, and who introduced her by saying to the patients, "Here is a young lady who has come to sing for you."

At the mere announcement, every face was aglow with

[1] Matthew xxv. 15.

animation, every eye was riveted upon her with expectant pleasure. She sang a few songs, commencing with the glorious "Star Spangled Banner." As the thrilling notes of that song rang through the apartment, one poor man, who had been given up by the physician as an almost hopeless case, raised himself in his cot, leaned his head upon his hand, and drank in every note like so much nectar. The effect was electrical. From that moment he began to amend, and finally recovered.

IV. EARLY IMPRESSIONS REVIVED.

A man was wounded on the first day of the fight at Shiloh, concerning whom an interesting fact was ascertained.

He lay all Sunday night in a tent held by the rebels, on the ground, in the mud, without sympathy or care. During that long and terrible night, amid the rain and the roar of artillery, there came vividly back to him the text and all the argument of a sermon he had heard twenty years before. The next day, when our troops were more successful, he was rescued, cared for, and taken to St. Louis, where he was found by certain members of the Young Men's Christian Association, and treated with the tenderness which he so much needed in mind and body.

The Holy Spirit brought home to his heart the impressions of that night; and the seed, buried for twenty years, and apparently lost, sprang up and brought forth fruit in his conversion. He lived six weeks to give testimony to God's goodness, and died in joy and hope. The last words he uttered were, "My God, my country, my mother!"

V. UNMARKED GRAVES.

Among the touching sights reported by those who explored the battle-field of Fair Oaks, in order to bury the dead and minister to the wounded, was the following:—

In one portion of the field, lying apart by themselves, were four dead soldiers. They had crept together and laid each a right hand upon that of his comrade, and thus died. A paper lay upon the breast of one of them, and a pencil near by on the ground, showing what their last work had been.

It is hard to think of leaving the world and having all trace of our fate hidden forever from those dear to us. To furnish the possible means of some information respecting them, one of the men had written on the paper, with a faltering hand,—

"Four dying soldiers. Be kind enough to give us a decent burial."

And then below these words were written the four names of the slain martyrs. We wept as we buried them together where they had lain; and, placing over them a tablet with the names they had so touchingly bequeathed to us, we enclosed the grave by a little railing, and left them to their last long sleep. "The sea shall give up its dead," and so, also, shall the battle-field, billowy with unmarked graves, — unmarked save by "His eye which seeth every precious thing."[1]

[1] Job xxviii. 10.

VI. SPIRIT OF SIRE AND SON.

The battle of Lexington was fought on the nineteenth of April, 1775, and the first Massachusetts volunteers were mobbed on the same day of the month, 1861, in the streets of Baltimore. They were the first men who responded to the call of the President for seventy-five thousand soldiers, after the capture of Sumter. Such was their promptitude that some of them left their homes at midnight, and, pressing their way through a storm of driving sleet, were in Boston under arms, awaiting orders to march, before another sun had risen, after their receiving the summons. That promptitude had much to do with saving the government. Without it, the boast of the rebels, when they planted their flag on Sumter, might have been made good. Before the end of May, that flag might have floated from the capitol at Washington, and the savage eye of the slave power have been glaring down upon us from the turrets of the captured city.

As one of these regiments was passing through New York, a gentleman of that city met one of its members on the street.

"Is there anything I can do for you?" said the New Yorker, whose heart warmed toward the representative of the brave Massachusetts militia who had been so prompt to shoulder the musket.

The soldier hesitated a moment, and finally, raising one of his feet, exhibited a boot with a hole in the toe, and, in other respects, decidedly the worse for wear.

"How came you here with such boots as those, my friend?" asked the patriotic citizen.

"When the order came for me to join my company, sir," replied the soldier, "I was ploughing in the same field at

Concord where my grandfather was ploughing when the British fired on the Massachusetts men at Lexington. He did not wait a moment; and I did not, sir."

It is needless to say that the soldier was immediately supplied with a full equipment for all his wants, and with a "God-speed" was sent forward on his way.

VII. THE UNKNOWN CHILDREN.

A gentleman from Philadelphia, who was at Gettysburg as a volunteer surgeon, obtained there a most touching relic of that terrible battle. It was a melainotype, or an ambrotype on iron of three children, and was taken from the hands of a dead soldier who belonged to the Union army. He had been mortally wounded, and crawled to a sheltered place, where his body was found, with the picture of his children so placed that his eyes could rest upon it in his dying moments. There was no clew to his name, or his regiment, or his former place of residence. He had evidently carried it with him into battle, and that image perhaps of a motherless group that must be cast henceforth upon God's fatherhood shows with what thoughts it was hardest for him to struggle in death.

Of the children in the picture, two were boys and one a girl, all of them with features of uncommon beauty. The oldest, a boy, is seated in the centre, the youngest, a boy, on the other's right hand, and a little girl on the left. The picture had a flat gilt frame, and probably had been sent to the soldier from home in a letter. It is to be hoped that it may find its way yet into the hands of some of the relatives of the deceased father.[1]

---

[1] Since this paragraph was laid aside for insertion here, the identity of the unknown soldier has been ascertained. His name was Humiston, and his widow and three children live at Portville, Cattaraugus County, New York. The publicity given to the circumstance led to this discovery.

VIII. A MOTHER'S LOVE.

It was early morning, on the first day of May, 1863, that the regiment of which the writer is a member left its bivouac in a thick grove of young oaks, and started at a quick step down a wide road leading to the famed city of Fredericksburg, Virginia.

A battle was expected. We felt that life was uncertain, and that ere another sunset, some of our number would be called to their long account; but stern duty beckoned us on, and we advanced to the intrenchments which the rebels had thrown up during the night to stop our progress.

Our regiment, which led the main column, immediately deployed as skirmishers, and advanced at a double-quick toward the battery which the confederates now opened on the line of battle forming behind us; while their skirmishers, concealed by fences and trees, poured a galling fire upon us.

Some few yards in front of my position stood a log-house, looking as thrifty as most Virginia houses. Just at this moment, while shells were screaming overhead, and the ground was torn with rifle-balls, a woman rushed out of this house and started toward our line. She had gone but a few steps, however, when she stopped; and then darting back into the building, against which the bullets now fell like rain, almost immediately reappeared with an infant in her arms, and again started toward the array of armed men who had now nearly reached the hut. Our men at this instant stopped the firing. Every one's eye was fixed with intense interest on the mother as she sped like a frightened deer toward a place of safety; and although the bullets fell like hail around her, and several (as I afterward learned) actually pierced her dress, she never faltered until she passed through our line, which closed behind her, and then she fell fainting to the ground, but was safe.

How strong must be that love which could urge a tender woman, unused to the horrible din of battle, through a fire which might appall the bravest! Yet her love for her child overcame every emotion of fear. It seemed as if an All-wise Hand turned aside the missiles of death which were hurtling by on every side, and permitted her to escape unhurt. The poetess was indeed right when she wrote,—

> "Over my heart, in the days that are flown,
> No love like mother's love ever hath shone." [1]

IX. THE VALUE OF SECONDS.

General Mitchell was well known as an eminent astronomer, in addition to his other merits. An officer with whom he had business to transact reported himself at a later hour than had been named for the interview.

"Sir, you are late," exclaimed the general.

"Only a few seconds," responded the officer.

"Sir, I have been in the habit of computing the value of a hundreth part of a second," retorted the general.

The subordinate felt the rebuke and was silent. The difference of a few seconds affects the movements of earth and sun and stars, and affects often as really the fate of armies and the destiny of nations and individuals, and that, too, in our interests future and eternal as well as present.

[1] First published in the *Zion's Advocate*, Portland, Maine.

X. OLD HUNDRED AT NIGHT.

During the Peninsular campaign several of us (says a correspondent of one of the public journals) were sitting in our tent, a few hours after sunset, on Sabbath evening, when one of the number, laying his hand on my knee, suddenly exclaimed, "Hark, what is that?"

In an instant the talking ceased, and every ear was bent forward to catch the sound which had fixed the attention of our comrade. A silence ensued for a moment, and then there was wafted across the air the music of that glorious anthem, "Old Hundred," in which it seemed as if a thousand voices participated.

All of us immediately sought the open air, and there stood until the last note died away upon our ear. Never before had we heard anything so magnificently grand as this same "Old Hundred" sung by the soldiers of the Union army on the plains of Yorktown. The air was made vocal with the music, and the woods around reverberated with the mighty strain. Beneath the canopy of heaven the soldiers gazed upward into the star-lit sky, and sang, all with one voice, —

> "Praise God from whom all blessings flow;
> Praise Him all creatures here below;
> Praise Him above, ye heavenly host,
> Praise Father, Son, and Holy Ghost."

It was solemn, soul-stirring, to hear these words thus chanted that have so often stirred the best, holiest emotions of man's heart. It was a scene not unfitted to inspire the genius of a Christian poet or artist.

XI. A PRECIOUS TESTIMONY.

My son (says Dr. Thompson)[1] had learned to trust in Jesus as a friend. I see him now as he stood with me alone in his chamber, strapping his knapsack for his journey to Wheeling — the parting interview. The day had been given to his outfit.

"Well, John," I said, "I believe I have procured everything that you will need. But there is one thing that you alone can care for. You are going upon a very serious business, with temptations and dangers, perhaps sickness and death, before you. You must keep near to Christ, my son, in prayer; never forget that."

Pausing for a moment in his preparations, he turned his large, loving eyes full upon me, looking his whole soul into mine, and answered, —

"Father, I think I'm all right there."

His religious habit was so reticent, so thoughtful, so sincere, that those few words expressed to me his whole inner life.

The well-thumbed Testament and knapsack manual for devotion, among his effects, bear witness to his fidelity; and the testimony borne by all to the pureness of his speech and manner, and to the Christian elevation of his whole life, prove how thoroughly he was right within.

XII. ANECDOTE OF GENERAL SEDGWICK.

I have seen a second lieutenant, (says one of our soldiers) in all the pomp and circumstance of a major-general, come dashing down the road, slashing at weary

---

[1] See the article on page 109.

stragglers with his sword, or swearing at those who were not quick enough in dragging themselves from under his horse's feet. One day, a soldier, one of our best, had fallen, exhausted by over-work and illness, and lay helpless in the road, when an officer came dashing along in evident haste to join his staff in advance. It was pitiable to see the effort the poor boy made to drag his unwilling limbs out of the way. He struggled up only to sink back with a look that asked only the privilege of lying there undisturbed, to die. In an instant he found his head pillowed on an arm as gentle as his far-away mother's might have been, and a face bent over him, expressive of the deepest pity, in every lineament. It is characteristic of our bravest boys, that they say but little. The uncomplaining words of the soldier in this instance were few, but understood.

The officer raised him in his arms and placed him in his own saddle, supporting the limp and swaying figure by one firm arm, while with the other he curbed the steps of his impatient horse to a gentler pace. For two miles, without a gesture of impatience, he travelled in this tedious way, until he reached an ambulance train, and placed the sick soldier in one of the wagons. It was our noble Sedgwick, our brave general of the Sixth Corps, pressed with great anxieties and knowing the preciousness of every moment.

We all know that great things are to be done, and well done, when we see that earnest figure in its rough blouse hurrying past, and never have our boys been disappointed in him. He works incessantly, is unostentatious; and when he appears among us, all eyes follow him with outspoken blessings. He saved his corps from utter annihilation at Chancellorsville by his bravery and good judgment.[1]

[1] Inserted in the *Christian Watchman*, Boston.

XIII. A BRAVE CONFESSION.

A visitor to a Philadelphia hospital, one of the women-workers in behalf of the invalid soldiers, says,—

In going my rounds, I stopped once to speak to a young man of a rather agreeable and pleasant expression of face, who seemed anxious to talk, and exhibited much intelligence, though without culture. At the battle of Newport News, he had been shot through the right leg, and had suffered terribly,—so much that he now looked the very shadow of a man, he was so dreadfully emaciated. His account of the battle was enthusiastic, and concluded with a long detail of the tortures he had to endure from hunger, thirst, and indeed almost every imaginable ill that could befall a soldier in the field, surrounded by enemies.

"I suppose you don't feel much like going back, do you?" I asked, when he had finished.

"Yes," he replied heartily. "If I knew I should have to suffer the same over again, I should want to go back. I want to get well chiefly to return to duty. There are too few honest patriots to spare even a single one, and if I have any pride, it is because I know I am one,—whole-souled and true. I haven't many virtues, but my fault will never be treachery to my native land. I'll die for her, if I can't live to defend her!"

XIV. THE SOLDIER'S LAST WATCH.

A lonely grave, a little apart from others, stands on the ground of one of the battles fought in the retreat from Richmond, in the summer of 1862, which bears on its wooden head-piece simply the name

The turf covers the remains of a youthful soldier who was not only brave and patient, but exemplary as a Christian. Those battles renewed from day to day and attended by so many hardships, destroyed many lives, in addition to those lost in conflict with the enemy. Hundreds and hundreds of our gallant men, worn out by marches, fighting, hunger, and loss of sleep, became discouraged, and either recklessly threw themselves into the jaws of death, or fell into the hands of the enemy, because they were unable to keep up with their more robust though not braver companions.

The circumstances of the death of one of these silent martyrs to their country were taken down from the lips of a soldier who was with him in his last hours. It is all that may be known, save to a few bleeding hearts, of one who, alas! like so many others, sleeps in that saddest of all places, a battle-field. The worn-out soldier, the day before his death, said to his lieutenant, "I am so weak and helpless, I do not know what I can do further."

He was told to lie down and get what rest he could on the battle-field. About ten at night, (said his tent-mate), as we were talking together, an officer of the company came up and told us we should retreat at two o'clock in the morning. He ordered us to stand guard till then, two hours each in turn.

We took straws and drew lots, to decide who should stand first. The lot fell on Trowbridge. I threw myself on the ground under a tree, with my blanket drawn over me, and was soon in a deep sleep. At twelve I was aroused, but said, "You must be mistaken; it cannot be five minutes since I lay down."

We had been ordered not to speak aloud, or to have a light; and he replied in a whisper, "Feel of the hands of my watch, — it is twelve."

I took his place, and he was soon asleep or seemed to be asleep. At half-past one o'clock, the order came to break up and move. I went to awake Trowbridge, but had no answer except that he groaned heavily once and then again. I tried to soothe him and awake him gently, but he turned aside his head, groaned once more and was gone. I struck a match in my possession and looked upon his features; they were set and ghastly in death. I placed his hand on my cheek, and asked him, if he was still conscious, to press it. There was no response; life was evidently extinct.

I made an attempt to find the surgeon or the chaplain, but they had both gone forward with the army. So, I searched his pockets, and taking from them six dollars for his mother, and a letter directed to himself, I replaced the envelope, that his name at least might be known to those who should find the body.

Several days after this, I was one of a number of men detailed to go back to that spot and bury the dead. On searching near the place where Trowbridge died, I found a grave with a wooden tablet bearing his name. Not far distant was a house at which I called and asked the inmates if they knew anything of that grave. The woman of the family then brought forward an envelope, the very one I had replaced, and said they had buried a soldier there, from whose pocket it was taken. It was a relief to know what had become of the body. Of course I wrote to his mother, sending the money, and giving an account of her son's last moments and his burial.

XV. POWER OF FORGIVENESS.

Governmental justice must follow law; it may not sacrifice the public interest for any private one. Even in cases where the judge may deal with the individual as such, we need wisdom to know whether lenity or severity will best answer the purpose. The apostle speaks of a difference: "Of some have compassion; and others save with fear, pulling them out of the fire."[1]

In one of the garrisons, a soldier, who had been guilty of some misdemeanor, was about to be brought before the commander of his regiment to receive his sentence and be punished. The officer who entered the soldier's name, on seeing it said, "Here is B. F—— again. What can we do with him? He has gone through almost every ordeal already."

The sergeant, with an apology for his freedom, spoke up and said, "There is one thing that has never been done with him yet, sir."

"What is that, sergeant?"

"Well, sir, he has never yet been forgiven."

"Forgiven!" said the colonel. "There is his case entered. It is too late."

"Yes, but the man is not before you, and you can cancel it."

The colonel reflected a few moments, and then ordered the delinquent to be brought in, and asked him what he had to say about the charges alleged against him.

"Nothing, sir," was the reply, "only that I am sorry for what I have done."

"Well," said the officer after a few prefatory words, "we have decided to forgive you."

---

[1] Jude 22, 23.

The soldier was struck with astonishment. The tears started to his eyes,— he wept. The colonel, with the adjutant and others present, were deeply affected when they saw the man so humbled. The grateful soldier thanked the colonel for his kindness and withdrew.

The author of these lines had a personal knowledge of the conduct of the pardoned culprit for two years and a half after this occurrence. During that time, no charge was brought against him, nor any fault ever found with him. He was a reclaimed and faithful man.

It was a triumph of mercy. The offender was won by kindness.

XVI. SEALS OF HIS MINISTRY.

A touching scene occurred at Camp Nelson, in Kentucky. A clergyman, who labored at that camp, as a delegate of the Christian Commission, relates the incident.

There was one man among those with whom I conversed there that I shall never forget. He was a soldier from Kentucky. He was unable to read and had a painful sense of his ignorance. One of his first questions was, "Don't you think a man can go to heaven if he has no learning?"

"Certainly, if he will only trust in his Saviour," I replied.

"That I have tried to do," said he; "and the last thing I did before leaving home was to pray with my sister."

As I sought to enlighten him, and encourage him to trust more and more in the Lord Jesus, he looked me intently in the eye and said, "Old gentleman — I confess, it is many years I have tried to serve the Master — what you say has done me more good than anything the doctors have done or can do for me."

The next Sabbath, I saw a soldier's funeral passing my

tent, with a fife and drum playing a funeral march. I joined the solemn procession, and, on reaching the grave, proposed to the officer in charge to make some remarks. He consented, and when the men were drawn up in order and the coffin was lowered into the grave, I began to speak. By the name on the little headboard, I discovered that I was standing at the grave of the man with whom I had recently conversed.

In my remarks, I alluded to that circumstance, not without tenderness on my part, and with evident effect on others. Prayer was then offered for the bereaved friends, for the sick in the hospital, and those present, and I closed. The word was given, and the soldiers fired the parting salute over the grave, then "Right about face, — forward, march!" and they were gone.

I can never forget this scene. I hope to see that youthful soldier again in another and better world. The remark of his that my conversation did him more good than anything the doctors could do has strengthened me for the rest of life. Those words of the honest, unlettered boy are the best credentials that I or any minister could have from human testimony.

XVII. A STEP ONWARD.

Yesterday (says a friend, who writes from Providence, R. I.) a battalion of colored soldiers, six hundred in number, came up to the city from the famed Dutch Island. They are on their way to New Orleans. The colored women of the city have procured a grand banner for them. To-day, December tenth, it was presented to these sons of liberty. The flag is a heavy silk, fringed; the whole very rich and elegant.

The presentation was made by Mr. Waugh, a freedman, who said he had never learned grammar, but who surprised those who listened to him, by his elegant, well-put and patriotic speech. The response was made by another freedman called to the duty ten minutes only before he was to perform it, and both of them showed that men of their race can frame a speech fitting and forcible, better than some who assume that duty whose opportunities have been vastly greater.

Our excellent Governor Smith is in the forefront of these patriotic plans for the redeemed children of oppression. His labor has for its first result above eighteen hundred colored troops, "armed and equipped." If any one can show a finer body of troops in vigor, in spirit, and in manners, let them go forward and serve their country.

But the colored women sending a battle-flag borne by such a regiment to a city and State where slavery has reigned with such uncurbed license! Is not this a step onward?

We are not at the end yet; but has not our flag now risen high enough to show which way its folds point?

XVIII. GENEROSITY OF A SLAVE.

A few weeks since, one of the most able and useful chaplains of the army spent a few days in Washington, and while there, was invited to preach in one of the colored churches of the city.

He had a large and interesting congregation. Among them were those who had been slaves as well as others. The speaker reminded them of the sudden change that has taken place in their condition and prospects. He urged them to show themselves worthy of the future which is opening before them. They had been scorned and oppressed. Now they had their own destiny, in some sense that of the country, in their hands. If they were meek and patient under injuries, they would overcome the malice of their enemies. Some were clamoring against them as unworthy of freedom. If they were temperate, industrious, and honest, they would silence such accusers. The preacher knew of instances in which colored men and women had, by their courage and generosity, won the esteem and gratitude of a multitude of officers and soldiers of our army. He illustrated the remark by an example.

After one of the battles of this war (said he) in northeastern Virginia, many wounded Union and Confederate soldiers were brought into the town of Winchester, and placed in the churches, school-rooms, and court-house, side by side.

The ladies of that place brought into the hospitals many things to nourish and tempt the languid appetite of the sufferers, but they gave everything to the Confederate soldiers; our men they passed by as unworthy of sympathy or notice. One day, a lady who had been a constant visitor, brought in a supply of fragrant tea. She went from one couch to another of her friends, but had no eye or heart of pity for others. One of our wounded men, who was very ill, thought that a cup of this tea might help him. He begged me to ask the lady for a taste of it. I went to her, and in a manner that I thought not offensive told her the soldier's request.

"No," said she, and her face flushed with anger; "not a drop of it; this tea is all for our suffering martyrs."

"Madam," I said, "I looked for no other answer. I beg pardon for having seemed to suppose for a moment that I should receive a different one."

My anger was aroused, I confess. At that moment, an

aged colored woman approached the surgeon and myself. She was lame, and could hardly walk under the weight of two large baskets which she bore on her arms, while a black boy followed her, carrying another basket.

Having come up to us, she set down her burden and said, —

"Master, I am a slave; my husband is a slave, and my children are slaves. Will you accept these things from a poor slave woman for the wounded men here? I do not want money. No, master, I could never look you in the face, if I took your money."

She then opened one of the baskets, and took up a roll of stockings, and said, —

"Master, months ago, I knew this war was coming; and when all were asleep in my cabin, I knit these that some poor sufferer might be warmed, — and will you allow a poor slave to give them to these men?"

Then taking up some papers of tea she said, "This tea I earned by my own work. I would not drink it myself, for I knew the day was not far off when some weak and fainting men would need it more than I do. Will you permit me to give it to you? And here," said she, lifting up some cans of fruit, "are the peaches, pears, and plums of my own garden; I saved them all for you. I could not eat them when my heart told me that suffering and dying soldiers would need them. Will you permit me, kind master, to give them to you for the poor men lying here?

And so other things she had brought — linen napkins, handkerchiefs, lint — she held up, and said, —

"Master, I have not stolen them. My own hands have earned them over the wash-tub and by house-cleaning. Permit me to give them to you. I wished to do something for those who are far from home, among strangers and suffering want."

As she talked, she grew more and more earnest. Tears rolled over her face, and fell on her hands as she lifted to me the treasures of her basket. I can never forget the earnestness and humility of her manner, as she said, again and again, "Permit me, master, permit me."

"Oh, yes, Aunty," I said; "we will not only receive them, but pay you for all you have brought."

"Oh, master," said she, "be not so unkind as to offer me money. I want the pleasure of giving these little things. Oh, I am sorry I have so little! If I had a thousand times as much, and better things, too, I should give them all."

Our sick and wounded men looked with wonder and admiration on the woman, and soon a hundred of them cried out, "Aunty, God bless you! You are the only white woman we have seen in Winchester."

Now (continued the chaplain), do you think those soldiers ever forgot that woman, and thought her skin was darker than that of their sisters and mother. Will they not ever remember her as a noble, true friend in need? And will not every one of them be kinder to every daughter of Africa who comes in his way, because one of them pitied and helped him when he was a stranger and half dead. I do not know what became of that generous woman. She may be still a slave; but certain I am that in long years to come, when the soldiers of the army meet in peaceful homes, we will talk of her, and ask God to bless her.

Go and do as she did. Be gentle; do good unto all men, even your enemies. Be not vain and proud, spending all you make in dress and pleasure; but deny yourselves to do good, and soon those who despise you will become your friends.

As the chaplain was relating these facts, he saw in the

congregation a woman whose face glowed and was wet with tears. And when he had ended the service, this person came up and said to him, "Master, I am the woman you spoke of this morning. I bless the good Lord I am free, and my husband and two children are all free and here in Washington, and we are now happier than ever in our lives."[1]

As they heard this, many gathered around her, to thank her again for her charity to the wounded soldiers. And the chaplain rejoiced to meet in freedom one who had shown herself to be so generous a woman and so true a Christian.

XIX. PRINCIPLE STRONGER THAN NATURE.

In one of the earlier stages of the war, a young officer fell in battle, as he was bravely leading on his troops against the insurgents. His body was brought home for burial. The venerable mother who was nearly, if not quite, four-score years old, stood gazing calmly on the remains of her son, who should have been her own stay and staff in the decline of life.

At last a movement was made by a friend to cover the face, and hide it from human sight forever. The noble woman put him gently aside, and, carefully performing the act herself, said, "My son, I have laid you to rest many a time before. Now I do it for the last time, and with the flag of your country."

[1] In the dialogue of the narrative we have, of course, the sense of the speakers, not the exact words. As to the facts of the narrative, the Rev. Dr. Marks, of Washington, reports them on the strength of his own personal knowledge.

XX. SIGHTS AFTER BATTLE.

On the twenty-seventh of the last month[1] a battle was fought beyond the Rapidan, which resulted in a victory for the national arms, but with a heavy loss on both sides. A letter, written at Alexandria, Virginia, December sixth,[2] describes some of the after-scenes of the conflict, which it is painful to read, and must have been still more painful to witness.

A week elapsed after the fight, and trains of cars, laden with the wounded and dying, began to make their appearance at Alexandria, from the "front."

The work of amputation, dressing of wounds, and preparations for removal, commenced on the spot the next morning after the battle. It was some distance to the nearest railroad, and the wounded, maimed, in some cases dying men, were put into ambulances, and sent forward to that point. The roads were so wretched that five or six miles a day was all the progress that could be made. It must be left to the imagination to conceive what they suffered under such circumstances, during so many wearisome days and nights.

On reaching Alexandria (says the eye-witness), every thing was done for their relief that could be done by the ministrations and sympathy of man. Agents of the Sanitary Commission, in anticipation of their arrival, met them at the station with hot coffee, and with suitable food. Several delegates of the Christian Commission, who were providentially there, lent their aid in transferring the suffering men to the several hospitals in that city. Between thirty and forty freight cars were filled with those living

[1] November, 1862.
[2] In the *Boston Recorder*, December 18, 1863.

relics of the slaughter. Seven hundred men, certainly not fewer, were brought hither in this manner. Ambulances and stretchers were in constant motion between the cars and the hospitals; but it was past midnight before the sad work was completed.

The scenes of that night it is impossible for any description adequately to portray. Some of the men had lost an arm, some a leg, some both legs. The wounds were of every conceivable sort, and in every part of the body, from the crown of the head to the sole of the foot. They had been shot in the head, in the face, in the neck, in the shoulders, the arms, the legs, and the feet. They had been shot through the chest, through the lungs, through the hips and through the thighs.

Yet let no one suppose it was all gloom, lamentation, and complaint here. It was otherwise, far otherwise. Sufferers they were, but, almost without exception, patient, cheerful sufferers. They gave the highest proof of courage that men can give. "Almost any one," said a great commander, "can be brave in battle under a good leader; but he is the real hero who can be brave when the battle is over." To look at some of these men might almost lead one to think that they were gathered there for some celebration or a festive scene.

They were grateful for our assistance (says the writer of the letter), but it was wonderful to see how disposed and able they were to help themselves. Some, indeed, could do nothing in their own behalf. But many of them, frightfully maimed and mangled as they were, with a little help from us, would descend from the cars and take their places in the ambulances, nearly as quick as if they had been well.

With such lights and shadows does the memory of that Friday night, December fourth, 1863, abide with me, and will abide forever. What pen but that of the recording angel can write its history? The stars in their courses looked down mildly and lovingly upon us, from the sweet canopy above, as if in sympathy with our hearts and work. With a silence almost as profound as theirs, unknown to those whom we ministered to, and they unknown to us, with musings in their hearts and ours known only to Him who "knoweth what is in man," we went forward with our sad work, thankful, if such work must be done, for the privilege of doing it, in the hope that we are following, at some humble distance, "Him who went about doing good."

But more remarkable than even that night were the two following days, Saturday and Sabbath which we spent in intercourse with these men. We visited them from ward to ward in the hospitals, conversed and prayed with them, extended to them, as far as we could, the kind and tender sympathy of loved ones far away, wrote letters for them, and supplied them with copies of the Word of God in the place of those they had lost in the service. Oh, what a field for pastoral work! No minister of Christ at home, in ordinary times, has one to be compared with it for a moment. Men at home, impenitent men, cannot be approached on the subject of their salvation as these men can. To say that they are "accessible" is not enough. Their hearts are all open. They speak freely and ingenuously even when not specially interested. Many of them are tender in their feelings,—the starting tear, the choked utterance reveal it. Some are anxious and seeking. They love to be conversed with and counselled. Some, with bitter regrets, confess their backsliding, and lament that they have not maintained that character in the army which they had hoped to maintain.

On the contrary, there are not a few shining examples

of what the grace of God can do for men in a situation usually so adverse to a religious life. Having unfurled their banner at the outset, having at the very first defined their position before their comrades, as friends of Jesus and soldiers of the cross, they have been able to hold on their way and to grow stronger and stronger.

Among the maimed and wounded were three who fell into our hands from the rebel army. Two of them belonged to a Georgia regiment, the third to a North Carolina regiment. No case (says the narrator) interested me so much, or appealed for sympathy so much as that of these prisoners. I had repeated interviews with them, and heard them talk about home, and the cause in which we are fighting. They are choice young men, and I think they are Union men. One of them requested me to write my name in the Testament I gave him.

If the churches at home could hear what some of these men in the hospitals say of the services of the Christian Commission in the field, if they could know how many lives it has saved, how many hearts it has strengthened and comforted, it would be the most effective appeal ever made to them for their prayers and their charities.

XXI. DYING FOR A BENEFACTOR.

In the battle which resulted in the capture of Fort Donelson, an orderly sergeant saw a rebel pointing a rifle at the captain of his company. The aim was perfect; the distance at which he stood left no room for escape. At that instant the soldier rushed forward, threw himself before the officer, received the bullet in his own breast, and fell dead in the arms of the man he had saved.

It was ascertained, as the explanation of this singular act, that the brave fellow had been reared and generously treated by the captain's father. He had declared when he enlisted in the army, that he would be happy to die to save the life of his benefactor's son. The affection shown to each other by Damon and Pythias did not exceed that of this nameless soldier.

It was an instance of that last degree of self-sacrifice of which the Scripture represents our imperfect nature as capable. "Scarcely for a righteous man"—one who is simply just—"will one die; yet, peradventure, for a good man"—one truly benevolent—"some would even dare to die."[1]

XXII. THE LAST VICTORY.

General N. B. Sanders, so honorably known as a brave and efficient commander, was wounded in one of the East Tennessee battles, near the end of 1863. He was a Kentuckian, educated at West Point, which he left in 1856. He had been shot in a close hand-to-hand fight with the enemy. He was not aware at first how serious the injury was. On being examined by the physician, the general asked,—

"Tell me, doctor, if my wound is mortal?"

The doctor replied, "Sanders, it is a fearful wound and mortal. I am very sorry to say it, my dear fellow, but the odds are against you."

The general calmly replied, "Well, I am not afraid to die. I have made up my mind upon that subject. I have done my duty, and have served my country as well as I could."

He lingered until the next day, and during that time was perfectly conscious. In the course of the morning, he

[1] Romans v. 7.

explained certain symptoms to the doctor, and asked him what they meant.

The doctor replied, "General, you are dying."

"If that be so," he said, "I would like to see a clergyman."

The Rev. Mr. Hayden, chaplain of the post, was sent for, who came; and in the presence of General Burnside, with some of his staff, Captain Harris, a classmate, and several others, the dying officer was baptized.

He remarked after this that it had always been the desire of his friends that he should be baptized. He meant that they had long ago urged him to take this step, and thought him a fit subject for the ordinance. He was too distrustful to seem to rely on his own judgment in such a matter.

The minister then commended him to God, and while the fervent prayer was offered, General Burnside and the others present were kneeling around the bed of the dying believer. He shook hands with his chief, who stood tearfully over him, as if loath to witness the flight of the brave spirit. It was a scene never to be forgotten.

After this, he was preparing to partake of the sacrament, when his strength suddenly failed, and he was gone. It was hardly possible to mark the change. As Dr. Jackson, the physician, said, "He went to sleep like an infant." In a moment, as we trust, he passed beyond the need of symbols into the heavenly rest.

Such was the end of one of the bravest and most unpretending men whom God has raised up to serve the country in this time of need.

XXIII. DO YOU REMEMBER ECKINGTON?

Passing through the hospital one day, a young man was pointed out to me who the nurse said was near his end. I approached, and kneeling by the side of his cot, took his hand in mine. As he opened his eyes and looked up into mine, a smile of recognition passed over his features.

"I know you, I know you," said he. "Do you remember Eckington Hospital? Not long since, you and a good lady were there. Under a grove of trees in front of the building, you preached to us about the Great Physician. Then the lady sang to us some sweet songs of Zion, and reading matter furnished by the Christian Commission was distributed among the men. Yes, chaplain, I was then a convalescent soldier, and a wicked young man. When I was a boy, my mother used to kneel with me at the bedside and teach me the little prayer, —

'Now I lay me down to sleep,'

and till I left home I was instructed how to live, but for all that, I never became a Christian.

"Well, sir, as I listened to the preaching, and the singing of those sweet songs, I began to feel that at last I ought to give my heart to God. I saw how good he had been to me all my life, and I felt that I had done nothing but sin against him while my heart was at enmity with him. I resolved to go to Jesus, and through him seek salvation. That night, I began to pray; and though for a time it seemed very dark, yet it was not long before I felt that Jesus was my Saviour. No sooner did I trust in Him, and commit my soul to God with all its interests, than I felt, yea, I knew, I was accepted and saved. Oh, the love that sprang up in my heart to Jesus in that moment! How I love him now!" he said, as floods of tears flowed from his eyes, "and how I long to be with him! I did not expect to die so soon. A few days only have passed since I had this hope; but,—thank God, I have improved the time."

I spoke of his mother.

"Mother I am sure will be happy," said he. "I had just as lief die as not, for I shall see her in heaven. Father has already gone there."

He was so much affected that I feared his tears and emotions would hasten his death, and said to him,—

"Be as calm as you can, my brother."

He only whispered back, "Jesus wept."

I left him with the light of heaven beaming through his pale features. I was told he dwelt upon the name of Jesus in faint whispers, with indescribable tenderness till his lips ceased to move.

XXIV. THE BOOK WILL TELL.

The brother of a sick soldier travelled two thousand miles to find him, watch over him, and, if it might be, restore him to his friends. But he arrived too late. Before the long journey was accomplished, the hand of death was laid upon the invalid, and had borne him beyond the reach of human care and sympathy. The brother, wishing to secure the few effects of the departed one as keepsakes, went to the camp where his regiment was stationed. A fellow-soldier (says one of the party) led us to a tent that was only large enough to contain two bunks and a small table. Beneath one of the bunks were two or three soiled and dusty knapsacks. The weeping brother proceeded to open one of these, and to examine its contents. Every little article of the scanty wardrobe was scrutinized as well as blinding tear-drops would permit. The brother was not certain, but thought he could recognize some of the articles as those of the loved one, of whom the most trifling token would be so dear to surviving friends.

At the bottom of the knapsack lay a Bible. The thought which seized me at this discovery (says the relator) was that also of our guide, who cried out instantly, "The book will tell."

The trembling hands of the bereaved brother grasped the Bible, and, unclasping it, we read, " Presented to —— by his brother, ——, N. Y., ——, 1862."

The doubt was solved. Here, indeed, were the effects that we had taken such pains to recover, and they were known by the testimony of the Bible, in which the hand of affection had written the owner's name. That exclamation, "The book will tell," is full of meaning. The Bible has been given as a keepsake to thousands and thousands of our soldiers, as they have gone forth to the dangers of the war, and has not been given in vain. Many of them, it is impossible to doubt, will be indebted to that gift for having their names enrolled in the Lamb's book of life. During this war, how often has the sacred volume, put into the knapsack of the departing soldier by mother or sister, been sent back to the lonely home as the only relic of the son and brother who has fallen in battle, or pined away in the camp or hospital. But one anxiety is left now, and respecting that they say to themselves, "The book will tell." With blinded eyes, with hope and fear, they open the returned Bible to see what evidence of its perusal they can find — what passages were marked, at what verse the last leaf was turned down.

The saying has a lesson for us all. The revelations of this book are to decide each one's destiny. The tests of character are prescribed there, to which all must be brought, in the presence of the Judge at last; and from that book in effect will issue the sentence, — "Come" or "Depart" — which awaits every probationer.

XXV. A SOLDIER'S POCKET DIARY.

It is very suggestive and very touching to look over the pocket diary, in which a brave soldier, in short, abrupt, terse sentences, with long omissions, gives hints of what is passing around and within him. Such glimpses of military life give us our best views of its hardships, and of the spirit of the men who endure them so cheerfully.

Oliver S. Currier[1] was a native of Maine, who enlisted, in the summer of 1862, in the Thirty-Fifth Massachusetts, Company K, of Roxbury. He was a disciple of Christ, and thoroughly conscientious in all that he did. He was unable at first to gratify his patriotic desires, as claims rested on him which he felt he was not at liberty to disregard. That obstacle at length was removed.

One night in July, a friend entered the chamber where he was sleeping, and awoke him to say that the way was now open for him to enlist as a soldier. There was no more sleep for him that night; he left his bed, went out at midnight, and signed the roll. He had been troubled about a mortgage, and was anxious to provide that his parents should not be turned out of their home in case he should fall in battle. A friend having assumed that responsibility for him, he started for Maine the next morning, and placed a deed of the little cottage and garden in the hands of his father; and on the fourth day returned, entered the ranks, and went with his company to camp.

[1] He was a grandson of the late Rev. Jotham Sewall, of Maine, "whose praise is in all the churches" as an eloquent and apostolic servant of Jesus Christ.

Under date of September fourteenth, he writes, at South Mountain, "I have been in my first battle. One man out of the company killed." This was three weeks after they left home.

Three days later, at Antietam: "We went in at about four o'clock. Our company lost thirteen killed and thirty-one wounded. Have seen hard work to-day. After we withdrew, I only found four of our company. Our regiment was second across the bridge. I feel sad, *sad*, SAD."

Well might he feel sad. The beloved commander[1] of his company was borne off the field with three severe wounds, and marks of twenty others, and every officer was wounded. The dear friend who called him to arms at midnight was among the dead, with so many others who had been accustomed to sing the songs of Zion with him in that strange land.[2]

But this sadness had no despondency in it. "Our roll-call has only thirty-nine names," he writes, a few days after. "We are small in number, but strong in determination to do all we can to help put down this great REBELLION."

We pass over references to long and exhausting marches, and come to the record of scenes just before the fatal battle at Fredericksburg.

"Nov. 22. Still lying opposite Fredericksburg; weather cold. We occupy a poor camp-ground. I am not very well; a poor appetite. I wish I had a good potato to eat."

"Sunday, 23d. Very cold. Listened to reading of the proclamation [for Thanksgiving] of the Governor of Massachusetts. I do not feel very well; have not any overcoat."

[1] Captain King of Roxbury, now a lieutenant colonel and military commandant of Lexington, Ky.

[2] It may not be obtrusive for the writer to say that a dear relative, a nephew and namesake, was one of these brave and Christian young men who fell in this battle at Antietam.

"Monday, 24th. I wish I felt better. Have no appetite. I would like to be at home a few days; spend Thanksgiving there!"

"Wednesday, a letter from home. How it cheers the sick soldier to hear from the dear ones at home! They long for my return. God grant my return."

"Thursday, 27th. My Thanksgiving consisted of a little parched rye and a small boiled potato. I never tasted anything so good as that potato."

How significant these brief sentences!

"Monday, Dec. 1. Letters from home. How precious they are!"

"Saturday, 6th. A cold snow-storm; oh, how cheerless! Wet ground to pitch our tents on, no straw to lie on, worn-out shoes, green wood, short rations. A sorry time we are having."

"Sunday, 7th. I got through the night, but it was tough. I liked to have frozen. I don't think I slept an hour; up most all night; wet feet."

How will those who enjoy the peaceful prosperity to secure which our heroic soldiers are enduring such hardships, a few years hence, read these sentences, and how will they honor the memory of these noble men!

"Monday, 8th. Very cold last night. I am poorly clothed; without overcoat. To-day it is warm and quite pleasant. Health good."

"Wednesday, 10th. Very pleasant. Cartridges dealt out to-day. There is to be fighting soon."

"Thursday, 11th. Received two months' pay, $26. Battle of Fredericksburg. We have been under arms all the forenoon, expecting to be ordered into action every minute. Cannonading is terrific — a continuous roar since daybreak. I am going to send uncle J—— $20 by ——."

These were the last words he wrote.

The regiment went into action immediately. A cannon-ball took off his leg; amputation was performed; but he died the same night, and his poor body, no more to suffer cold or hunger, lies buried in a pleasant garden in Fredericksburg.

The comfort of knowing how he was carried off the field, and how he was sustained, and what his last messages were, and all the particulars of his dying moments, is denied to his friends. The comfort of knowing that one like the Son of God was with him, and that his grace was sufficient, and that in peaceful and joyful triumph he fell asleep,— this blessed assurance his friends have. His religious character was so simple and natural, so consistent and unpretending, that we have no doubt what the closing scene was, and what heavenly joy he entered upon. And may God grant to every soldier like precious faith![1]

> "'Twere sweet indeed to close our eyes,
> With those we cherished near,
> And, wafted upward by their sighs,
> Soar to some calmer sphere:
> But whether on the scaffold high,
> Or in the battle's van,
> The fittest place for man to die
> Is where he dies for man."

XXVI. GENTLE AS WELL AS BRAVE.

The late Major-General Buford was offered a major-general's commission in the rebel army when he was in Utah, at the beginning of the Rebellion. He crushed the treasonable paper in his hand, and declared that he would live and die under the flag of the Union.

No commander, probably, was more loved by his soldiers

[1] Abbreviated from a Tract for Soldiers.

than he was. A striking instance of his thoughtful regard for the feelings of others is mentioned in connection with his death. A few hours before that event, while suffering from delirium, he roundly scolded his negro servant, but during a brief, lucid interval, understanding what he had done, he called the negro to his bedside and said to him,—

"Edward, I hear I have been scolding you. I did not know what I was saying. You have been a faithful servant, Edward."

The poor negro sat down and wept as though his heart was broken.

General Buford was promoted to the rank of major-general after he had received his fatal wound. On having his commission brought to him, he exclaimed,—

"Now, I wish I could live."

His last intelligible words, uttered during an attack of delirium, were,—

"Put guards on all the roads, and don't let the men run back to the rear."

It was an illustration of the ruling passion, strong in death. It was remarked of him that nothing so moved his scorn as to see men skulking or hanging on the rear. This gallant officer had been trained in a noble school of patriotism, that of the lamented Admiral Foote.[1]

How brief the interval! Death separated them; death has united them.

XXVII. PICKET DUTY.

The nature of this perilous service is not understood by every one. It is described briefly, but vividly, in the following sentences. The writer is a clergyman, who relates to us his own experience:—

[1] See page 90, where the two are mentioned together.

Picket duty at all times is arbitrary, but at night trebly so. No monarch on a throne, with absolute power, is more independent, or exercises greater sway for the time being, than a simple private soldier stationed on his beat with an enemy in front. Darkness veils all distinctions. He is not obliged to know his own officers or comrades, or the commanding general, or the highest officer in the land, only through the means of the countersign. With musket loaded and capped he walks his rounds, having to do with matters only of life and death, and at the same time clothed with absolute power.

It is a position of fearful importance and responsibility, one that always made me feel solemn and terribly earnest. Often, too, these posts are in thick woods, where the soldier stands alone, cut off from camp, cut off from his fellows, subject only to the harassings of his imagination and sense of fear. The shadows deepen into inky night. All objects around him, even to the little birds that were his companions during the day, are gathered within the curtains of a hushed repose; but the soldier, with every nerve and faculty of his mind strained to the utmost tension of keenness and sensibility, speaks only in low whispers; his fingers tighten round the stock of his musket as he leans forward to catch the sound of approaching footsteps, or, in the absence of danger, looks longingly up to the cold, gray sky, with its wealth of soft and flaming stars.

And what an hour for noble, lofty thought, in connection with the subjects of death, eternity, and the future world!

XXVIII. LOCK OF HAIR FOR MOTHER.

It was just after the battle of Williamsburg,[1] where hundreds of our brave fellows had fallen, never to bear arms again in their country's cause, and where hundreds more were wounded, that a soldier came to the tent of a delegate of the Christian Commission and said, "Chaplain, one of our boys is badly wounded, and wants to see you right away."

Hurrying after the messenger, says the delegate, I was taken to the hospital and led to a bed, upon which lay a noble young soldier. He was pale and bloodstained from a terrible wound above the temple. I saw at a glance that he had but a few hours to live upon earth. Taking his hand, I said to him, —

"Well, my brother, what can I do for you?"

The poor dying soldier looked up in my face, and placing his finger where his hair was stained with his blood, he said, —

"Chaplain, cut a big lock from here for mother! for my mother, mind, chaplain!"

I hesitated to do it. He said, "Don't be afraid, chaplain, to disfigure my hair. It's for mother, and nobody will come to see me in the dead-house to-morrow."

I did as he requested me.

"Now, chaplain," said the dying man, "I want you to kneel down by me and return thanks to God."

"For what?" I asked.

"For giving me such a mother. Oh! chaplain, she is a good mother; her teachings comfort me and console me now. And, chaplain, thank God that by his grace I am a

[1] In the Peninsula, May, 1862.

Christian. What would I do now if I was not a Christian? I know that my Redeemer liveth. I feel that his finished work has saved me. And, chaplain, thank God for giving me dying grace. He has made my dying bed

'Feel soft as downy pillows are.'

Thank him for the promised home in glory. I'll soon be there, — there where there is no war, nor sorrow, nor desolation nor death, — where I shall see Jesus, and be forever with the Lord."

I knelt by the dying man, and thanked God for the blessings he had bestowed upon him, — the blessings of a good mother, a Christian hope, and dying grace, to bear testimony to God's faithfulness.

Shortly after the prayer, he said, "Good-by, chaplain; if you ever see that mother of mine, tell her it was all well with me."

XXIX. THE YOUNG COLOR-SERGEANT.

At once a color-bearer in the army of his country and in the army of Jesus, — what prouder position than this for a young Christian soldier! He was General Kilpatrick's color-bearer, and a mere boy. His comrades all said he was a brave fellow. The main artery of one of his legs had been cut off by a Minie ball. The wound had bled several times while in the hospital, and he was fast sinking. He whispered to an attendant who was bending over him:

"Jesus has a home in heaven for me."

"How do you know?"

"Because God loves me. He loves his Son Jesus, and he loves me too."

These were almost his last words. A few hours before

his death, his father came, truly a broken-hearted man. "For he was his youngest boy, — his Benjamin, — and how could he spare him?"

"I didn't want him to go; and how, how, shall I go home without him? Oh! I am afraid it will be too much for the mother."

The boy was laid in his coffin, and the ladies and little children of Hagerstown where he died trimmed the body with flowers, — though he himself was the brightest flower of all, destined assuredly to bloom and flourish forever in the Paradise above.

XXX. NOT YET TOO LATE.

Among the wounded at the battle of Stone River, in Tennessee, was a young man. Over the mortally wounded son hung the anxious mother, in the deepest sorrow that he gave no evidence of fitness for eternal scenes. But the words the dying youth uttered, severely as they condemned himself, showed clearly his own convictions of the shame and wrong of those who neglect God till life is drawing to a close, and hope then to obtain his favor.

To a Christian appeal, he replied, — "If I live to get well, I will be a Christian; but I will not throw the fag-end of my life in the face of the Almighty." He immediately expired.

The poor fellow certainly mistook the gospel mode of salvation, for faith in Christ can avail in other cases as it did with the dying thief in his last moments. The "fag-end" of his life was distinguished by an act which opened to him the gates of Paradise. The time may be short, but much may be done often in a short time.

The striking language of the dying soldier contains a

stinging rebuke to all those who practically claim the best of life for themselves, while they venture to put off their Maker with the little that remains when they are about to sink into the grave.[1]

XXXI. SOLDIER, ARE YOU HUNGRY?

Be kind to the soldiers. What they need is good cheer for the mind as well as the body, assurance of sympathy, proof that our hearts are with them as they go forth to peril their lives for us by land and sea. Brave men appreciate such tokens of interest in them and their work. Even a child may show to them kindness, the remembrance of which will strengthen their hearts and nerve their arms in the day of battle.

A writer from Baltimore illustrates this trait of the soldier's character. About eighteen months ago, a northern regiment passed through this city on the way to Washington. They had occasion to halt a short time in one of our streets, for rest and refreshment. While they were doing this, a little fellow approached one of the men and said, —

"Soldier, are you hungry?"

"Yes, — I am," he replied; upon which the boy invited him to go with him to his home near by, and there, on his making known the case, the family set before the hunger-bitten soldier a bountiful repast.

A few weeks ago, this regiment, having served out their term of enlistment, passed through Baltimore again, on their way home. The soldier referred to had distinguished himself on the field, and had risen from a private to the rank of captain. He had not forgotten the kindness of

[1] From the *Congregationalist*.

his little friend in Baltimore. He knew where he lived, sought him out, and presented to him a handsome photographic album filled with likenesses of all the prominent generals in the Union army. Inscribed upon the back of the album in beautiful gilt letters, were the words, — "Soldier, are you hungry?"

This little boy is the son of a Lutheran minister in the city of Baltimore.

XXXII. OUR GOOD-HEARTED PRESIDENT.

"I have observed more than once," says Daniel Webster, in his eulogy on honest Zachary Taylor, "that the prevalent notion with the masses of mankind for conferring high honors on individuals is a confidence in their mildness, their paternal, protecting, prudent, and safe character. The people naturally feel safe where they feel themselves to be under the control and protection of sober counsel, of impartial minds, and a general paternal superintendence."

Such titles to popular confidence and favor we recognize, also, in the man on whom it has devolved to guide our ship of State through the present crisis. The people trust him because he has made them feel that he is unselfish and honest. They believe he has sought to do his duty according to the best of his knowledge and ability, and that conviction at the bottom of their hearts has been our sheet-anchor; it has held us together, has buoyed up the nation's faith, has kept us from drifting into anarchy and ruin. It is a quality of character and a means of power not inconsistent with genius, but which genius alone does not confer; it is worth infinitely more to us, in a time like this, than any glare of military reputation, or brilliancy of intellect, or diplomatic skill.

The way to be thought upright and faithful and earnest for the public welfare, is to be so in truth, and it is by that art of arts that Mr. Lincoln has so won to himself the hearts of the great mass of the nation.

Incidents like the following bring out the character of an individual in a natural manner, and leave us in no doubt how we are to understand him.

On Monday last (says a visitor at Washington),[1] I dropped in upon Mr. Lincoln, and found him busy counting greenbacks.

"This, sir," said he, "is something out of my usual line; but a President of the United States has a multiplicity of duties not specified in the Constitution or acts of congress. This is one of them. This money belongs to a poor negro who is a porter in one of the Departments (the Treasury), who is at present very ill with the small pox. He is now in hospital, and could not draw his pay because he could not sign his name.

I have been at considerable trouble to overcome the difficulty and get it for him, and have at length succeeded in cutting red tape, as you newspaper men say. I am now dividing the money and putting by a portion labelled, in an envelope, with my own hands, according to his wish;" and his Excellency proceeded to endorse the package very carefully.

No one who witnessed the transaction could fail to appreciate the goodness of heart which would prompt a man in his situation, borne down by a weight of cares almost without parallel in the world's history, to turn aside thus and befriend one of the humblest of his fellow-creatures in sickness and sorrow.

---

[1] Who published the incident in the *Chicago Tribune.*

XXXIII. BROUGHT BACK TO THE FOLD.

On the evening of the battle of Rappahannock Station, my friend, Dr. R——, of the Third Division of our corps, came to me, saying a man in their hospital wished to see a chaplain. Accompanying him, I found a young man about twenty years old, a member of the Tenth Massachusetts, with his leg crushed and mangled by a piece of shell. The shock had been so severe that amputation was useless, and he was sinking rapidly.

Expressing himself glad to see me, I inquired his religious history. It was the same old story, — a bright hope — active church-membership — army life — army irregularities, and the abandonment of his profession.

"And now," said he, "if there can be forgiveness for such a wanderer, pray for me."

I confess I felt more backwardness than was right. A circle of coarse soldiers stood there, surveying the solemn scene with mere morbid curiosity. Another group stood there, more educated and refined, — a knot of surgeons, some of whom, I knew, had no belief in God or eternity, and considered my interview with the dying man as at best but amiable officiousness. But there lay the sinking sufferer, and I wore the uniform of a minister of Christ, and bending over the table where he lay, I asked the Good Shepherd to give assurance of pardon to the wandering sheep. I dared not remind the boy that he was dying the noblest death that mortal man can die, but held up his case merely as that of a lost sinner, whose redemption must come, not from that horrid shell-wound, or the blood that, for his country's sake, was trickling from that mangled limb, but from the blood shed upon Calvary, and the wounds of a slain Redeemer. Throughout the prayer, his murmured responses and fervent ejaculations disclosed his own earnestness in the petition, and the smothered hope revived again; and, faint at first, but growing brighter and brighter, there finally beamed in full radiance on his soul that faith which supports in the stern hour.

Meanwhile, there stood beside the table a noble-looking young fellow, a little older than the dying soldier, moistening his lips, and affectionately smoothing the hair from his brow, but so perfectly calm and collected, I supposed he was merely one of the hospital attendants. A remark of some one present started my suspicion, and I asked, —

"Is this a friend of yours?"

Said he, "It is my younger brother."

So calm was his voice, and so composed his manner throughout the whole, that the thing seemed impossible, except that often those who feel most deeply manifest it the least.

He said to his brother, "S——, what shall I tell mother for you?"

"Tell her I died for my country," was the prompt and noble reply.

"Give me a kiss for her," said the other; and the bronzed face bowed down to the pale lips as tenderly as if they had been those of an infant. More than one in the tent turned to hide his tears, and the two brothers seemed most moved of all.

The dying boy sank rapidly, but the clouds vanished from his mind, and his faith grew bright and strong. I repeated, "I know that my Redeemer liveth;" "The Lord is my Shepherd, I shall not want;" "In my Father's house are many mansions;" and still other passages. I recited, also, the beautiful hymn: —

"Rock of ages, cleft for me,"

and those lines, especially dear when the couch of dissolution was a rough board table in a dark, cold tent, with merely a knapsack to rest the head upon, —

"Jesus can make a dying bed
Feel soft as downy pillows are."

The hymns of Zion had been familiar to him at home, and he tried to repeat, —

"Jesus, lover of my soul."

That was always a favorite hymn of mine, and I repeated it to him entire. It seemed to give him a great deal of comfort, and to strengthen him even more than the rest had done.

But his voice was already beginning to fail. Said he, "There's — a — silver — pencil — in — pocket ——."

He evidently wished to send it to some one for a keepsake, and it was with the deepest sorrow we saw he was unable to speak friendship's last message. There was but one friend of whom he had power to speak now. He had lain for some minutes perfectly motionless. I thought all was over. But all at once he roused up and said, —

"'Jesus, lover of my soul.' Oh, repeat that again!"

My voice choked up so that I could hardly speak. With broken utterances I once more went through with the beautiful stanzas. But I know not if he heard me, for I could not have got to the last verse before "the storm of life" was over; "the haven" was reached, and "the billows" had died away in eternal peace.[1]

[1] From the N. Y. Examiner.

XXXV. THE CURRENT BETWEEN HOME AND CAMP.

Some of the marks fastened on the blankets, shirts, and other gifts sent to the Sanitary Commission for the soldiers, show the thought and feeling at home. Thus, on a homespun blanket, worn, but washed as clean as snow, was pinned a bit of paper, which said, "This blanket was carried by Milly Aldrich (who is ninety-three years old), down hill and up hill, one and a half miles, to be given to some soldier."

On a bed-quilt was pinned a card, saying, "My son is in the army. Whoever is made warm by this quilt, which I have worked on for six days and the greater part of six nights, let him remember his own mother's love."

On another blanket was this: "This blanket was used by a soldier in the war of 1812; may it keep some soldier warm in this war against traitors."

On a pillow was written: "This pillow belonged to my little boy, who died resting on it; it is a precious treasure to me, but I give it for the soldiers."

On a pair of woollen socks was written: "These stockings were knit by a little girl five years old, and she is going to knit some more, for mother says it will help some poor soldier."

On a box of beautiful lint was this mark: "Made in a sick-room, where the sunlight has not entered for nine years, but where God has entered, and where two sons have bid their mother good-by, as they have gone out to the war."

On a bundle containing bandages was written: "This is a poor gift, but it is all I had; I have given my husband and my boy, and only wish I had more to give; but I have not."

On some eye-shades was marked: "Made by one who is blind. Oh, how I long to see the dear old flag that you are all fighting under!"

XXXVI. HOME-LINKS OF THE WAR.

The Rev. Robert J. Parvin, a laborer for the Christian Commission, related the following history, at a recent meeting of that Association, in the Hall of Representatives at Washington.

At Gettysburg (said he), in the Fifth Corps Hospital, of which I had charge in the Christian Commission's work for a few weeks, I had occasion to see how many home-links there are between our work and the last hours of dying soldiers. I remember well a captain from the State of Maine, of the 20th Maine Volunteers, who was brought into that old barn, where were sixty-five of the worst cases in the whole corps. Oh, they were all sadly wounded! The brave fellow had some of his own men lying on the floor not far from him. He loved them with a father's love. As one after another they died around him, it worked so upon his mind that he became a raving maniac, until it took four or five to hold him. With great difficulty we got him away from his men who were dying, — in a room by himself, — and he rallied. The surgeon went in to see him. He came out and I passed in. The surgeon had told me he could not live. If he had had a primary amputation — an amputation, that is, on the field — he might have recovered, but he could not now.

I took him by the hand. His first words were, "Chaplain (for such they call us), what did the surgeon say?"

"Why, captain, you are in a critical case."

"I know that, chaplain; but does the surgeon think I can live?"

"He thinks it is hardly possible that you will live, captain."

"My wife, chaplain, — have you heard from her since your message yesterday?"

"No; we have received no answer. The lines are in the hands of the Government, which needs them; perhaps that is the reason we cannot get an answer at once. We hope she will be here."

"Does the surgeon say I cannot live long, chaplain?"

"Yes; but you are a Christian man, Capt. Billings?"

"Yes, chaplain, I have no fears. I left my place in the Sabbath school for my place in the army. My hope is in the Lord Jesus Christ. I have tried to serve him in the army, and he will not forsake me now. I would like to see my wife," he continued, as his thoughts recurred to that dear one.

"Well, captain, if you have anything to say, will you give the message to me?"

He asked me to give her his knapsack and sword, and other little things that he mentioned; and if she came, the message he wished me to deliver; and then he seemed to dismiss all these things from his mind, as he lay there calm, peaceful, a dying man as well as a dying soldier, and, above all, a dying Christian.

"Now," said he, at length, "don't stay longer with me. Go and minister to the boys, and run in here as you can to read a few words of Scripture to me, and kneel down and pray with me."

After I had prayed with him, he said to me, "Could you have my body embalmed and sent home? I lost my money on the field?"

"Certainly, captain, it shall be done; give yourself no further thought about that."

At no other time did he refer to it, but passed away as a dying Christian, triumphing over all the horrors of war, over all the sad circumstances around him. It was in the morning at eleven o'clock that he passed away. At five o'clock that afternoon his body was sent to the embalmer's. At ten o'clock that night, as I was busy writing letters from memoranda, taken through the day, a knock was heard at my door. "Walk in," I responded. A man stepped in, inquiring, "Is Captain Billings, of the 20th Maine, here?"

What a question for us to meet! But I thought of the home-link. "Who are you?" I asked.

"I am his brother. I have his wife with me! I have buoyed her up this long way with the hope that we would find the captain in good condition. *Where is he, sir?*"

"You have not brought the captain's wife out here with you to-night?" The corps hospital was four miles from Gettysburg.

"No; I left her in town for to-night."

"Oh, it is well; the body of your brother was sent to the embalmer's at five o'clock this afternoon!"

"Oh! oh!" said he, "I cannot tell her! I cannot tell her! I cannot trust myself to tell her, or even to see her again, to-night!"

The poor man seemed overcome. "I cannot see her," he continued; "I have brought her on, all the way to Gettysburg, and now *you* must, *you must* tell her all."

And so our duty was to see the wife and deliver to her the messages and the tokens of dying love of her husband, and speak to her words of comfort in the name of the Lord! His body was carried on to the State of Maine to repose with those of his kindred there.

XXXVI. A PLEA FOR THE CHRISTIAN COMMISSION.

Some account of General Howard, of Maine, has been given on a previous page.[1] This gallant officer and decided witness for Christ was one of the speakers at the great meeting in Philadelphia, on the 28th of January, the second anniversary of the United States Christian Commission. Such a man has a right to be heard. No words could be more appropriate to place here, as the last words to linger on our ears as we bring these pages to an end, than the following sentences from the speech of this Christian patriot, on that occasion.

I may be allowed (said he) to speak freely to the friends who are here to-night. Let me tell you one thing which I need not suppress, if I could, and that is, that I feel in my heart a deep and abiding interest in the cause of my Redeemer. I know that this is also the cause of the Christian Commission, and, therefore, I love it, and identify myself with it; and I doubt not that you love it, and will do everything you can for it, for a like reason. And now, I ask you — as I am to go back to the field to take up my cross anew, and to stand up night and day, evening and morning, for the cause of him that I love — that your earnest, importunate prayers may follow me, and that God would bless the soldiers, that evil may be repressed among them, and that when they go into battle they may go without a fear, because they know in whom they have believed.

My friends, I heard a general once say (he was not a Christian General), in reference to General Magruder, on the other side, that he could not be a very brave man, nor have true courage, because he was such a profane and wicked man, and delighted to lead the young into shame and

---

[1] See Chapter III, page 78.

degradation. I am sure he was right. I assert that the highest type of courage is Christian courage. When your spirit yearns up to God in the prayer, "O, Lord, be my protector, and in this peril let me run under the shadow of thy wing," then you will fear no evil, though you walk through the valley of the shadow of death.

My friends, these things are realities with me. By the blessing of God, by his Spirit, he has enabled me to have a clear conviction that, should he take me away, I shall go to be with him. Not because I am good or holy or righteous; but because I have a Saviour, an all-sufficient Saviour, who is able to save even the chief of sinners unto the uttermost. Therefore I am able to say that I can go into the battle fearing no evil. And would to God, for their sakes, that every officer in the army and every soldier in the ranks could declare, in sincerity from the depths of his heart, that God had done such great things for him!

These to me are settled, solemn convictions, and I speak them freely and frankly, as I am encouraged to do on this auspicious occasion. It may seem to some that it is expressing one's private feelings too publicly; but I think it well for me to bear such testimony in a work like yours, which contemplates this great and all-important result, — the promotion of heart-religion and the salvation of souls. And especially do I feel this, in these times of excitement and terror, over the mere temporal accessories of war, the dreadful sacrifice of lives, the horrible sights of wounds, the caring for the wounded and sick, the lamentations for the dead, — amid all this I fear that the still, small voice has not always been listened to, the silent and beautiful, though wonderful work of the Spirit of God has not been seen, and its importance felt as it should be in our land. This the Christian Commission is striving to accomplish; it seeks to keep alive the spirit of Christianity among our soldiers.

Their agency is the leaven in our armies. May they leaven the whole lump! It is this only that will prepare us for our liberties. This bond, the bond of Christian love, is the true bond, after all, that shall permanently unite us. There is no other. We speak of the chains of commerce and trade, of corn and cotton, that will unite the sections of our country, — but these are temporary, fluctuating, perishing links. The religion of Jesus Christ is the lasting bond that connects not only Maine with Massachusetts, and Massachusetts with Connecticut, but Maine with Texas, and Florida with Wisconsin.

We boast of being an asylum for all nations. From England, Ireland, France, Germany, Russia, and almost every country beyond the ocean, come men, women, and children, who settle down in the midst of us. How shall we cause them to assimilate to us? How shall we ever make them good and useful citizens? Will it be, think you, by merely giving them land on which to settle? Will they become one with us, because they grow in material wealth and prosperity? No, no! Nothing but an education, a true education of heart and morals, such as the religion of Jesus Christ imparts, can ever truly and safely assimilate all these heterogeneous elements, and enable us to be truly one people.

The gospel has its victories to achieve for us as well as the sword. Many of the rebels hated us more before the war than they do now. They respect us much more than they once did, after seeing that we are not afraid to expose our bodies to be burned, if necessary, in a just cause, — the cause of our country that we love, — that we shrink from no sacrifice of money, time, or life, in order to maintain and perpetuate the beautiful government that our fathers bequeathed to us.

But this is not all. They have felt, too, the power of

the spirit of kindness and love, of which the religion of Jesus has borne so many fruits in this struggle. They have been astonished at the kindness which has been shown to them when they have fallen into our hands. It was this that demoralized them at Vicksburg. In the West the rebels are not so violent as they were. When they come into our lines now, they say they were forced to fight, that they are Union men, and always were Union men. And they are coming in every day. We have just heard that since General Rosecrans took command of the Cumberland Army, eight thousand have delivered themselves up to us. And do they hate us? No! We have melted them down by Christian kindness and love. And, my friends, this is the way to disarm them. I believe, and say it with emphatic assurance, that if we all have the spirit of the Master in our hearts we shall demoralize them wherever we find them!

I do not advocate any shrinking back, or checking of the terrible steeds of war. No! Fill up the ranks. Make them full. Make the next campaign more vigorous than any that has gone before it, so that it shall be, by the divine help, perfectly impossible for the rebels to keep the field. But let us wield this power along with the alleviating and saving influences of the religion of Christ. Let these, as diffused by the Christian Commission, and in other ways, follow our armies everywhere, blessing friend and foe alike, and we shall then cause the enemy to come into our lines, not only by the eight thousand, but by the sixteen and the sixty thousand. It is this that will ruin their cause, and finally break down their opposition.

This terrible revolution has been brought upon us, by the overruling hand of a wise Providence, among its other effects, to tear out from among us the roots of prejudice, — prejudice of the bitterest kind, that of races. But nothing is too hard in the end for Christian love and charity and truth; and that 'spirit assuredly will prevail, and we shall yet come together and be one people, whose God is the Lord. Let us resolve anew, as we go hence, that, as for us, we will all do what we can for our country, our soldiers, and the cause of Christ.

> "Lord, while for all mankind we pray,
>   Of every clime and coast,
> Oh, hear us for our native land,—
>   The land we love the most.
>
> Oh, guard our shores from every foe;
>   With peace our borders bless,—
> Our cities with prosperity,
>   Our fields with plenteousness.
>
> Unite us in the sacred love
>   Of knowledge, truth, and thee,
> And let our hills and valleys chant
>   The songs of liberty.
>
> Lord of the nations, thus to thee
>   Our country we commend;
> Be thou her refuge and her trust,—
>   Her everlasting Friend."

INDEX.

SOME matters are set forth here not represented in the general Table of Contents, at the beginning of the volume. Names of persons and places are given somewhat fully, because they suggest to many readers the points of chief interest in the book.

Adams, an Illinois soldier, 166.
Album of our generals, 237.
Aldrich, Milly, the gift of an old man, 242.
Allen, C. A., chaplain from Indiana, 138.
Alvord, Rev. J. W., Secretary of the Tract Society, communications from, 49, 79, 123, 131, 166.
Ambrotype of unknown children, 201.
Anderson, Major, abandons Fort Moultrie, 182; his speech to a Sunday school, 191.
Andrew, B—, of Brooklyn, N. Y., 79.
Andrews, Lorin, President of Kenyon College, 16.
Angel of the hospital, 150.
Angels, an object of interest to, 54.
Antietam visited after battle, 173; the slaughter there, 228.
April 19th, henceforth doubly memorable, 200.
Army Hymn, why so popular, 189.
Articles of Faith, 129.

B——, Rev. Mr., one of the chaplains, 161.
Ball's Bluff, an exploit in the battle of, 196.
Barrows, W., Rev., interesting letter of, 44.
"Banner of the Covenant" quoted, 26.
Banks, General, campaign in Virginia, 169.
Baptism, the nation's, 33.
Bartimæus, of whom the type, 45.
Baton Rouge, letter from, 47.
Bass, Rev. Mr., N. Y. chaplain, 58.
Bethune Dr., lines of, 183.
Bealton Station, where the chaplains met, 147.
Bentley, Wm. C., of Rhode Island, 111.
Berry General, at Williamsburg, 23.
Bibles, donation of, 26; the best protectors, 92; found on the battlefield, 186.
Bible-men, 28.
Billings, Captain, of Maine, his death at Gettysburg, 243.

INDEX.

Billy, the drummer-boy, 162.
Birch, Major, with Gen. Mitchell, 148.
Bomb-proof, a place of prayer, 34.
"Boston Recorder" cited, 132, 218.
Bradley, Rev. D. M., a patriotic missionary, 193.
Broadhead, Colonel, his last words, 31.
Brown, Robert A., chaplain, 28.
Buford, Colonel. 90; his last words, 231.
Bull Run battle, incidents of, 65.
Burnside, General, his character, 184, 223.

C.

Camp Nelson, Ky., the unlettered soldier-boy, 211.
Canada steamer, scene on board of, 92.
Canfield, Herman, Colonel, his triumph in death, 61.
Carney, William H., heroic defence of his flag, 115; his history, 116.
Carolina city, letter from, 25.
Catholic woman's piety, 127.
Cavaliers, English, 185.
Cemetery, National, at Gettysburg, 195.
Chadlow, Rev. Mr., circumstance mentioned by, 161.
Chain bridge, on the Potomac, 74.
Charley, how he died, 117.
Chase, John W., and his brother, of Rhode Island, 25.
Chase, Chaplain, of Maine, 151.
Chase, Secretary of the Treasury, letter of, 194.
Chicago Sanitary Commission, 67.
"Chicago Tribune," cited, 104, 238.
"Christian Advocate," article from, 38.
Christ's soldiers in battle, 77.
Christmas night of 1860, for what memorable, 182.
Church members in the army, 22.
Churches, regimental, 123.
"Cincinnati Gazette," referred to, 37.
Clark, Chaplain, of Swampscot, Mass., 95.
Clark, Rev. Bishop, of Rhode Island, statement of, 184.
Collins, quotation from, 99.
"Congregationalist," referred to, 236.
Connecticut Ninth, Colonel Cahill, 68.

Conscience of the country aroused, 15
Contrabands, preaching to, 148.
Colton, Chaplain, of Indiana, 48.
Congress, frigate, destruction of, 102.
Courage, moral, example of, 17.
Cromwell's motto, 185.
Cross how made easy, 82.
Cumberland, fate of that vessel, 102.
Currier, Oliver S., his diary, 227.

D.

"Daily Advertiser," Boston, referred to, 103.
Davis, Commodore, commended, 54.
Decision, Christian, 16.
De Soto, scene on board of, 56.
Devereux, Lieut.-Colonel, Mass., 177.
Donelson, Fort, incident there, 85.
Douglas Hospital, death of a soldier in, 158.
Duffield, Mrs., letter to the Christian Commission, 135.
Duffield, H. M., adjutant, 135.
Dying for one's enemies, 222.

E.

Eagerness for religious reading, 141.
Eckington Hospital, 224.
Elkhart, Michigan, home of a brave soldier, 37.
Ellsworth's avengers, 51.
Evans, Rev. Mr., of Connecticut, 30.
Emancipation proclaimed, 189.
"Examiner," New York, referred to, 241.
Example, personal, power of, 79.

F.

Faith in Christ, its power, 42, 110, 122.
Fair Oaks, battle of, 110.
Fifty-fourth Mass., colored troops, 113.
Flag, next to the cross, 18.
Flag, which way it points, 213; used as a pall, 217.
Flag-raising at Sumter, 183.
Flag-ship Benton, scene on board of, 54.

INDEX.   253

Foote, Admiral, his death, 57; a praying commander, 89.
Forgiveness, illustration of, 148.

G.

Gaylord, ———, chaplain of the Mass. Twelfth, 188.
Gettysburg, battle of, 186.
Gilder, Chaplain, New York, 151.
Gospel, ameliorating spirit of, 91.
Gospel, designed for all, 211.
Gough, Mr., his speech, 100.
Graton, Edward R., of Clapville, Mass., 142.
Graves, "lonely," 99.
Griffith, Captain, his peaceful end, 61.
Gustavus Adolphus, his army, 185.

H.

Harrison, Colonel, of the Seventieth Indiana, 138.
Hagerstown, Md., a funeral there, 235.
Hamiston, father of the Portville children, 201.
Hampton Roads, sea-fight there, 102.
Havelock's Highlanders, 49.
Henry, John, of Indiana, the Sabbath-school teacher, 40.
Hero, the true one, 219.
Holmes, Dr. O. W., his "Hymn," 189.
Hope for the bereaved, 128.
Hopkinton, N. H., soldier from, 47.
Hospitals, labors in, 69.
Houses of Congress, their vote for a fast, 187.
Howard, General, of Maine, his character, 78; at a friend's death-bed, 60; his speech at Philadelphia, 246.
Hymn, the last on earth, 85.

I.

Illinois Eighty-third Regiment, bravery of, at Fort Donelson, 166.
Iowa First Regiment, drummer-boy of, 106.
Indiana Thirteenth, an experience of their chaplain, 27.
Ironsides, who they were, 27.

J.

Jackson, Stonewall, in the Shenandoah, 169.
James, Rev. Mr., chaplain, Mass., 143.
"Jamie" they called him, 161.
"Journal," Boston, extract from, 22.

K.

Keepsakes of the dead, 226.
Kenyon College, Ohio, its patriotic President, 16.
Kilpatrick, General, his color-bearer, 233.
Kindness, effect of, 210, 249.
King, Captain, of Roxbury, Mass., his bravery, 228.
Knapsack, its contents, 157; sent home as the last gift, 244.

L.

Lasher, chaplain of the Connecticut Fifth, 188.
Leasure, D., Colonel of the Ninth Pennsylvania Regiment, 27.
Lee, Edward, the Tennessee drummer-boy, 104.
Lee's Mill, battle of, 75.
Lexington, Mass., the battle there, referred to, 200.
Life's "fag-end," 235.
Lincoln, President, attempt to assassinate, 180; proceeds to Washington, 181; remarks of, at Steubenville, 182; appoints a fast, 187; proclaims emancipation, 190; reply of, to the Synod, 192; anecdote of, 237.
Lock and key found at the right moment, 51.
Long Bridge, station of the Mass. Thirteenth, 34.
Lord's Prayer, how expressive, 98.
Lutzen, in Germany, battle of, 185.
Lyceums in the army, 52.

INDEX.

M.

Macauley's character of the Puritans, 185.
Magruder, the rebel general, 246.
Mahon, Rev. Mr., of Michigan, 28.
Malvern Hill, an incident there, 53.
Martyrology of the church, 42.
McIlvaine, Bishop of Ohio, discourse of, 16.
Marks, Rev. Dr., describes a revival, 128.
Martyrs, unnamed, 199.
Massachusetts Second, at Stoneman's Station, 45.
Massachusetts Nineteenth, crossing the Rappahannock, 177.
Massachusetts Twenty-second, prayer-meeting of, 83.
Means, Rev. J. O., of Roxbury, sermon by, 175.
Memphis Hospital, 83.
Michigan Seventh, at Fredericksburg, 121.
Midnight summons, 227.
Mind triumphant over the body, 64.
Ministry, mark of a true one, 212.
Mitchell, General, as a preacher, 44; account of his death, 154; striking remark of, 203.
Morris Island, attack on the fortress there, 112.
Monitor, the, decides the victory, 103.
Mothers, how much they suffer, 60; influence of, 146; prayers of, answered, 146; dying testimony to, 198, 234.
Moultrie, Fort, abandoned, 182.

N.

Nantucket, Mass., its brave soldier, 98.
Newburyport, Mass., its unnamed soldier, 120.
Newcomb, Edgar M., of Boston, his character and death, 175.
New England Rooms in New York, 53.
"New London" gunboat, at work, 69.

New York Seventh, on the way to Washington, 72.
New York Fortieth Regiment, its history, 151.
North Mountain, Virginia, a death there, 109.

O.

Ohio Ninth Brigade, at Shelbyville, Tenn., 44.

P.

Pantomime of a battle, 93.
Paragraph, remarkable one in a will, 24.
Park St. Church, Boston, a funeral there, 172.
Parvin, Rev. J., touching recital of, 243.
Pastor chosen captain, 21.
Patent Office Hospital, a death there, 168.
Peck, Solomon, D.D., a communication from, 27.
Pennsylvania Sixth, with its church, 124; Sixty-third, a scene in the camp of, 152.
Phelps, Captain, on board the Benton, 55.
Pohlman, the missionary in China, 20; his son slain in battle, 21.
Pollard, W. S., of the Thirteenth Mass., 144.
Prayer how answered, 146.
Prayer and work, 35.
Prejudice of races, how inveterate, 249.
Psalm, nineteenth, applied, 73.
Putnam, W. Lowell, of Boston, his heroism, 95.

Q.

Quint, A. H., Chaplain of the Mass. Second, 126; his address to the soldiers, 188.

INDEX. 255

R.

Rappahannock, crossing of, 177.
Rebels, kind to a Union soldier, 85.
Reed, chaplain of the Penn. Thirtieth, 188.
Repentance, never too late, 235.
Rhode Islanders, 56.
Richmond, the prison in, 64.
Rock used as a pulpit, 44.
Russel, Colonel, of Connecticut, his conversion and death, 72.

S.

S——, of the Mass. Tenth, 240.
Sabbath, how spent at Beaufort, S. C., 29.
Safford, Mary, her hospital labors, 66.
Simpson, Bishop, his sermon at Chicago, 17.
Sanders, General, his death, 222.
Savage, Rev. Mr., a workman for Christ, 88.
Scorner, reproved, 43.
Scott, William, pardoned by the President, 75; circumstances of his death, 75.
Scripture, power of, 73, 84.
Sedgwick, General, anecdote of, 206.
Sewell, Rev. Jonathan, of Maine, 227.
Servants of Christ, their reward, 41.
Shaw, Robert G., Colonel, circumstances of his death, 112.
Shiloh, an event of the battle there, 18.
Ship Island, the first Sabbath there, 68.
Sidney, Sir Philip, at Zutphen, 96.
Smith, J. M., of Maine, his talents and heroic end, 22.
Smith, Governor, of the State of Rhode Island, 213.
Smith, Joseph, Lieut., killed on board the Congress, 103.
Stars at night, the teaching of, 19, 63.
Statesmanship, what is essential to it, 180.
Steadman, Levi, of the Sixth Wisconsin, 134.

Stoever, Prof., of Gettysburg, articles from, 60, 125.
Strickland, Rev. Mr., at Gen. Mitchell's death-bed, 148.
Stuart, George H., President of the Christian Commission, 135.
Sublimity of suffering, 110.
Sweetser, Francis, of the Massachusetts Sixteenth, 111.

T.

Taylor, Zachary, eulogy on, 237.
Tennessee, East, sermon preached on its mountains, 44.
Thompson, John H., the collegian, 169.
Tract Society, American, report of, 89.
Trowbridge, the dying sentinel, 207.
Twentieth Maine Volunteers, an officer of, 243.
Twenty-second Mass., prayer-meeting of, 45.
Twenty-fourth New York, Christian men in, 49.

U.

Unadilla, New York, its noble soldier 58.
Union of the States, worth dying for, 32.
Union, the true bond of, 248.
Union soldiers, graves of, at Fredericksburg, 122.
Uniontown, Ky., skirmish there, 40.

V.

Van Shaick, George, the pastor's son, 58.
Vermont Third Regiment, one of their heroes, 74.
Vermont Twelfth Regiment, their Sabbath school, 137.
Veterans in the service, 152.
Vicksburg, the siege of, 91.
Victory over the fears of death, 244.
Volunteer, the first one in Ohio, 16.
Volunteers, the Fifty-ninth, of New York, 20.

W.

War, "tearful," 59.
War, what it costs, 175.
Warren, Charles, of Massachusetts, his fortitude, 96.
Washington, Captain, of Dubuque, Iowa, 91.
Webster, Daniel, a remark of, 237.
Western churches, how fully represented in the army, 22.
Weston, Rev. Dr., New York, chaplain, 73.
William B——, of Massachusetts, his last prayer, 157.
William J——, of Maine, his last request, 125.
Williams, Captain, died at Beaufort, S. C., 155.
Williamsburg, Va., incidents of the battle there, 23, 101, 234.
Winchester, Va., suffering of our wounded there, 214.
Wisconsin Sixth Regiment, death of one of its soldiers, 133.
Woman, the only white one at Winchester, Va., 216.
Woman, gift of our blind, 243.
Women benevolent labors of, in hospitals, 66.
Wounds, how various, 219.

Y.

Yorktown, attack on, 24.
Yorktown, relics of the Revolution there, 75; music heard by night, 204.
Young, the, advice to, by General Anderson, 190.

Z.

Zeal, patriotic, signal instance of, 21.
Zion, hymns of, their power, 224, 241.
"Zion's Advocate," article accredited to, 203.

THE END.

Valuable Works,

PUBLISHED BY

GOULD AND LINCOLN,

59 WASHINGTON STREET, BOSTON.

CHRISTIAN'S DAILY TREASURY; a Religious Exercise for every day in the year. By Rev. H. TEMPLE. 12mo, cloth. $1.00.

WREATH AROUND THE CROSS; or, Scripture Truths Illustrated. By Rev. A. MORTON BROWN, D. D. 16mo, cloth. 60 cents.

SCHOOL OF CHRIST; or, Christianity Viewed in its Leading Aspects. By REV A. R. L. FOOTE. 16mo, cloth. 50 cents.

THE CHRISTIAN LIFE, Social and Individual. By PETER BAYNE, M. A. 12mo, cloth. $1.25.

THE PURITANS; or, The Church, Court, and Parliament of England. By Rev. SAMUEL HOPKINS. In 3 vols., octavo. Vol. I., cloth, *ready.* $2.50.

MODERN ATHEISM; under its various forms. By JAMES BUCHANAN, D.D. 12mo, cloth. $1.25.

THE MISSION OF THE COMFORTER; with copious Notes. By JULIUS CHARLES HARE. American edition; Notes translated. 12mo, cloth. $1.25.

GOD REVEALED IN NATURE AND IN CHRIST. By Rev. JAMES B. WALKER. 12mo, cloth $1.00.

PHILOSOPHY OF THE PLAN OF SALVATION. New, improved, and enlarged edition. 12mo, cloth. 75 cents.

YAHVEH CHRIST; or, The Memorial Name. By ALEX'R MACWHORTER. Introductory Letter by NATH'L W. TAYLOR, D.D. 12mo, cloth. 60 cents.

SALVATION BY CHRIST: Discourses on some of the most important Doctrines of the Gospel. By FRANCIS WAYLAND, D D. 12mo, cloth. $1.00.

THE SUFFERING SAVIOUR; or, Meditations on the Last Days of Christ. By FREDERICK W. KRUMMACHER, D. D. 12mo, cloth. $1.25.

THE GREAT DAY OF ATONEMENT; or, Meditations and Prayers on the Sufferings and Death of our Lord. 75 cents.

EXTENT OF THE ATONEMENT IN ITS RELATION TO GOD AND THE UNIVERSE. By THOMAS W. JENKYN, D.D. 12mo, cloth. $1.00.

THE IMITATION OF CHRIST. By THOMAS À KEMPIS. With a Life of à Kempis, by Dr C. ULLMANN. 12mo, cloth. 85 cents.

THE HARVEST AND THE REAPERS. Home Work for all, and how to do it. By Rev. HARVEY NEWCOMB. 16mo, cloth. 63 cents.

Gould and Lincoln's Publications.
(RELIGIOUS.)

LIMITS OF RELIGIOUS THOUGHT EXAMINED. By HENRY L. MANSEL, B D. Notes translated for American ed. 12mo, cl. $.100.

THE CRUCIBLE; or, Tests of a Regenerate State. By Rev. J. A. GOODHUE. Introduction by Dr. KIRK. 12mo, cloth. $1.00.

LEADERS OF THE REFORMATION. Luther — Calvin — Latimer — Knox. By JOHN TULLOCH, D. D. 12mo, cloth. $1.00.

BARON STOW. CHRISTIAN BROTHERHOOD. 16mo, cloth. 50 cents.

———————— FIRST THINGS; or, the Development of Church Life. 16mo, cloth. 60 cents.

JOHN ANGELL JAMES. CHURCH MEMBER'S GUIDE. Cloth. 33 cts.

———————— CHURCH IN EARNEST. 18mo, cloth. 40 cts.

———————— CHRISTIAN PROGRESS. Sequel to the Anxious Inquirer. 18mo, cloth. 31 cents.

THE GREAT CONCERN. By N. ADAMS, D. D. 12mo, cloth. 85 cents.

JOHN HARRIS'S WORKS. THE GREAT TEACHER. With an Introductory Essay by H. HUMPHREY, D. D. 12mo, cloth. 85 cents.

———————— THE GREAT COMMISSION. With an Introductory Essay by WILLIAM R. WILLIAMS, D. D. 12mo, cloth. $1.00.

———————— THE PRE-ADAMITE EARTH. Contributions to Theological Science. 12mo, cloth. $1.00.

———————— MAN PRIMEVAL: Constitution and Primitive Condition of the Human Being. Portrait of Author. 12mo, cloth. $1.25.

———————— PATRIARCHY; or, The Family, its Constitution and Probation. 12mo, cloth. $1.25.

———————— SERMONS, CHARGES, ADDRESSES, &c. Two volumes, octavo, cloth. $1.00 each.

WILLIAM R. WILLIAMS. RELIGIOUS PROGRESS. 12mo, cloth 85 cts.

———————— LECTURES ON THE LORD'S PRAYER. 12mo, cloth. 85 cents.

THE BETTER LAND. By Rev. A. C. THOMPSON. 12mo, cloth. 85 cents

EVENING OF LIFE; or, Light and Comfort amid the Shadows of Declining Years. By JEREMIAH CHAPLIN, D. D. 12mo, cloth. $1.00.

HEAVEN. By JAMES WILLIAM KIMBALL. 12mo, cloth. $1.00.

THE SAINT'S EVERLASTING REST. BAXTER. 16mo, cl. 50 cts.

Gould and Lincoln's Publications.
(BIOGRAPHICAL.)

LIFE OF JOHN MILTON, in connection with the Political, Ecclesiastical, and Literary History of his time. By DAVID MASSON, M. A. 3 vols., 8vo. Vol. I., cloth. $2.75.

LIFE AND CORRESPONDENCE OF REV. DANIEL WILSON, D. D., late Bishop of Calcutta By Rev. JOSIAH BATEMAN. With portraits, map, and illustrations. One volume, royal octavo. $3.00.

LIFE AND CORRESPONDENCE OF THE LATE AMOS LAW-RENCE. By W. R. LAWRENCE, M. D. 8vo, cloth. $1.50. 12mo, cloth. $1.00.

DR. GRANT AND THE MOUNTAIN NESTORIANS. By Rev. THOMAS LAURIE, his surviving associate. 12mo, cloth. $1.25.

MEMOIR OF THE LIFE AND TIMES OF ISAAC BACKUS. By ALVAH HOVEY, D. D. 12mo, cloth. $1.25.

LIFE OF JAMES MONTGOMERY. By Mrs. H. C. KNIGHT, Author of "Lady Huntington and her Friends" 12mo, cloth. $1.25.

MY MOTHER; or, Recollections of Maternal Influence. By a New England Clergyman. 12mo, cloth. 75 cents.

MEMOIR OF ROGER WILLIAMS. By Professor WILLIAM GAMMELL. 16mo, cloth. 75 cents.

LIFE AND CORRESPONDENCE OF JOHN FOSTER. By JOHN E. RYLAND. 2 vols. in one, 12mo, cloth. $1.25.

PHILIP DODDRIDGE. His Life and Labors. By JOHN STOUGHTON, D. D. 16mo, cloth. 60 cents.

MEMOIR OF ANN H. JUDSON. By Rev. J. D. KNOWLES. 18mo, cloth. 58 cents.

MEMOIR OF GEORGE D. BOARDMAN. By Rev. A. KING. Introduction by W. R. WILLIAMS, D. D. 12mo, cloth. 75 cents.

LIFE OF GODFREY WILLIAM VON LEIBNITZ. By JOHN. M. MACKIE. 16mo, cloth. 75 cents.

THE TEACHER'S LAST LESSON; A Memoir of MARTHA WHITING, of Charlestown Female Seminary. By C. N. BADGER. 12mo, cloth. $1.00.

MEMOIR OF HENRIETTA SHUCK, the first Female Missionary to China. By Rev. J. B. JETER, D. D. 18mo, cloth. 50 cents.

MEMOIR OF REV. WILLIAM G. CROCKER, Missionary to West Africa. By R. B. MEDBURY. 18mo, cloth. 63 cents.

THE KAREN APOSTLE; or, Memoir of KO-THAH-BYU, the first Karen Convert. By Rev. F. MASON, D. D. 18mo, cloth. 25 cents.

MEMORIES OF A GRANDMOTHER. By a Lady of Massachusetts 16mo cloth. 50 cents.

Gould and Lincoln's Publications.

(LITERARY.)

THE PURITANS; or, the Court, Church, and Parliament of England. By SAMUEL HOPKINS. 3 vols., 8vo, cloth. $2.00 per volume.

HISTORICAL EVIDENCES OF THE TRUTH OF THE SCRIPTURE RECORDS, STATED ANEW, with Special Reference to the Doubts and Discoveries of Modern Times. Bampton Lecture for 1859. By GEORGE RAWLINSON. 12mo, cloth $1.00.

CHRIST IN HISTORY. By ROBERT TURNBULL, D. D. A New and Enlarged Edition. 12mo, cloth. $1.25.

THE CHRISTIAN LIFE; Social and Individual. By PETER BAYNE. 12mo, cloth. $1.25.

ESSAYS IN BIOGRAPHY AND CRITICISM. By PETER BAYNE. Arranged in two series, or parts. 2 vols., 12mo, cloth. $1.25 each.

THE GREYSON LETTERS. By HENRY ROGERS, Author of the "Eclipse of Faith." 12mo, cloth. $1.25.

CHAMBERS' WORKS. CYCLOPÆDIA OF ENGLISH LITERATURE. Selections from English Authors, from the earliest to the present time. 2 vols., 8vo, cloth. $5.00.

MISCELLANY OF USEFUL AND ENTERTAINING KNOWLEDGE. 10 vols., 16mo, cloth. $7.50.

HOME BOOK; or, Pocket Miscellany. 6 vols., 16mo, cloth. $3.00.

THE PREACHER AND THE KING; or, Bourdaloue in the Court of Louis XIV. By L. F. BUNGENER. 12mo, cloth. $1.25.

THE PRIEST AND THE HUGUENOT; or, Persecution in the age of Louis XV. By L. F. BUNGENER. 2 vols, 12mo, cloth. $2.25.

MISCELLANIES. By WILLIAM R. WILLIAMS, D. D. 12mo, cloth. $1.25.

ANCIENT LITERATURE AND ART. Essays and Letters from Eminent Philologists. By Profs. SEARS, EDWARDS, and FELTON. 12mo, cloth. $1.25.

MODERN FRENCH LITERATURE. By L. RAYMOND DE VERICOUR. Revised, with Notes by W. S. CHASE. 12mo, cloth. $1.25.

BRITISH NOVELISTS AND THEIR STYLES. By DAVID MASSON, M. A., Author of Life of Milton. 16mo, cloth. 75 cents.

REPUBLICAN CHRISTIANITY; or, True Liberty, exhibited in the Life, Precepts, and early Disciples of the Redeemer. By E. L. MAGOON. 12mo, cloth. $1.25.

THE HALLIG; or, the Sheepfold in the Waters. Translated from the German of BIERNATSKI, by Mrs. GEORGE P. MARSH. 12mo, cloth. $1.00.

MANSEL'S MISCELLANIES; including "Prolegomina Logica," "Metaphysics," "Limits of Demonstrative Evidence," "Philosophy of Kant," etc. 12mo. *In press.*

Gould and Lincoln's Publications.

(SABBATH SCHOOL.)

POPULAR CYCLOPÆDIA OF BIBLICAL LITERATURE. Condensed, by JOHN KITTO, D. D. Numerous Illustrations. 8vo. $3.00.

THE HISTORY OF PALESTINE; with Chapters on its Geography and Natural History, its Customs and Institutions. By JOHN KITTO, D. D. With Illustrations. 12mo. $1.25.

ANALYTICAL CONCORDANCE TO THE HOLY SCRIPTURES; or, The Bible under Distinct and Classified Topics. By JOHN EADIE, D. D. 8vo. $3.00.

CRUDEN'S CONDENSED CONCORDANCE. By ALEX. CRUDEN. 8vo. Half boards, $1.25. Sheep, $1.50.

COMMENTARY ON THE ORIGINAL TEXT OF THE ACTS OF THE APOSTLES. By H. B. HACKETT, D. D. 8vo. $2.25.

ILLUSTRATIONS OF SCRIPTURE. Suggested by a tour through the Holy Land. With Illustrations. New, Enlarged Edition. By H. B. HACKETT, D. D. 12mo, cloth. $1.00.

PROF. H. J. RIPLEY'S NOTES.

―――――――――― *ON THE GOSPELS.* For Teachers in Sabbath Schools, and as an Aid to Family Instruction. With Map of Canaan. Cloth, embossed. $1.25.

―――――――――― *ON THE ACTS OF THE APOSTLES.* With Map of the Travels of the Apostle PAUL. 12mo, cloth, embossed. 75 cents.

―――――――――― *ON THE EPISTLE OF PAUL TO THE ROMANS.* 12mo, cloth, embossed. 67 cents.

COMMENTARY ON THE EPISTLE TO THE EPHESIANS. Explanatory, Doctrinal, and Practical. By R. E. PATTISON, D. D. 12mo. 85 cents.

MALCOM'S NEW BIBLE DICTIONARY of Names, Objects, and Terms, found in the Holy Scriptures. By HOWARD MALCOM, D. D. 16mo, cloth. 60 cents.

HARMONY QUESTIONS ON THE FOUR GOSPELS, for the use of Sabbath Schools. By Rev. S. B. SWAIM, D. D. Vol. I. 18mo, cloth backs. 13 cents.

SABBATH-SCHOOL CLASS-BOOK. By E. LINCOLN. 13 cents.

LINCOLN'S SCRIPTURE QUESTIONS; with Answers. 8 cents.

THE SABBATH-SCHOOL HARMONY; with appropriate Hymns and Music for Sabbath Schools. By N. D GOULD. 13 cents.

EVIDENCES OF CHRISTIANITY, as exhibited in the writings of its apologists, down to Augustine. By Prof. W. J. BOLTON, Cambridge, England 12mo, cloth. 80 cents.

Gould and Lincoln's Publications.
(RELIGIOUS.)

GOTTHOLD'S EMBLEMS; or, Invisible Things Understood by Things that are Made. By CHRISTIAN SCRIVER. Tr. from the 28th German Ed. by Rev. ROBERT MENZIES. 8vo, cloth, $1.00 Fine Edition, Tinted Paper, royal 8vo, cloth, $1.50.

THE STILL HOUR; or, Communion with God. By Prof. AUSTIN PHELPS, D. D., of Andover Theological Seminary. 16mo, cloth. 38 cents.

LESSONS AT THE CROSS; or, Spiritual Truths Familiarly Exhibited in their Relations to Christ. By SAMUEL HOPKINS, author of "The Puritans," etc. Introduction by GEORGE W. BLAGDEN, D. D. 16mo, cloth. 75 cents.

NEW ENGLAND THEOCRACY. From the German of Uhden's History of the Congregationalists of New England. Introduction by NEANDER. By Mrs. H. C. CONANT. 12mo, cloth. $1.00.

EVENINGS WITH THE DOCTRINES. By Rev. NEHEMIAH ADAMS, D. D. 12mo, cloth.

THE STATE OF THE IMPENITENT DEAD. By ALVAH HOVEY, D. D., Prof. of Christian Theology in Newton Theol. Inst. 16mo, cloth. 50 cents.

FOOTSTEPS OF OUR FOREFATHERS; what they Suffered and what they Sought. Describing Localities, Personages, and Events, in the Struggles for Religious Liberty. By JAMES G. MIALL. Illustrations. 12mo, cloth. $1.00.

MEMORIALS OF EARLY CHRISTIANITY. Presenting, in a graphic form, Memorable Events of Early Ecclesiastical History, etc. By Rev. J. G. MIALL. With Illustrations. 12mo, cloth. $1.00.

THE MISSIONARY ENTERPRISE. The most important Discourses in the language on Christian Missions, by distinguished American Authors. Edited by BARON STOW, D. D. 12mo, cloth. 85 cents.

THE RELIGIONS OF THE WORLD, and their Relations to Christianity. By FREDERICK DENISON MAURICE, Prof. of Divinity in King's Coll., London. 16mo, cloth. 60 cents.

THE CHRISTIAN WORLD UNMASKED. By JOHN BERRIDGE, A. M., Vicar of Everton, Bedfordshire. With a Life of the Author, by Rev. THOMAS GUTHRIE, D. D. 16mo, cloth. 50 cents.

THE EXCELLENT WOMAN, as described in the Book of Proverbs. With an Introduction by W. B. SPRAGUE, D. D. Twenty-four splendid Illustrations. 12mo, cloth. $1.00.

MOTHERS OF THE WISE AND GOOD. By JABEZ BURNS, D. D. 16mo, cloth. 75 cents.

THE SIGNET-RING, and its Heavenly Motto. From the German. Illustrated. 16mo, cloth, gilt. 31 cents.

THE MARRIAGE-RING; or, How to Make Home Happy. From the writings of JOHN ANGELL JAMES. Beautifully Illustrated edition. 16mo, cloth, gilt. 75 cents.

(32)

Gould and Lincoln's Publications.

(EDUCATIONAL.)

LECTURES ON METAPHYSICS. By SIR WILLIAM HAMILTON. With Notes from original materials. 8vo, cloth. $3.00.

LECTURES ON LOGIC. By SIR WILLIAM HAMILTON. With an Appendix, containing the author's latest development of his new Logical theory. 8vo, cloth.

ELEMENTS OF MORAL SCIENCE. By FRANCIS WAYLAND, D. D., late President of Brown University. 12mo, cloth. $1.25.

THE SAME, Abridged for Schools and Academies, half morocco. 50 cents.

ELEMENTS OF POLITICAL ECONOMY. By FRANCIS WAYLAND, D. D. 12mo, cloth. $1.25.

THE SAME, Abridged for Schools and Academies, half morocco. 50 cents.

MENTAL PHILOSOPHY; including the Intellect, the Sensibilities, and the Will. By JOSEPH HAVEN, D. D. 12mo, cloth. $1.50.

MORAL PHILOSOPHY; including Theoretical and Practical Ethics. By JOSEPH HAVEN, D. D. 12mo, cloth. $1.25.

THE EARTH AND MAN; Lectures on Comparative Physical Geography in its relation to the History of Mankind. By ARNOLD GUYOT. 12mo, cloth. $1.25.

THE ELEMENTS OF GEOLOGY; adapted to Schools and Colleges. With numerous Illustrations. By J. R. LOOMIS, President of Lewisburg University. 12mo, cloth. 75 cents.

PRINCIPLES OF ZOÖLOGY; for the use of Schools and Colleges. With numerous Illustrations. By LOUIS AGASSIZ and AUGUSTUS A. GOULD, M. D. 12mo, cloth. $1.00.

PALEY'S NATURAL THEOLOGY. Illustrated by forty Plates. Edited by JOHN WARE, M. D. 12mo, cloth. $1.25.

GUYOT'S MURAL MAPS; A series of elegant colored maps, exhibiting the Physical Phenomena of the Globe.

MAP OF THE WORLD, mounted. $10.00

MAP OF NORTH AMERICA, mounted. $9.00.

MAP OF SOUTH AMERICA, mounted. $9.00.

MAP OF GEOGRAPHICAL ELEMENTS, mounted. $9.00.

GEOLOGICAL MAP OF THE UNITED STATES AND BRITISH PROVINCES; with Geological Sections and Fossil Plates. By JULES MARCOU. 2 vols., 8vo, cloth. $3.00.

GOULD AND LINCOLN,

59 WASHINGTON STREET, BOSTON,

Would call particular attention to the following valuable works described in their Catalogue of Publications, viz.:

Hugh Miller's Works.
Bayne's Works. Walker's Works. Miall's Works. Bungener's Work.
Annual of Scientific Discovery. Knight's Knowledge is Power.
Krummacher's Suffering Saviour,
Banvard's American Histories. The Aimwell Stories.
Newcomb's Works. Tweedie's Works. Chambers's Works. Harris' Works.
Kitto's Cyclopædia of Biblical Literature.
Mrs. Knight's Life of Montgomery. Kitto's History of Palestine.
Whewell's Work. Wayland's Works. Agassiz's Works.

Williams' Works. Guyot's Works.
Thompson's Better Land. Kimball's Heaven. Valuable Works on Missions.
Haven's Mental Philosophy. Buchanan's Modern Atheism.
Cruden's Condensed Concordance. Eadie's Analytical Concordance.
The Psalmist: a Collection of Hymns.
Valuable School Books. Works for Sabbath Schools.
Memoir of Amos Lawrence.
Poetical Works of Milton, Cowper, Scott. Elegant Miniature Volumes.
Arvine's Cyclopædia of Anecdotes.
Ripley's Notes on Gospels, Acts, and Romans.
Sprague's European Celebrities. Marsh's Camel and the Hallig.
Roget's Thesaurus of English Words.
Hackett's Notes on Acts. M'Whorter's Yahveh Christ.
Siebold and Stannius's Comparative Anatomy. Marcou's Geological Map, U. S.
Religious and Miscellaneous Works.
Works in the various Departments of Literature, Science and Art.

www.ingramcontent.com/pod-product-compliance
Lightning Source LLC
Chambersburg PA
CBHW032107220426
43664CB00008B/1163